# Recipe for Life

# Recipe for Life

MARY BERRY

MICHAEL JOSEPH
*an imprint of*
PENGUIN BOOKS

MICHAEL JOSEPH

Published by the Penguin Group

Penguin Books Ltd, 80 Strand, London WC2R ORL, England

Penguin Group (USA) Inc., 375 Hudson Street, New York, New York 10014, USA

Penguin Group (Canada), 90 Eglinton Avenue East, Suite 700, Toronto, Ontario, Canada M4P 2Y3
(a division of Pearson Penguin Canada Inc.)

Penguin Ireland, 25 St Stephen's Green, Dublin 2, Ireland (a division of Penguin Books Ltd)

Penguin Group (Australia), 707 Collins Street, Melbourne, Victoria 3008, Australia
(a division of Pearson Australia Group Pty Ltd)

Penguin Books India Pvt Ltd, 11 Community Centre, Panchsheel Park, New Delhi – 110 017, India

Penguin Group (NZ), 67 Apollo Drive, Rosedale, Auckland 0632, New Zealand
(a division of Pearson New Zealand Ltd)

Penguin Books (South Africa) (Pty) Ltd, Block D, Rosebank Office Park,
181 Jan Smuts Avenue, Parktown North, Gauteng 2193, South Africa

Penguin Books Ltd, Registered Offices: 80 Strand, London WC2R ORL, England

www.penguin.com

First published 2013
001

Set in 13.5/16pt Garamond MT Std
Typeset by Jouve (UK), Milton Keynes
Printed in Great Britain by Clays Ltd, St Ives plc

A CIP catalogue record for this book is available from the British Library

HARDBACK ISBN: 978–1–405–91284–6
TRADE PAPERBACK ISBN: 978–0–718–17889–5

www.greenpenguin.co.uk

I dedicate this book to my husband Paul and also my loving and supportive family – always there for me and always with me.

# List of Permissions

All photos are from private collections apart from the below.

**Endpapers**
Mary at the *Bake Off* Fête © The Original Fête Company
The *Bake Off* team on set © Sam Beddoes
Mary and the *Bake Off* team at the BAFTAs © Dave M. Benett/Getty
Mary in the car © James Hemming
Mary, Mel and Sue at the BAFTAs © Stephen Butler/BAFTA/ Rex
    Features

**Prelims**
Mary cooking with her children © Hart/Evening News/Rex Features
Mary in stripey apron © Fremantle Media
Mary standing by BAFTA © Jonathan Hordle/Rex Features

**Integrated**
Mary on the see-saw © Mirrorpix
Mary with The Duchess of Cambridge © www.childbereavementuk.org
Lucy and Mary © Joe Plimmer, Camera Press London
Mary with Lucy and Lucinda © Megan Taylor
Mary and Paul hugging © The Cake & Bake Show
Mary on *The Graham Norton Show* © Ian West/PA Wire/Press Association
    Images
Mary and Paul at the BAFTAs © David Fisher / Rex Features
Mary standing by window © Charlotte Murphy

**Inset 2**
Mary baking with Annabel © Fremantle Media

**Inset 3**
Mary standing beside the Aga © David Woolford

**Inset 4**

Mary with Paul, Mel and Sue at the BAFTAs © Pacific Coast News

Paul and Mary on *Loose Women* © Ken McKay/Rex Features

Mary with Sue, Paul and Mel on *Bake Off* © Love Productions

Mary and Paul on the Easter *Bake Off* © Love Productions

The *Bake Off* tent © Love Productions

Mel with *Bake Off* sign © The Original Fête Company

Mary in floral jacket © Love Productions

Mary, her husband and children at the investiture ceremony © WPA Pool/Getty

Mary and her family at her investiture lunch x 2 © Edward Lloyd/ Alpha Press

Mary's collection of books © James Hemming

Mary and her family © Love Productions

Mary in electric-blue dress © David Fisher/Rex Features

**Recipes**

**Mexican Spicy Lamb** © *Cook Now, Eat Later* by Mary Berry, published by Headline Publishing Group, 2002.

**Smoked Haddock Bouillabaisse** © *Cook Now, Eat Later* by Mary Berry, published by Headline Publishing Group, 2002.

**Slow Roast Shoulder of Lamb** © *Mary Berry's Family Sunday Lunches*, published by Headline Publishing Group, 2011.

**Watercroft Chicken** © *Mary Berry's New AGA Book*, published by Headline Publishing Group, 2011.

**Pasta Al Fresco** © *Mary Berry's New AGA Book*, published by Headline Publishing Group, 2011.

**Canterbury Tart** © *Mary Berry's New AGA Book*, published by Headline Publishing Group, 2011.

**Baked Salmon with Parmesan and Parsley Crust** © *Mary Berry's New AGA Book*, published by Headline Publishing Group, 2011.

Every effort has been made to trace copyright holders. The publishers will be glad to rectify in future editions any errors or omissions brought to their attention.

# Acknowledgements

I have been immensely blessed to have Lucy Young, my assistant, by my side for twenty-three years, sorting me out, organizing my life and being my friend. We write books together and think alike, with never a cross word, and will have many more years together I hope.

Louise Moore at Penguin commissioned this book and it has been a sheer joy to work with her – she was so encouraging as each chapter evolved. Her energy and enthusiasm were infectious and I felt like I was her only author, which is a real skill when she looks after so many people. Thank you for being lovely.

Catherine Woods turned my wavering voice into my story, memories and events. Catherine became one of the family, gently encouraging me to spill the beans with kindness and laughter.

Tamsin English edited the book with such care and interest in my story; choosing the photos with her was a wonderful trip down memory lane.

# I

In the words of my father, my birth caused no end of trouble. I arrived on 24th March 1935, two weeks before I had been expected, on the day that my parents, Alleyne and Margery Berry, had been scheduled to move house. Not at all convenient, as you can imagine! When my mother went into labour in the bedroom of their maisonette on Park Street in Bath, the removal men had to be sent packing and the disgruntled new tenants persuaded, by Mum's doctor, to delay their own move. Years later, in his memoirs, my father would record my birth as follows: 'After coming to Bath, for a short time we lived in a converted half-house [maisonette] and Mary had the confounded cheek to be born there when she should have arrived a fortnight later.' It was certainly not be the last time that my father would have cause to despair of his only daughter's flightiness.

Thanks to the inconvenient timing of the arrival of Mary-Rosa Alleyne Berry it was a week behind schedule that my family moved into their new home at 5 Park Lane, opposite Bath's Victoria Park. My father, who was a surveyor, had designed the house himself to accommodate his growing family, which as well as troublesome week-old me also included my five-year-old brother Roger. My younger brother, William, would arrive four years later, and one of my earliest memories is of seeing him as a chubby baby sitting in a high chair in the kitchen at Park Lane, tied in with a loop of woolly blue fabric of the type used in school to show whether you were in the red team or blue team. In those days it was thought to be clever financial planning to have your children spaced so widely apart, but it's not a bit good growing up as you have absolutely nothing in common with your siblings. We're the greatest of friends these days, but as a child I was just beaten up all the time by my big brother.

Blowing bubbles with Roger.

Although we only lived there until I was seven, I still have vivid mental snapshots of the house at Park Lane: the steep drive, the nursery painted with lions, tigers and elephants that gave you the thrilling feeling of sleeping in a zoo, the tiny family bathroom and the enamel-topped kitchen table with the crank-handled mincer screwed to its edge, which was used to grind Sunday's Roast Beef into mince for Tuesday's

Cottage Pie. But it is the garden that I remember the most clearly, almost down to each individual plant, as we played outside endlessly. I would spend hours building dens amongst the tangle of shrubs at the bottom of the garden. My friends and I would huddle together in our makeshift camp: talking, planning and making up stories. By the time we had moved to our next house, South Lawn, our dens had become so sophisticated that we could cook in them. We'd build a fire at the back of the den and fry whatever we could get our hands on in a little pan. Usually bread, but we sometimes went up to the hens and would sneak an egg. One of our dens even had its own supply of hot water. We would light a fire, contain it within a border of bricks and run a curved pipe through the middle. You poured water in one end then it came out the other into a bucket, warmed by the flames. Can you imagine what the Health and Safety police would have to say about that these days? I'm not sure if our parents even knew about it!

At Park Lane we were great friends with the Dakin children who lived next door – Tony, Bobby and baby Janet – and whose garden was linked to ours with a five-bar gate. My mother would often send me through the gate with messages for Mrs Dakin. On one occasion it was Mr Dakin who greeted me and told me that 'Ivy's in the bath.' That seemed so funny to me, because I never knew Mrs Dakin as Ivy!

The boys would often beat me up; one time I remember Bobby Dakin pushing me into our ornamental fishpond – I emerged spluttering amongst the dark green water lily leaves. But having grown up with brothers I was a bit of a tomboy and would sometimes give as good as I got. I once challenged my younger brother to a boxing match, convinced I would win – although William managed to get in the first punch and landed the biggest whack on my nose. I just stood there, too stunned to cry, as the blood gushed from my nose. I remember my horrified fascination at seeing it splatter on to my jumper, shockingly bright against the pale blue wool. The tears came soon enough, though; I made an awful fuss about it because the only way to get any attention from the grown-ups was to make a huge scene. And so it was William who got the ticking off, even though I was the one who had started it.

At the back of the house Dad had built an aviary to keep budgerigars, one of his many hobbies, and there were always chickens for eggs. Dad used to cook up potato peelings and kitchen waste, to mix with bran to make chicken feed, in an industrial-sized pressure cooker he kept in the garage – a huge contraption that looked like a giant's saucepan. One day, without warning, the cooker suddenly exploded while my big brother Roger was nearby. He was rushed to Forbes Fraser Hospital, and I remember going to visit him and being immensely shocked because my brother seemed to have turned purple. At some point someone must have explained to me that he had been covered with ultra-violet blue – a bluish-purple lotion that was used to treat burns at the time.

Another awful drama occurred when Dad set up an incubator to hatch a clutch of the eggs. Every day we went to look at them, to check how they were doing, but the heat from the lamp must have been too fierce and to my horror some of those dear little chicks got burnt and died. Gosh, it was traumatic. You really remember the childhood dramas, don't you?

If we weren't running around in the garden we would be across the road in Victoria Park, playing on the swings, or on an afternoon walk with Mum. And when anyone came to visit, whatever the weather, we would go on picnics. That was a real treat. Mum would pack egg-and-cress sandwiches, sausages and biscuits – perhaps a bit of cake if you were lucky – and there would be games and friends and running about.

We would usually picnic with a purpose. On the early days of spring we would go primrosing, gathering up posies of the pale yellow flowers, while in summer the picnic activity would be swimming. We would often drive to a village called Freshford where there was a weir, and I remember slipping down its mossy side into the green depths, my knitted woollen swimming costume soaking up water like a sponge and dragging me down. In autumn we would hunt for wild mushrooms and scour the hedgerows for blackberries, taking home whatever fruit escaped our mouths to be made into jam.

Another favourite destination for family picnics was the village of Lacock, famous for its grand house, Lacock Abbey, where we would set out our feast by the most beautiful stretch of the River Avon. Dad was a keen photographer and every time we went there he would tell us about a former resident, the Victorian photography pioneer Fox Talbot. 'The first ever photograph was taken of this very window,' he would say, pointing at the house. And we would all line up on the bridge and look obediently over towards the famous window, even though we'd done it dozens of times before.

I suppose one of the reasons we spent so much time outside when we were young was because there wasn't a great deal of incentive to stay indoors. I had toys, of course: my rocking horse and a Little Black Sambo doll were particular favourites. But I was never the sort of child who would sit prettily and read a book or do a spot of needlework. When we got back from school we would always cluster around the radio at five o'clock to listen to classic stories like *Robinson Crusoe* and *Swallows and Amazons* on *Children's Hour*, but in those days, like most people, we didn't have a television. I still remember the excitement when, in my mid-teens, our friends the Wills family acquired a television set. On alternate Sunday evenings we would go to their house to sit in reverent silence in front of a quiz programme called *Animal, Vegetable or Mineral?*, which consisted of art historians and archaeologists trying to identify museum artefacts. It was a hugely popular programme and one of the panellists, Sir Mortimer Wheeler, became quite a star. I can't imagine a moustachioed archaeologist being named 'TV Personality of the Year' today, as he was in 1954!

Another compelling incentive to stay outside, particularly in my early childhood, was the grim spectre of Nanny. In that era it was very usual to have help in the house and so we had a maid to take care of the housework and a succession of nannies to take care of us children. They were at best tolerated and at worst despised. The only one I can remember with any clarity, probably because she was the worst of the bunch, was Nanny Denier. Banish any thoughts of a rosy-cheeked Mary Poppins and her spoonful of sugar: Nanny Denier was an ogre of a woman, fiendishly strict and relentlessly bossy, whose sole purpose in life was to keep her charges silent and spotless. 'You must always wear clean underwear in case you get run over by a bus,' she would boom. We had as little to do with her as possible.

To be fair, we probably tested Nanny Denier to her limits: I have been told I was quite a naughty little girl. We would often get smacked, although not brutally, just a tap on the leg – if they could catch you, that is! While life inside our home was quite strictly regulated, you could get up to all sorts of mischief in the garden and most of the time nobody would find out. My parents never came out into the garden to check on us. They would shout out to us for meals, but they wouldn't have ever come down the garden to ask what we were up to; they just let us get on with it. Nowadays everybody seems to want to know what children are doing the whole time. We had a goat shed at South Lawn where I tried smoking my first cigarette, supplied by Roger, but it was so disgusting I never did it again. Another time, bored at home during the school holidays, I spent a whole morning picking flowers from the garden and tying them into bunches, then set up a stall outside our front gate to sell them, with no permission whatsoever. Well, everybody was out or busy, so why not? The maid or someone would have been meant to be looking after me, although most probably they'd have been chatting in the kitchen. Business was brisk and I was doing really rather well – until Dad arrived home unexpectedly. He was not in the least bit happy about my business venture and as punishment sent me straight round to one of our neighbours, Miss Jackson, who raised money for charity, and made me donate all my profits to the Red Cross, which I grudgingly did.

We were really very frightened of Dad. If I was naughty my mother's warning – 'I'll tell your father' – was usually quite enough to get me to behave. Apart from reading us the occasional bedtime story (a particular paternal favourite was *Tom Brown's Schooldays*), Dad had very little to do with our day-to-day care; in fact, I'm sure he viewed us as a bit of a nuisance. For a while Mum had to give him breakfast in bed, as he would get so exasperated by our time-wasting and general sloppiness first thing in the morning. He would address me as 'Mary-Rosa' in a stern voice if I was naughty and call me 'Scruffy' whenever I appeared from the garden looking like I'd been dragged through a hedge backwards, which more often than not I probably had been.

Dad was very strict and seldom affectionate; praise and encouragement were equally rare. The only time I can remember him rewarding me for anything was when I made a rag doll. 'Where did you get that from?' he asked. When I told him that I'd made it myself he was clearly impressed and gave me a shilling – about 5p – and I was really chuffed about that. But I think Dad was immensely disappointed that I wasn't at all academic, and in the early days of my career, I was very much motivated by a need to win his approval. Even nowadays I often think, 'Well, Dad would be pleased,' when there's been some achievement or success in my career.

My father was a great man who was awarded an OBE for his services to Bath. As the city's Chairman of Planning, and later Mayor, he was a key figure in Bath's development and was instrumental in establishing the University at Claverton Down, from where he would be awarded an honorary MA degree for his efforts. Without his determination and vision, there probably wouldn't be a university there today. A newspaper report on his retirement from the council paid tribute to Dad's work: 'He has been a controversial figure, but even those who have not loved him cannot deny that he has been the most outstanding figure in Bath's local government in the last fifty years. For a quarter of a century he virtually directed the city's planning policy. He has always done what he believed to be right, no matter how unpopular that might be.' I think that last comment leaves little doubt as to his single-mindedness!

My father was born in 1904, the son of a vicar, Arthur Berry, who would go on to become Canon of York. His

Today, Pa's portrait hangs in the Guildhall in Bath.

mother, Annie, died when he was only two, leaving him in the care of housekeepers, nannies and maids. Dad wrote in his memoirs: 'Mother, I gather, never recovered from my birth and was confined to a couch upstairs in the drawing room for the next two and a half years, the remainder of her life . . . I scarcely remember anything of her, but was always told she was a very beautiful, artistically accomplished woman. I only remember three things connected with my mother: Father peeling grapes for her, making soup in the best brown dinner service and my building sandcastles with prayer books at her funeral.'

When my father was five, a governess joined the Berry household. Years later Dad recalled their first meeting: 'Miss Atton, as most unmarried women of the upper classes, had to be a governess, and she happened to be out of a job . . . I met her at the station and we walked to the vicarage hand in hand, exchanging information and starting a relationship, which influenced my life for some forty years. She was never more than a housekeeper, although gradually she assumed the duties of a vicar's wife. Father was faithful to his Annie until his death.' Miss Atton was a devout Christian and one of the many ways in which she took up this role was by organizing sewing days with other ladies to make tea cosies, patchwork blankets, pin cushions and aprons for church sales when at Drypool Vicarage in Hull with Grandpa.

Despite his bond with Miss Atton, growing up without a mother must have been terribly hard for Dad, as his own father didn't understand children at all. Although my father was a Christian man, he never went to church because my grandfather had always made him go when he was young. Indeed, my own memory of Grandpa Berry, who came to live with us in a cottage at the back of our house after his retirement (together with Miss Atton, who lived with him until his death, although their relationship was only ever purely platonic), is of a terribly stern, Victorian figure dressed all in black with a dog collar, who was of the firm belief that children should be seen and not heard – preferably neither seen nor heard. He was very remote, not warm in any way. While he was still working he would sometimes take services at St Stephen's, our local church on Lansdown Road, when he came to stay, and his sermons were notoriously severe. I remember Mum asking us one Sunday, 'Would you like to go to church? Grandpa will be preaching today.' And my little brother William replying, quick as a flash, 'No thank you, Mother, I've already been.'

Later, when Grandpa Berry lived with us, I spent very little time with him. Although I would often visit the cottage to play the card game bezique with Miss Atton, the only time I remember going there with the sole purpose of seeing Grandpa was when I was given a homework project to create an 'illuminated' alphabet, in which the letters were embellished with flowers and intricate designs of the sort you'd see in religious manuscripts. 'You'd better go and see Grandpa, he'll be good at that,' Dad told me; sure enough we spent a long time working on that together and it was one of the rare times I felt relaxed around him.

Me on my first pony, Susan, with Grandpa and Miss Atton.

My parents first met at a mutual friend's twenty-first birthday party in St Albans and for my father at least – who recalled declaring to friends that he had just seen the girl he was going to marry – it was love at first sight. For her part, my mother, Margery, remembers her first encounter with her future husband in rather less starry-eyed terms than he: 'Alleyne said he would give me a box of chocolates if I spelt his name correctly and I did. From then on presents kept arriving, from pheasants to a doll which he had won in a raffle by correctly naming it Margery.'

I barely remember Granny Wilson, my mother's mother, who died just after we moved to South Lawn, but her father, William – Grandpa Wilson – would sometimes come to stay with us. Through my childhood eyes I remember an extremely tall and very sporty man; it seemed to me that he played golf all the time. He was quite hearty and always wanted us to go on walks, but I wasn't very keen on walking anywhere unless there was motive, like blackberry picking. When I was young, walking for walking's own sake was to be avoided if at all possible. Grandpa Wilson wasn't keen on small, rowdy children and I remember he would reward whichever of us was the best behaved at the breakfast table with the first spoonful from the lid of his boiled egg.

As well as my grandfathers, my parents' maiden aunts often came to stay. There were quite a lot of these middle-aged, unmarried ladies in my family, and they always seemed to come in pairs. On my father's side there was Gertie Hawes (my godmother), who lived with Anne, and Mabel, who lived with Winifred; I believe these four were all cousins and worked as teachers. There were three more maiden aunts on my mother's side but I'm afraid I can only remember the name of Reebie, who also worked as a teacher while the other two stayed at home to keep the house and look after her, as they would have done a husband.

Whenever a pair of aunts came to stay they would take us for walks and play snakes and ladders or cards with us. I don't remember them being stern or unapproachable, but they weren't warm and cuddly either. They were just . . . nice. And, to a tomboy like myself, a little bit boring.

In 1929, my parents were married in Manchester Cathedral

and three years later they settled in Bath, where Dad became partner at a surveying firm called Powell and Company based in the back of an old post office on George Street. The early thirties was a bleak time for Britain: the Slump saw profits plunge and unemployment skyrocket as the effects of America's Great Depression spread worldwide. There wasn't much money about and people weren't buying houses, so Powell and Company were struggling, but under Dad's leadership over the following years the business would flourish and eventually became a successful estate agency, valuation and auctioneering firm called Berry, Powell and Shackell. At the age of eighty-five he was still going to his office on most days, in his words, 'occasionally to advise, but mostly for a cup of coffee'.

By the time I was old enough to remember it, Dad's company had taken over the whole of the old post office. It was a big operation that employed around forty people (all of whom used to come to our house for a Christmas party every year, for which Mum would do all the catering). Dad's office was on the first floor at the top of an awfully long flight of slate stairs and I can see him in there now, working away at his imposing antique partners' desk, the wall directly behind him covered in framed family photos. There were numerous other offices arranged over several floors and at the top were the living quarters of the housekeeper and her caretaker husband. My favourite place to visit, however, was a tiny, narrow room at the back of the building that smelled of sawdust and glue. Along with all its other services, Dad's firm also sold furniture and so there were a number of craftsmen based at the Old Post Office, including Mr Maynard, who was a carpenter. I used to love going to that little room to watch him at work while I was waiting for Mum or Dad to finish whatever they were doing. Mr Maynard always kept a can of runny glue (that reminded me of golden syrup) sitting in a bucket of water on the side and would give me off-cuts of wood to stick together to make little boats and shapes. He was such a dear man and a wonderful craftsman. Every Christmas he would make a piece of furniture as a present for my mother; I remember one year he made a beautiful tray with a hand-painted surround. It sat on her dressing table for years, but I'm sorry to say I have no idea where it is now.

Perhaps as a result of his own difficult childhood, my father absolutely adored my mother. Not that he was particularly demonstrative – especially in front of us children – but he never liked to leave Mum's side. He was passionately possessive of her; she had been a keen amateur actress when she was young, playing leading roles in musical comedies at the Manchester Opera House and Prince's Theatre, but as soon as they were engaged my father immediately put a stop to it, wanting to keep her all to himself. In 1951, Dad was invited on a three-week trip to America as part of his mayoral duties to open the Pump Room in Chicago's Ambassador Hotel (named after the famous Pump Room in Bath), but he told them he never went anywhere without his wife – and, to my mother's incredulous delight, they agreed to pay for her to go too!

By Dad's own account, this was an incredibly lavish trip during which he was deemed an important enough guest to appear on TV chat shows, be ferried around by Rolls Royce and attended by the President's own bodyguard. He wrote in his memoirs: 'We found ourselves in one of the old piston planes on our journey to the United States where we were treated like royalty, taken into the cockpit, went downstairs for drinks and went to bed in sheets . . . The highlight of our visit was a special affair called "Two Hundred Years Late for

Lunch". Millionaires only were invited and everybody was issued with eighteenth-century costume. All the plate, mugs, cutlery, etc., were in gold. During lunch an enormous pigeon pie was brought in which, when opened up, released a bevy of white pigeons which flew around the room and the guests made efforts to catch them in the nets provided.' I can't imagine Americans going to such a special effort for the mayor of Bath today!

If Dad was the head of our household, my mother was its heart. A slim and very beautiful woman, she was the one who I'd go to if my brothers were beating me up, or I'd been scared by a creaking floorboard at bedtime. I can vividly remember that wonderful feeling of security and content-ment at being tucked up in bed listening to Mum reading *Peter Rabbit* to me: 'Once upon a time there were four little rabbits, and their names were Flopsy, Mopsy, Cottontail and Peter . . .'

Mum was always beautifully turned out, even in wartime when clothes were rationed along with everything else. She refused to wear flat shoes to her dying day, which annoyed me immensely as she grew older because I was so afraid of her falling. I would take her shoe shopping and pick out a really pretty pair of flats, but she would always insist on heels, which I'm sure you can appreciate wasn't entirely sensible at the age of 105! Along with her pride in her own appearance, she always made sure that the house was looking the best it could too. Although my own domestic standards aren't quite as exacting, like Mum I can't bear a house without fresh flowers in it and I wouldn't dream of getting out of a bed without making it soon after.

My mother was always busy. On Fridays she worked in my father's office, doing the staff wages, otherwise she was looking after us – and, of course, a large part of her time was spent in the kitchen. There were few gadgets in those days – mincers, sharp knives and that was about it – so a lot of work went into preparing meals. My mother wasn't a cook by trade, but we always had home-cooked everything. I was a chubby child because Mum made such good meals: boiled salt beef and carrots, steak and kidney, and hot ham with mustard sauce. From a young age I enjoyed helping her in the kitchen: chopping vegetables, laying the table, mincing orange and lemon peel for the marmalade. Nowadays when I have that first, fresh taste of my new season's marmalade it always takes me back to the days of Mum making her own. Before she got started, she would always spread out sheets of news-paper to protect the table and would usually get distracted by a story on one of the sheets and end up reading the whole thing. I remember Dad teasing her, saying, 'It always takes your mother far longer than it should to make jam because she has to catch up on last week's news first.'

Mum ran a tight ship. Bedtimes were strict and non-negotiable, and every meal was taken at the dining-room table with all of us together (apart from Dad's breakfast-in-bed period) with my father, as leader of the family, always served first. She would never dream of eating in the kitchen – and would certainly never eat on the hoof. One of the changes to society that I think is a huge sadness is that more families don't eat their meals together these days. It's very important to enjoy food together as a family. When you all sit round the table and children's tummies are full, they feel content and relaxed enough to talk to you about their lives; you miss out on those special moments if you're eating in front of the television. I appreciate that it isn't always possible because we're all so busy, but Friday night or Sunday lunchtime should be designated as a time to have a meal together, as it can be the only opportunity in the whole week you have to sit down together and talk. Without this, it's no wonder families break down. As you can probably tell, this is something I feel very strongly about, and I was heartened to see that Chris Evans, who I think is a wonderful man, and great on the radio in the morning for cheering the day, recently dedicated his newspaper column to this very subject. He wrote: 'Dining room or not, we need to maintain the tradition of having dinner properly: opposite each other, not in front of the telly (at least, not too often). My wife and I make a point of doing this at least five times a week.' Well said, Mr Evans!

While Dad might not have been the most affectionate of parents, he was wonderful at doing things with us. A hugely practical man, he always had a hobby; if he wasn't working he was busy building or creating. One summer he built a rowing boat and I remember watching him steaming the timbers so they were pliable enough to be bent into shape for the hull. We kept the boat on the river just outside Bath and would go out on it every weekend, taking a packed lunch and a Primus stove so we could boil the kettle for tea. In order to get the Primus going you had to use a little gadget – a sort of fine wire with a small handle that we referred to as the 'pricker' – to clear the hole that the gas came out through. This was frequently lost, amid much bad language from Dad. That was great entertainment.

Photography was Dad's great love: he had a real talent and took some wonderful pictures, although it's a shame that because he was usually behind the camera, he doesn't feature in many of them. Our family outings were regularly punctuated by Dad herding us into a group, saying, 'For goodness sake smile, you lot!'

Some years ago I was shopping for a birthday card and as I looked along the racks in the High Wycombe branch of John Lewis I was amazed to see a very familiar image. It was a black-and-white picture of a woman crouched on a beach with a makeshift see-saw on her back, on either end of which sat a laughing boy and a very chubby, giggly little girl in a knitted swimsuit. I recognized it instantly, because it was a photo my father had taken of my mother, Roger and I on the beach at Tenby, which had subsequently won first prize in the *Daily Mirror*'s Photograph of the Year competition in 1938. The prize was £100, quite a lot of money in those days, and Dad was delighted. Mirror Group Newspapers owns the copyright of the photo, but I still have the original framed in my kitchen and it brings back such happy memories every time I look at it.

Sunny-side up: Dad's award-winning photo.

We always had assorted pets because Dad absolutely adored animals. I think it was animals before children, really! Dad was Secretary of the Bath RSPCA – his father before him was Chairman of the Hull branch – and it was quite a part of his life. First thing every morning he would draw up a list of jobs for the day, which the uniformed RSPCA inspector would then come to his office on George Street to collect, and on Saturdays I would usually go with him to the kennels at Claverton Down (which he designed himself and are still there) to check on how the strays were being cared for. At home there was usually a stray cat or two, and we always had a dachshund. Rupert was the first; I remember Dad setting off on his motorbike for work every morning – in wartime there was no petrol for a car – and as he roared off this little dog would be tucked inside his Harris Tweed jacket with just his head poking out, the bottom two buttons done up to keep him secure. Rupert was extremely well behaved and whenever any clients came into Dad's office he would always wait at the top of the long flight of stairs in his basket and wouldn't come down until it was time for Dad or one of the secretaries to take him out. Dad always came home for lunch, and would take Rupert back with him then.

Later we had a miniature dachshund that had back problems and lost the use of its hind legs, so Dad bandaged its legs in old socks to protect the skin as they dragged along the floor. He then came up with the bright idea of taking the dog swimming to try and develop its muscles. As he was Bath's Chairman of Planning at the time, Dad was very involved with the city and had free access to the Roman Baths. He gave Mum the keys to the Great Bath, the magnificent central pool that was the jewel of the ancient complex – now too precious for public use – and every day she smuggled in the dachshund when no one else was around, to give it swimming lessons. Under the gaze of the statues of Roman Emperors and Governors that lined the historic hot pool, our little dog would furiously paddle away in the warm water until gradually it regained use of its legs and started to walk again.

# GINGER AND TREACLE SPICED TRAYBAKE

My mother used to make a version of this cake when we were growing up and it is still one of my favourites today. Treacle can be difficult to weigh accurately as it tends to stick to the scale pan. Weighing the treacle on top of the sugar overcomes this problem. This traybake freezes very well un-iced and in fact it improves with freezing.

*Makes about 15–20 slices*

- 225g (8 oz) soft unsalted butter or baking spread
- 175g (6 oz) light muscovado sugar
- 200g (7 oz) black treacle
- 275g (10 oz) self-raising flour
- 2 level teaspoons baking powder
- 1 teaspoon ground mixed spice
- 1 teaspoon ground allspice
- 4 large eggs
- 4 tablespoons milk
- 3 bulbs of stem ginger from a jar, chopped finely

### for the icing
- 75g (3 oz) icing sugar, sieved
- about 3 tablespoons stem ginger syrup from the jar
- 3 bulbs of stem ginger from a jar, chopped finely

Preheat the oven to 160°C/Fan 140°C/Gas 3. Cut a rectangle of non-stick baking parchment to fit the base and sides of a 30 x 23 x 4cm (12 x 9 x 1½ inches) traybake tin or roasting tin. Grease the tin and then line with the paper, pushing it neatly into the corners of the tin.

Measure all the ingredients for the traybake into a large bowl and beat for about 2 minutes until well blended. A hand-held electric mixer is best for this but, of course, you can also mix it by hand with a wooden spoon.

Turn the mixture into the prepared tin, scraping the sides of the bowl with a plastic spatula to remove it all. Level the top gently with the back of the spatula.

Bake in the preheated oven for about 35–40 minutes until the traybake springs back when pressed lightly with a finger in the centre and is beginning to shrink away from the sides of the tin. Allow it to cool a little, then remove the cake by easing the paper away from the sides of the tin. Turn on to a cooling rack, remove the lining paper and leave to cool completely.

To make the icing: mix the icing sugar and syrup together in a small bowl until smooth and of a spreading consistency. Pour the icing over the cake, spread gently to the edges with a small palette knife and sprinkle with the chopped stem ginger to decorate. Allow the icing to set before slicing the traybake to serve.

## 2

My early childhood years, from the ages of four to ten, were set against the backdrop of the Second World War, the start of which coincided with the birth of my brother William in 1939. But while the adults in my family must have been fearful over our country's uncertain future, the war barely encroached on day-to-day life in my own happy, secure little world. There were occasional air-raid sirens that would send us scurrying under the kitchen table or later into the air-raid shelter that Dad had built in the garden, but to me this felt more like a game. Our air-raid shelter at Park Lane looked like a giant molehill and had steps leading down to a small chamber with just enough room to fit beds for us children. The roof leaked, so whatever the weather it was always cold and wet when you were inside. When the siren sounded we would be wrenched from our beds, swaddled in layers of clothing and then hurried through the darkness to the shelter. You'd lie beneath the scratchy blankets, the dank wet-earth smell almost heavy enough to taste, listening to the muffled wail of sirens and the zoooooooom of aeroplanes overhead. Nowadays if I hear those sounds on a film or television programme I am instantly transported back to my childhood, but it doesn't stir up a feeling of fear, rather a sort of nostalgia, a sense of: yes, I remember that. I was never the least bit scared when we went down to the shelter, it was actually rather fun. As long as your mother and father were there too you felt perfectly safe;

I was far more troubled by the damp than I was the German bombers.

The sirens always turned out to be false alarms until the night of 25th April 1942, when many hundreds of bombs and countless incendiary devices rained down on Bath for two nights as part of Hitler's 'Baedeker' raids on British cultural centres, which were a reprisal for the RAF bombing of the German port of Lübeck a month earlier. By this time we were living at South Lawn, where there was no need for an air-raid shelter as we could just go down to the cellar. Again, I don't remember feeling at all frightened, but my mother must have been frantic with worry – not least because my father was out on the streets during both nights of the Bath Blitz. At the start of the war he had been thirty-five, too old for the army, but everyone was expected to undertake some form of voluntary service so he joined the Special Constabulary. He was responsible for going out at night, checking for fires and making sure people had blackout material up in their windows, and by chance he was on duty during the Blitz. He described those terrifying nights in his memoirs: 'I was seconded to the main control room in Weston Park and the first bomb fell in the grounds, smashing all the windows and destroying the telephone. The Chief Constable, as controller, was therefore cut off from the whole city and he ordered me to go out and see what the conditions were. I can tell you I have seldom been more afraid in my life. With bombs falling I took my car round and found that destruction was mainly confined to residential property . . . I called on my family to make sure they were safe and found them cowering in the basement. The bombing was again very acute on the following evening and 400 people at least were killed by machine-gun bullets from the planes as well as the bombs.'

South Lawn, where I grew up.

When we eventually emerged from the cellar I remember seeing shards of shattered glass all over the floor from where our windows had been blown out by the force of the explosions, and when we ventured outside there were craters and holes all over the road. Having been blithely unaware of what was going on while we had been in the cellar, it was a huge shock to me. Official figures show that 900 buildings were completely destroyed and another 12,500 were damaged during those two nights. It was the first moment that I had any inkling of the true horror of war.

After the Blitz two of Dad's employees, Mr Kelly and Mr Bailey, came to live with us at South Lawn with their families because their homes had been damaged, so for a while the three families were all squashed up together. I remember all the women working together in the kitchen to feed the many mouths. My father's business owned a furniture depository and that too had been bombed, so temporary homes had to be found for all the contents. We had a huge second drawing room at South Lawn that was given over to storing pianos from the damaged warehouse; there must have been at least thirty in there. The piano room, as it was thereafter known, was always kept locked, but my brothers and I often managed to sneak in and would spend many happy hours running in and out and over the tops of the pianos.

Shortly after the Bath Blitz it was decided that we children should get out of the city, as nobody had any idea if the bombers would make a return sortie, and so my parents sent me to stay with my second godmother and her husband in their new home in Trowbridge, just outside the city. My god-mother's name was Auntie Peter. I'm not sure what she was christened, but in the thirties it was the fashion for avant-garde ladies to call themselves by men's names. My memory is of a slim, very elegantly dressed woman with a fox-fur stole draped around her neck, the creature's little beady-eyed head still dangling from one end and its tail from the other.

Before the war I didn't see a lot of Auntie Peter, but always looked forward to her visits since she would occasionally come bearing presents. I can still remember my delight when, at the age of five, she presented me with the most beautiful pale yellow party dress, smocked in voile with a little spray of silk primroses and violets tied at the sash. Clothes were on ration when I was young: I had my school uniform, a set of clothes for best and the rest of the time it was woolly Fair Isle jumpers and grey serge skirts or hand-me-downs from my big brother Roger. So to have this brand new dress was just wonderful! I thought I was the bee's knees, and have had an absolute thing for primroses ever since. As I grew older, Auntie Peter would mark my birthday by giving me the same number of thrupenny bits as years I had reached, so I would get eight of the octagonal brass coins on my eighth birthday and so forth.

One morning, a few days after the Bath Blitz, Auntie Peter came to collect me in what we children called her 'blowy car', a Morris Eight convertible. (Goodness knows how she got the petrol, as that too was strictly rationed during the war.) As we drove off, my hair whipping about my face, I thought it was all terribly exciting. I was seven and it was my first time away from home on my own; young children never really had sleepovers in those days. But a few miles into the journey the road – known locally as Sally in the Woods – plunged into a tunnel of trees, the branches arching over and blocking out the light, and as we sped into the sudden darkness it occurred to me: 'I'm going away from home and I don't know when I'll be coming back.' I felt alone and a little scared, feelings that intensified when I walked through the front door of Auntie Peter's house to be greeted by a full-sized tiger-skin rug complete with head, the poor beast's jaws stretched open menacingly wide. For a small child with an active imagination, away from her parents for the first time, gosh, it really was the stuff of nightmares!

Auntie Peter was kind, but very strict. In my late teens her husband, Uncle Bill, became principal of Harper Adams agricultural college in Shropshire and to my delight I would be invited to the end-of-term balls. However, Auntie Peter would spend the whole evening watching me with eyes as beady as those on her fox-fur stole to check I didn't get up to mischief – and would then march me back to the house the moment the ball was over.

As food was strictly rationed during the war and my father refused to get anything on the black market, my parents transformed our garden at South Lawn into a model of self-sufficiency. Dad turned the grass and flower beds over to growing fruit and vegetables, and we kept pigs for meat and goats for the milk. Some of Mum's friends were really quite sniffy about the fact that we drank goat's milk at home, as it was thought to be something that people in foreign countries did, but with milk rations limited to just two or three pints a week it proved invaluable. Mum would let the goat's milk sit and then skim the cream off the top, which she would put in a jar and keep shaking vigorously until it formed butter, which was a great bonus – although you got very little butter from a quarter of a pint of cream. The pig would be fattened and then taken for slaughter, after which Dad would bring it home to butcher. I assume we must have shared the meat amongst our neighbours or sold it to the local butchers, as there were no freezers in those days.

Offal was one of the few things not to be rationed, so we ate a great deal of it. Mum was very good at doing delicious things with the bits of animals that people usually ignore these days, like tongue, kidneys and oxtail. I think it's a shame people don't eat more ox tongue, as it's really very simple to prepare: you simmer it for three or four hours until tender, then skin it, cut it in half and press it into a six-inch round cake tin, put some weights on top and let it go cold. It's very cheap, very delicious and everybody will love it. My particular favourite, though, were sweetbreads, and I remember asking Mum to cook them for me even when I was married. She would toss sweetbreads in seasoned flour and fry them, or serve them in a creamy sauce. During the war we would still have a Sunday roast, but it would be a cheaper cut like a shoulder of lamb. To this day I never buy a leg of lamb as I think the shoulder has more flavour, but I cook it for much longer than my mother did. Back then she wouldn't have wanted to keep the oven on for too long, as that would have been an extravagance. Economy was so much part of the household routine: I can remember being endlessly ticked off for not turning off the lights after leaving a room, and, of course, every scrap of leftover food was scrupulously used up. You'd start with a joint of meat, then you'd have cold meat, then mince and the bones would be used for stock that would then be turned into soup, so you could get almost a week of meals from just one joint. We would eat whatever vegetables were in season in the garden, be that sprouts, cabbage or carrots, and Dad bought a canning machine so we could preserve any surplus. Mum would layer runner beans with salt in a stone jar to keep them fresh, then you would just rinse off the salt when you were ready to eat them. I didn't like them so much, though, because they would still be very salty!

As sugar was in particularly short supply, Mum sat us all down at the start of rationing and said: 'There won't be any cakes or puddings if you don't give up sugar in your tea.' We didn't need telling twice! She would save up our sugar ration and once a week we would be able to have a pudding. It would usually be on a Saturday; we would gather round to watch it come out of the oven and breathe in those wonderful baked aromas. It was such a treat. Bread and Butter Pudding was a particular favourite – and, conveniently, an ideal way to use up leftover stale bread – and a few years later when I spent some time in France and wanted to cook the family a typical English dish it was Mum's Bread and Butter Pudding that I made them, and they thought it was wonderful.

To make the most of our rations, Mum would bake things that didn't use much sugar such as Rock Cakes, which are just flour, a little butter, raisins and not much else. In those days raisins always came with the seeds still in them and our local grocer had a machine – it looked like a revolving cylinder lined with spikes – to remove them. You would pour the raisins in the top and they would come out the bottom, a little squished but seedless nonetheless.

My mother became quite slim during the war, because she'd always give herself smaller portions to make sure there was enough for the rest of us and so we never felt at all deprived. Every Saturday we would visit Mr Maynard's sweet shop on Lansdown Hill to choose our weekly ration of sweets, which we'd then scrupulously share out into piles. If one of us wasn't able to go on our weekly outing – say Roger was playing in a school rugby match, for instance – then your siblings would choose the sweets for you, and that always ended up in a bit of a rowdy debate. You can imagine how it would go: 'What do you mean, you chose humbugs? You know I don't like humbugs!'

Going to see Mr Maynard in his sweet shop was an absolute ritual and a much-anticipated weekly outing. Callard & Bowser Toffees were a particular favourite of mine. I honestly think we had more sweets during rationing than we did after it was over! In fact, it wasn't until after the war had ended that we realized how fortunate we had been. Bath had close links with Alkmaar in Holland; there was a civil exchange programme that, as a councillor, my father was very much part of. My parents became life-long friends with a number of Dutch families, including one called the DeWolfe-Beerbohms who would come to stay with us in Bath – and us with them in Alkmaar. When they talked about the war they explained how they never had enough to eat. We would listen in horror as they told us about people eating tulip bulbs because food was so scarce – and this was quite a wealthy family! It was shocking to hear their stories of having starving children from the town to stay for a week at a time to feed them up. Until that point, secure in our little bubble, we really had no idea that people in other countries had suffered so much during the war.

In later years we would visit Holland as well, but our family holidays were usually spent at the seaside in places like Devon, Cornwall and Tenby in Wales. We would take a cottage (it would never have entered anyone's head to go to a hotel) or stay on a farm. I remember one particularly blissful holiday in Cornwall, where this wonderful farmer's wife would give us clotted cream and marmalade for breakfast. We would spend the day on the beach and then as soon as we got back we would help on the farm. There would often be other families staying on the farm as well and those children might not want to get dirty, but the three of us would be out there feeding the cows or helping to catch the horses until it was time for high tea around seven o'clock, when you would sit down to a Shepherd's Pie or Beef Stew. They were such happy times, filled with laughter, ice cream and sunshine; in my memory it never rained once when we were on holiday.

The first time I ever went to a hotel was just after the war ended, at the age of eleven, when Dad took us all up to London and we stayed for three nights at the Cumberland Hotel near Marble Arch. It was a magical trip: we went to the Houses of Parliament, to the theatre to see *The Mousetrap* and we visited Harrods – not to buy anything, just to stare at the wonderful displays and, the biggest thrill of all, to ride the escalator. I'd never even seen one before, but here there were seven floors of them! I think the most exciting part of the trip for my brothers and I was staying in the hotel. Being able to pick up the phone in our own room, to run down those wondrously long carpeted corridors and ride up and down in the lift, taking turns to press the buttons. And every morning, going down to breakfast in a posh room filled with chandeliers and black-suited waiters! It was so exciting.

When I was twelve, we went to France to visit chateau country, travelling around and staying in village hotels en route. We went to Versailles, to Tours – a glittering succession of chateaux, each one more magnificent than the last. I have some very vivid memories of this holiday, although they have little to do with sightseeing; in fact by the end we never wanted to see another chateau ever again – not that we would ever have dreamt of saying so to our parents! No, my memories are rather more prosaic. There was the time I walked out of our hotel to be hit by the smell of drains, which in those days was pretty common in rural areas as the sewers outside the large towns weren't quite up to scratch. Another memory is of the strap breaking on my shoe and my father telling me, 'There's a shoemaker down the road – take it to him to be repaired.' I remember my nervousness as I wandered around this strange village, trying to remember the French word for 'cobbler' and wishing I'd paid more attention at school. (I found the place in the end and asked, in halting schoolgirl French, something like: '*S'il vous plaît, vous recommendez mon soulliere? Il est kaput.*' Not exactly textbook, but I got my shoe fixed and felt very proud for managing it on my own.) But for me, the real revelation of this holiday was the French food. I'd never tasted anything like it. We weren't staying in luxurious hotels – these would be little places in tiny villages, with room only for a few guests – but Madame would produce plate after plate of the most beautiful food. Mealtimes were just so exciting. There would be wonderful casseroles served with *pomme purée*, so smooth and buttery and luxurious and nothing like the mash we had at home, which was just squashed potatoes with milk, pepper and salt. Very often we would have a tomato salad for the first course, which we thought was really very odd, but absolutely loved it. At some places there would be delicious puddings, in others it would be a choice of fruit – *'pêche, poire ou abricot?'* – and the fruit was always so fresh and bursting with flavour that we didn't really miss dessert. My father always used to admire the way French restaurant tables would be covered with a sheet of white or checked paper instead of a cloth, as it meant you always ate off a clean one. 'Why don't they do that in England?' he'd say – although I think Mum would have preferred a nice linen cloth!

When we set out for the day we would often be given a picnic, but this had little in common with English packed lunches. There would be a big box filled with pies, charcuterie, a melon that had been cut up and meticulously assembled into a whole again – so many wonderful and delicious things that we couldn't wait for lunchtime. It was such a revelation to me and really sparked my interest in cooking and ingredients. I think that holiday probably marked my awakening to the amazing potential of food.

I was only ten years old when the war ended, but I can remember VE Day very well. There were flags everywhere – rather like last year's Diamond Jubilee celebrations, except in those days you couldn't buy the bunting so you had to make your own – and even at that young age I was very aware of a tremendous feeling of joy and relief on the streets. We had a family tea party at South Lawn, with a table laid outside covered by a lace cloth with the best china and all sorts of cakes and treats. I still have a photo of us all sitting outside together: Auntie Peter and her husband are there too, and

I'm wearing a triangular hat made out of newspaper and a dress instead of my usual scruffy shorts. We hadn't celebrated anything for years and it was just so exciting and jubilant.

Cutting the victory cake: VE Day tea with the family and Auntie Peter.

My parents were very sociable and loved entertaining. South Lawn was quite a sizeable house and they would throw the most wonderful parties and fill the place with people. Before the big night, Dad would issue each guest with secret instructions: he might tell one to paint one of their finger-nails red, another to wear glasses with one of the lenses popped out or to come wearing odd shoes. Then, as every-one arrived, all the guests had to go round and try to work out what thing was different about each person. It was a very clever way to break the ice and encourage everyone to get to know each other. As the night went on, Dad would arrange all sorts of quizzes, charades and wonderful games, while Mum would play the piano. Of course, we were all supposed to be in bed, but we would sometimes sneak out of our rooms and sit hidden in darkness at the top of the stairs to watch what was going on. It was very exciting to peek through the banisters at the brightly lit scene below and see all the grown-ups dressed in their finery. Occasionally, if we thought we could get away with it, we would even tiptoe downstairs and scurry around between the guests, trying to sneak something to eat from the enticing-looking plates before we were caught.

My parents' socializing stepped up a gear during the year that my father was mayor. With the mayoral salary just £600, out of which the candidate was supposed to cover all their expenses ('and all past mayors had grumbled that the mayorship had ended up costing them a lot of money,' Dad noted) my mother was put in charge of organizing the numerous social functions that came with the post – and I would often be on hand to help.

'When Alleyne became Mayor he told me he intended to entertain many modestly rather than lavishly to a few,' Mum remembered. 'I was given a ration of tea and margarine for guests in the parlour. In those days there were few glasses as stock-in-trade, and no linen, silver or china. With the aid of two parlourmaids, I held endless tea-parties and coffee mornings.'

My mother was a keen card player and would often organize bridge evenings with our neighbours the Dakins and Auntie Peter and Uncle Bill. Dad would be wearing a jacket and tie and Mum would be in a dress; I thought it was all terribly glamorous. On these occasions the food was almost as important as the game itself. I'd watch Mum preparing it in the afternoon, laying everything out on beautiful lace cloths: there would be tiny 'bridge rolls' (finger-shaped bread rolls) filled with egg and cress, sandwiches, slices of cake and whole bananas dipped in chocolate with chopped pistachio nuts sprinkled across the middle. I've been trying to recreate those ever since, but the wetness of the banana always makes the chocolate slide off so I've never quite succeeded!

On our birthdays we would have a party at home for all our school friends, with musical chairs, ring-a-roses and a treasure hunt in the garden, and there would be a wonderful tea with sandwiches, biscuits and a candle-decked birthday cake: a Victoria Sandwich with your name and age iced on the top. A special treat on birthdays, however, was my mother's chocolate crispies. These weren't at all unusual – they're still a staple of children's parties today – but I remember them in particular because there was a bit of a ritual to making them. My mother would mix the cornflakes with melted chocolate then split open the waxed paper bag from inside the cereal box, spread it on a tray and spoon the chocolate-coated cornflakes into mounds on top of that. It wouldn't work these days, because the bags inside cereal boxes are now made of polythene rather than waxed paper, but back then it was yet another way to make sure nothing went to waste.

Although food wasn't endlessly discussed in the way it is today, being viewed in a more functional light, special occasions were still always marked with particular dishes – and helping my mother to prepare these was almost as exciting as the celebration itself. Every November she would make the Christmas cake and puddings and we'd stir the spice- and citrus-scented mixture with great excitement because it meant the countdown had begun. As the big day approached we would all decorate the house together, arranging branches of holly on sideboards and over mantelpieces and making paper chains, doily angels and snowflakes for the tree. Then, on Christmas Eve, Mum would make her Fish Pie for supper – a tradition I continue in our family to this day.

When you woke on Christmas morning, the first thing you would do was to scramble down to the end of your bed to retrieve your stocking. I made stockings for all of my children and if they are home for Christmas I still use them! By today's standards, when children seem to be given everything they have asked for over the previous six months, the contents of my childhood stocking were very modest: a stick of rock, small sweets, some little games and puzzles of the sort you'd find in a cracker today and, at the bottom, a tangerine in the toe.

As much as my parents enjoyed entertaining, on Christmas Day it was usually just the five of us, perhaps with one other guest – who Mum used to fondly refer to as our 'Lame Duck'. This would be someone who otherwise would have been on their own for Christmas, such as Miss Clayton, an elderly lady who lived in The Manor, the big house next door to ours. Later on Mum started a group called the Friends of the Royal United Hospital and became very friendly with the hospital's Matron, who also lived on her own. She was a lovely, round, sensible lady called Jenny Burgess, and Dad was also particularly fond of her. On Christmas morning once she had finished her ward rounds and wished all the patients a Merry Christmas he would go to pick her up from the hospital and then she'd spend the rest of the day with us.

We always had a bird for lunch – it wasn't usually turkey, but often a capon – stuffed with my mother's lemon-and-thyme sausagemeat stuffing (again, something I still make today) and served with sprouts, roast potatoes and leeks in parsley sauce. When lunch was finished we would all gather around the radio to listen to the Queen and then – finally! – we were allowed to open our presents from under the tree. The first Christmas present that I remember really well was a pair of fur-backed leather gloves that I was given when I was nine. I'm not sure why, but when I opened them I was so thrilled that I burst into tears – although I do get very cold, so perhaps I was just glad to have warm hands for once! A couple of years later I was lucky enough to receive something even better than the gloves: a pony, which I called Susan.

As a child, I lived and breathed ponies. We had stables at home in South Lawn and rented a field just below Lansdown Crescent, where I would spend hours going around the jumps that I had set up. On Christmas Day I would always have to excuse myself from the celebrations to give my pony her own 'Christmas lunch' of a carrot or apple. I adored Susan, a pretty bay, but she was small and stubborn and not very suitable for the gymkhanas that I had started to enter, so then my father bought me Kerry Lass, who was already well trained for showjumping.

Together we entered all the local gymkhanas and did quite well, winning plenty of rosettes. The first prize was always a pound, and, as it cost a pound to get four horse shoes fitted, on the whole I could pay for any shoeing from my winnings. You hacked everywhere – none of this horse-boxing to and fro – and I'd think nothing of hacking five miles to the blacksmith in Kelston or nearly ten miles to a gymkhana in Peasedown St John.

When I was fifteen, I begged my parents to let me go to Pony Camp, run by Beaufort Pony Club at the Highgrove estate in Gloucestershire, which nowadays of course is the Prince of Wales' private residence but back then was owned by the Morgan Jones family. Despite its name, Pony Camp wasn't residential – you would attend classes with your pony during the day and then go home at night – but we lived a good thirty miles from Highgrove and it would have been impossible for me to hack there and back every day. My parents asked the Morgan Jones family if it would be possible for me to camp in the grounds for the week. All highly irregular, but thankfully they agreed and so, together with my friend Lizzy Dobbs (whose mother was in charge of Bath Pony Club), we pitched a tent on the front lawn of Highgrove. The Morgan Jones family were very welcoming to us and it was a wonderful week: a cross-country course had been set up for us and we learnt dressage. I have no idea what Lizzy and I did for food – we must have had a little stove with us – and as far as I remember there were no washing facilities, since nobody had been expecting campers. I think Mrs Morgan Jones must have felt sorry for us in our little tent, as one day she invited us into the house to get cleaned up. 'You must come and have a bath,' she said. I remember it so clearly because it was one of those huge baths that instead of a plughole had a central brass column with a handle at the top that you'd turn one way to let out the water and the other to keep it in, so you could drain the bath without getting your sleeves wet. I often think about that enormous bath, and wonder if Prince Charles still uses it today!

# MY MOTHER'S BREAD AND BUTTER PUDDING

This is a great family favourite as a pudding following a weekend lunch. I have to admit the recipe is not economical, just delicious! Ideally use a rectangular dish simply because the bread fits it better. If you are not keen on sultanas, you can easily leave them out.

*Serves 6–8*

- 150g (5 oz) mixed sultanas and raisins
- 75g (3 oz) caster sugar
- grated rind of 1 lemon
- ½ teaspoon mixed spice
- 8 thin slices white bread, crusts removed
- 100 g (4 oz) butter, melted

### for the custard
- 2 large eggs
- 300ml (½ pint) double cream
- 150 ml (¼ pint) milk
- 2 tablespoons demerara sugar

You will need an ovenproof dish of about 1½–1¾ litres (2½–3 pints) or 18 x 23 x 5cm (7 x 9 x 2 inches). Use some of the melted butter to grease the dish.

Preheat the oven to 180°C/Fan 160°C/Gas 4.

Combine the dried fruit, sugar, lemon rind and spice together in a bowl and toss to mix well.

Cut each bread slice into 3 strips. Take sufficient strips to cover the base of the dish and dip one side of each in turn in the melted butter. Lay the strips in the dish, buttered-side down. Sprinkle with half the dried fruit mixture. Repeat the dipping and layering, but this time laying the bread strips buttered-side up. Sprinkle over the remaining dried fruit. Lay the third and final layer of bread strips on top, buttered-side up.

Beat together the eggs, cream and milk in a bowl and pour over the pudding. Sprinkle with the demerara sugar, then leave to stand for about 1 hour if time allows.

Bake in the preheated oven for about 30–40 minutes, or until the top is golden brown and crisp and the pudding slightly puffed up. Serve hot, although there are some who insist that it is delicious cold!

## 3

They say your schooldays are the happiest of your life, but for me quite the opposite was true. While my brothers were packed off to public school, I went to Bath High School, an independent day school for girls on Lansdown Road, a short walk from our home, and from the very start I absolutely hated it. Every morning I would dress in the smart school uniform of a navy skirt, green jumper and striped tie as slowly as possible, with a heavy heart at the prospect of the day ahead. I wasn't in the least bit academic and had absolutely no interest in sitting in a classroom with my head in a book. At the beginning of each term, I would try to get the desk right at the back of class by the window so I could see what was going on outside and where, with any luck, I would avoid the teacher's eye and avoid getting asked any questions. At least the food at school wasn't too awful, although they used to slice the meat cold and then heat it up in gravy, so it was always grey.

In my early years at the school the only subject I enjoyed – and consequently put any effort into – was PE. While I regarded most teachers as The Enemy, I liked the games mistress, Miss Bolton, who would let us play Shipwreck at the end of each term (where you set out all the gym equipment and have to get from one end of the hall to the other without touching the floor). Miss Bolton, who is still alive today, was also the leader of our Girl Guide troop and I remember how thrilled I was when she made me Patrol Leader of the Kingfishers, because she was the first teacher to look beyond my disastrous academic performance and entrust me with a position of responsibility. (I had tea with Miss Bolton recently and she told me that the school's headmistress Miss Blackburn never once came to watch a single sports game.) But all in all, during my school days I felt pretty inadequate. My brothers weren't particularly academic either and I know our lack of success at school frustrated Dad tremendously. Over the years he had sailed through all his exams without any effort, both at school and in his career, and he just couldn't understand why his children were struggling. Mum was far less strict with us, but even she seemed disappointed with me at times. She was a talented musician and played the piano beautifully, but I couldn't even manage that. I used spend my piano lessons eating chocolates with the teacher!

Uninterested in Maths or English and uninspired by the teachers, I put all my energies into being a real monkey. I never did anything terribly bad, but I was rowdy and untidy, always late for class and rarely finished my homework. For me, the best time of the day was break, because that was when I could run around and get into trouble. We would always try to keep out of the way of the teachers as much as possible during break, so a group of us used to play Kick the Can in the farthest part of the school field, which basically involved booting a can over a certain distance. That was terrific fun – and very noisy!

We were never caned, but the teachers did used to get very cross with me indeed. I would often be put in detention for minor misdemeanours, which involved sitting in a classroom after school for an hour or so with any other offenders (our desks well spaced out so we couldn't try to communicate) to do pointless exercises like writing lines, while the teacher – who would also clearly rather be anywhere else than there – sat at the front reading a book. I would fill page after page with lines such as: 'Empty vessels make the most noise.' I mean, what an absolute waste of everyone's time! Why on earth didn't they get us doing something constructive, like tidying the library? Copying out lines achieved nothing and – although I would be bored out of my mind – it certainly wasn't enough of a deterrent to prevent me from misbehaving again. Far scarier was the prospect of what happened to you when you were really naughty: a visit to the headmistress's office.

From what I understand today, Miss Blackburn was a great woman who was a champion of education for girls at a time when it was still viewed as something rather frivolous. So I can only assume that she must have decided I was a lost cause from the very beginning, as in my experience she was a terrifying dragon to whom I seemed to be a constant disappointment. She certainly had no time for those of us who weren't academic, focusing instead on the brightest girls. She selected one of her favourites from our year, Mary something-or-other, to take part in a quiz programme on *Children's Hour*, and I remember listening to this girl's appearance on the radio and being astonished when she was asked the simplest of questions, something that was really just common sense and to which I knew the answer immediately, and she got it wrong, and yet she was absolutely lauded with glory by Miss Blackburn! I thought it was so unfair.

On this subject, last year I agreed to appear on the BBC1 quiz show *Celebrity Pointless* alongside my fellow *Bake Off* judge Paul Hollywood, which was a very stupid thing to do because – and this is nothing to with age – I am absolutely useless at answering quick-fire questions. But I was full of

confidence because I was with Paul, who is very knowledge-
able and never short of something to say. Anyway, when I'm
doing things like this in the public eye I'm quite fussy about
making sure that I look decent, as that gives me confidence,
and I had therefore watched an episode beforehand so I'd
know what to wear. The contestants had all been in track-
suits and homely clothes so I wore a cardigan and skirt for
our appearance on the show. But when I arrived everyone
was terribly dressed up. Our opponent Jennie Bond was
wearing the most beautiful strappy red shoes, while I looked
like I was off to cook Sunday lunch! So I felt totally inadequate from the start and Paul ended up answering all the
questions for me, more or less, until it came to the final
decisive one (something about racehorses) when he was
stumped. 'The only racehorse I know is Red Rum,' I said –
and it was the right answer, so we won the game. If only Miss
Blackburn had been alive to see it! I've learnt my lesson
though: I'm never going on another programme of that sort.
I'm no good at thinking on my feet – or doing anything else
on them either, so *Strictly Come Dancing* is out as well. Even
Ann Widdecombe is a better dancer than me.

When our school buildings were damaged during the Bath
Blitz in 1942 my first thought was: 'Brilliant, school's been
bombed!' With our classrooms reduced to rubble I had glee-
fully assumed that the school would be forced to close, but I
had underestimated Miss Blackburn, who certainly wasn't
going to let the Luftwaffe stop her girls from getting their
education. It was decided that classes would be temporarily
re-housed in the homes of school parents, among them my
own family. When I learnt that a class would be temporarily
moving into the drawing room at South Lawn I felt a little

less disappointed about the fact that school hadn't been shut down. At least I'd be able to roll out of bed late in the morning and go straight to class, and sneak off to the kitchen to raid the fridge for elevenses . . . But, of course, in the event it wasn't my class that came to South Lawn, which I remember feeling at the age of seven was quite monstrously unfair! Instead, my year was assigned to a house about a quarter of a mile away down Lansdown Hill (a fifteen-minute walk that I used to do by myself) and so my plans were thwarted and it was business as usual – albeit with a different window to stare out of for a term or so.

My great partner in crime when I was at school was Jenny Chapman; seventy years later and we're still friends today. Jenny lived in a big house called Combe Grove on the other side of Bath in Monkton Combe; I could catch the number two bus at the bottom of my road and it would take me straight there. Jenny was a very attractive, sporty girl – one of the best tennis players in the school – and, like me, was far happier running around outdoors or riding her pony than sitting inside with a book. The pair of us used to come up with some great games. Her house sat at the top of a hill with an extremely steep front path bordered by box hedges that led straight down to the road. One day, Jenny's brother David made a little cart that could be attached to the family's spaniel, Butch, and we would take turns sitting in the cart and letting the dog pull us at breakneck speed down that perilous path. Highly dangerous, but enormous fun!

I would sometimes go to stay the night with Jenny and her family (we never called them sleepovers though) and we would sit up all night talking. Jenny's father was frightfully stern, but as he was a naval officer he was often away: the Admiralty had moved the majority of their operations from

London to Bath during the war, making his office much closer to home, and so he would usually either be there or at sea. As a result, Mrs Chapman was in charge – and I thought she was wonderful. She had a special ring she called her 'Genie's Ring' that she claimed could help solve any problem. I used to love hearing her tales about how she had come by that magical ring and was always thrilled to give it a little rub and make a wish. I found her mesmerizing. Jenny phoned me the other day and said: 'Do you remember Mum's ring?' It turns out that she has kept the ring and now tells the same tales to her own grandchildren.

Such was my dislike of school that when I woke one morning in early October 1948, at the age of thirteen, complaining of a headache and sore throat, my parents immediately assumed it was an attempt to get out of class. It wouldn't have been the first time that I had tried! It soon became apparent, however, that I was genuinely ill. This was no mere sniffle: I was confined to my bed with a raging temperature and muscle aches with what looked like a bad case of 'flu. All our bedrooms at South Lawn had fireplaces, but you were only allowed a fire when you were properly ill and so when my mother lit a blaze in the little Victorian grate in the corner of the room I realized that whatever I had was serious.

As I dozed in bed, Mum and Dad sat by my bedside, nursing me and reading me stories. As ill as I was, I can clearly remember feeling really rather special that I had both my parents' full attention focused on me, but over the next few days my condition worsened and my mother decided it was time to call the doctor. (In those days you only consulted your GP if you were really ill, and they would then automatically come to your house. Mum wouldn't have dreamt of calling the doctor if she didn't believe it was truly necessary. I find it incredible nowadays that people will go to their GP's surgery for the most minor things; they seem to think it is just part of their rights, but it's a waste of everyone's time.)

And so Dr Main, who was known locally as 'the Young Doctor', arrived at South Lawn to examine me. Even in my poorly state I could tell that he was concerned: I can recall his whispered conversation with my parents in the corner of the room and my mother's anxious glances over to me in bed as they talked.

From then on, everything happened very quickly. I was rushed to the Bath Isolation Hospital – now long gone – and put in a glass-sided room that contained only a bed and a small bedside table. Having dropped me off my parents disappeared almost immediately and I was left lying in my little glass cubicle, just feeling really awful, with absolutely no idea what was going on. Nobody had explained what was wrong with me and I was too weak and scared to ask the people who kept popping in and out to check on me. I was given drinks in a special cup with a spout as I couldn't hold anything or lift my head, although at this point I don't think I had really registered that I couldn't move my limbs; I felt so terrible that all I wanted to do was stay in bed. It wasn't until my third day in hospital that I finally managed to ask one of the nurses what was wrong with me. She picked up the chart on the end of my bed, scanned through the notes, and said briskly, 'You have got infantile paralysis.'

She then bustled out, the conversation obviously closed, and I just lay there thinking, 'Infantile paralysis? What's that then?' It meant nothing to me as I'd never heard of it – and I doubt that I would have been any the wiser if she had used the disease's more common name: polio.

Now that polio has been eradicated in our country thanks

My parents' wedding in 1929.

My baptism in 1936, presided over by my grandfather, Canon Berry. On either side of him are my mother and Miss Atton (holding me) with Roger in front.

Bathtime fun with Roger.

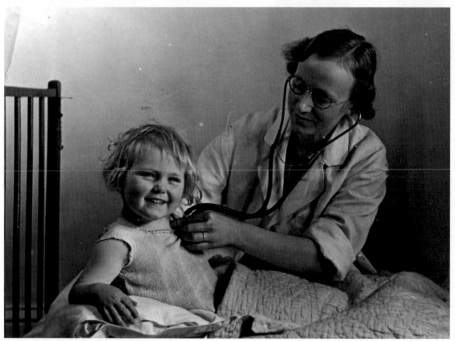

Mummy playing doctor.

My father won a competition with this photo. To make the cat drink, he placed a scrap of meat on top of the straw.

Here I am (bottom left) engrossed by Donald Duck on ciné film at my brother's birthday party.

Having the time of my life on the homemade swing, held up by Mummy and Cousin Anne.

Digging a sandpit with my younger brother, William, at Tenby.

Hard at work with William on one of our farm holidays in Devon.

We always had a collection of pets at home. Here I am giving Rupert a bath.

Winning prizes with Kerry Lass.

With the troops at Girl Guide camp at Watchet.

Me (bottom right) during my college days – what awful hats!

One of my earliest teaching jobs. Here I am giving a healthy-eating demonstration.

to immunization it's difficult to imagine the fear and panic that this highly contagious virus, which attacks the nerves of the brain and spinal cord leading to paralysis of the muscles, once provoked. While there is no cure, in some cases the affected nerves can be brought back to life with physical therapy, but if the nerve cells are completely destroyed then the result will be permanent paralysis or death. You can understand why polio was one of the most dreaded infections of my generation. In the forties and fifties there was a series of devastating outbreaks that swept through Britain, affecting thousands of children, and it was at the height of one of these epidemics that I contracted polio – although there had been few cases in Bath so my illness was deemed newsworthy enough to be reported in the local newspaper.

I was confined to that glass isolation room for a month, although I was so poorly I had little concept of the days and weeks passing. Alone and feeling terrible, the one thing I wanted was my mum, but my parents had to stay on the other side of the glass, only able to smile at me and mouth words of reassurance, and it took all of my strength just to tilt my head so I could see them. During their visits I would be in floods of tears: I just couldn't understand why Mum wasn't coming in to give me a cuddle, to talk to me and comfort me. It must have been terribly upsetting for them.

I gradually started to show signs of improvement and it was a huge relief when I was deemed well enough to move to the Bath and Wessex Orthopaedic Hospital, which is now part of the Royal United Hospital, where to my delight I was put on a ward with other children. Company at last!

My first impressions of the room that would be my home for nearly ten weeks were two rows of single metal beds and a highly polished floor, but the main thing that struck me as soon as I arrived was that it was immensely cold. The ward was designed for patients with the respiratory disease tuberculosis, for which treatment in those days was exposure to fresh air, so it had glass sliding doors along one side that were kept fully open to the elements as much as possible – and usually throughout the night. There were a few of us polio people mixed in with the TB lot and so we just had to pile on the blankets and put up with it. One morning in December I reached over to get my toothbrush out of the mug of water on my bedside table to find that it had frozen solid! It didn't do us any harm, though, and besides, finally to be able to cuddle up to Mum again after all those weeks stuck behind glass was just wonderful.

Visiting hours were frustratingly restricted: you were only allowed visitors on the last Saturday and second Sunday of the month, between the hours of two and four o'clock in the afternoon. I believe the reason for this was that since the hospital admitted patients from all over the county and there wasn't the public transport there is now, it was deemed unfair to those with families who lived further away if the Bath-based patients had more frequent visitors. On visiting day I used to watch the clock all morning, my excitement mounting as the hand edged ever closer to the magical hour of two o'clock when I could finally see my parents. On one of these glorious occasions I was thrilled to discover that I had a surprise visitor: my pony, Kerry Lass. My father had walked her the four miles from our own home to the hospital and as the sliding doors were open I could lie in bed stroking her velvety nose while she nuzzled me, clearly as delighted to see me as I was her. Can you imagine that happening in a hospital today? I remember being so thrilled on that day, not just because seeing Kerry Lass gave me hope that I'd get out of there, but at the thought of Dad taking the trouble to walk that pony all the way from home to see me. I was chuffed to bits.

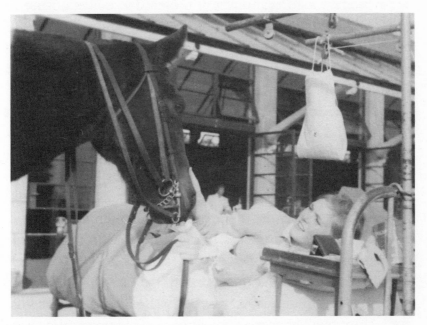

Kerry Lass's visit to the Orthopaedic Hospital.

There were no toys or other entertainments on the ward, but while I could cope pretty well with the boredom, the absolute worst part of it was that as my health improved they expected me to start lessons from my bed. I had thought the one consolation about being stuck in hospital was that there was no school! At least the teacher who came to see me was Miss Bolton, the games mistress. One time she kindly brought me a packet of dried figs, which I was very grateful for, but which struck me as a rather strange thing to bring.

Over the next ten weeks I was mostly confined to bed, although with regular physiotherapy I gradually started to regain the use of my limbs. The nurses were all very kind and warm, but the atmosphere on the ward changed in an instant whenever the surgeon, Miss Forrester-Brown, did her rounds. Maud Forrester-Brown was Britain's first female orthopaedic surgeon and was considered to be the authority on polio at the time; whenever I saw her striding down the corridor there would be a flock of people in white coats fluttering nervously in her wake. My memory is of a small and decidedly plain-looking person with short, straight hair, of whom everyone, even the redoubtable Matron, appeared to be terrified. I could tell when she had entered the ward even with my eyes shut as any chatter ceased instantly. Miss Forrester-Brown was a formidable character: not only was she a pioneer in the surgery of damaged nerves, she spoke five languages, rode her horse to hospital in the summer and skied there in the winter. We had just a handful of encounters, and I was grateful that they were brief.

Despite my frustration at being ill, I wouldn't have dreamt of complaining because I was well aware that I was one of the lucky ones. My nearest neighbour on the ward was a little girl called Buffy, who was confined to an iron lung – a tank-like machine that was used in cases where the chest muscles had been paralysed by the polio virus leaving the patient unable to breathe. Whenever I woke in the night I could hear this enormous contraption clanking rhythmically away. Buffy was about my age, but she was so terribly thin that she seemed far younger; she looked like a little withered skeleton, with just her head poking out the side of the iron lung. Although she hadn't the energy to talk, Buffy would always make the effort to smile at me throughout the day, even though she was so weak. I can remember her family gathering around her on visiting days, struggling to mask their concern behind jolly chatter. Then one night I woke briefly and was struck by an unfamiliar silence, and the following morning Matron told us that poor Buffy had died in the early hours. I knew that she had been seriously ill, but it was still a horrible shock and made me realize just how fortunate I had been.

I was finally discharged from hospital on 28th December, although to my delight I'd been allowed home for Christmas Day. I was still a long way from having made a full recovery – my left side was particularly weak, due to a lot of muscle wastage there – but I was permitted to go home on the condition that I kept my left hand secured above my head to encourage healing. There was a photograph of me with my father in the local newspaper the day after I was discharged and in it you can clearly see my hand is held up in a brace attached to a band around my head. I am staring into the camera with a rather surly expression on my face, but my dad is looking directly at me with such tenderness that when I first saw this photo a few months ago I was moved to tears. My father was never openly affectionate, but you can see from the look on his face just how worried he must have been. His concern is also apparent in his memoirs, in which he describes paying frequent visits to me while I was having physical therapy sessions at the Baths. He wrote of this time: 'Mary went to the High School and unfortunately got polio and at one time was not able to even raise a cup to her lips. Miraculously she recovered slowly and was put in the Orthopaedic Hospital. Visiting hours in those times were infrequent, but I managed to see her regularly on my visits to the Treatment Baths.'

For the next few months I had to go to the Orthopaedic Hospital twice a week to have massage on my left side (during this period I wasn't able to go to school on a regular basis), but I made a good recovery. I still have a slightly weaker left side and a curvature of the spine – although that is really only visible if I have a swimsuit on – and my left hand is smaller and a little misshapen, as if from arthritis, but it's never been a real disadvantage. I manage well, and have the perfect excuse never to darn socks!

I returned to daily school around the same time that my year had to select which subjects we would be studying for School Cert. (School Certificate Examinations were the fore-runner to O-Levels, which then became today's GCSEs.) Well, I say 'select', but you actually didn't get any choice in the subjects you would take: you were just shoved one way or the other according to your ability, or – in my case – lack of it. So while the clever clogs did Latin, Maths and History, the dim ones were left with Art, Cookery and Needlework. Even without losing a good chunk of my schooling to polio I clearly hadn't been a model pupil, so I'm sure it will come as no surprise to learn that I fell into the latter group.

Yet while I had been consigned to the academic scrapheap, this was to prove something of a turning point in my for-tunes at Bath High School. One of the subjects that we dummies were expected to take for School Cert was Home Economics, in those days known as Domestic Science. Although I had often helped my mother in the kitchen, chop-ping vegetables or stirring a cake mixture, I had never actually cooked anything myself, so I was feeling far from confident when I stepped into the shiny new Domestic Science class-room in a purpose-built mews on Lansdown Crescent, far away from the main school buildings (and the terrifying spec-tre of Miss Blackburn). Yet by the end of the very first class, I was brimming with excitement and longing for the next les-son. Forget learning about historical dates or wrestling with algebra: here was a subject that was fun, exciting and useful. Suddenly for the first time in my life I felt like I could do something! And, as it would turn out, do it rather well . . .

# CANTERBURY TART

This is a wonderful tart, one of my absolute favourites – like a *tarte au citron* but with apple as well. This freezes well too. If time is short, use bought sweet shortcrust pastry.

*Serves 10*

### for the pastry
- 100g (4 oz) butter, cubed
- 225g (8 oz) plain flour
- 40g (1½ oz) icing sugar
- 1 large egg, beaten
- 1 tablespoon water

### for the filling
- 4 large eggs
- 225g (8 oz) caster sugar
- grated rind and juice of 2 lemons
- 100g (4 oz) butter, melted
- 2 large Bramley apples, peeled and cored (about 350g (12 oz) in weight)
- 2 dessert apples, peeled, cored and thinly sliced
- about 25g (1 oz) demerara sugar

Preheat the oven to 200°C/Fan 180°C /Gas 6.

First make the pastry. Measure the butter, flour and icing sugar into a food processor. Process for a few moments until it forms a crumble mixture, then add the egg and water. Process again until the dough holds together. If making the pastry by hand, rub the butter into the flour and icing sugar until it resembles fine breadcrumbs. Stir in the beaten egg and bring together with the water to form a dough.

Roll out the dough thinly and line a round 28cm (11 inch) flan tin about 4cm (1½ inches) deep. Form a lip of pastry around the edge. Chill for 30 minutes whilst making the filling, then bake the pastry case blind for about 20 minutes in the pre-heated oven.

For the filling, beat the eggs, caster sugar, lemon rind and juice together in a large mixing bowl until blended. Stir in the warm melted butter then coarsely grate the Bramley apples directly into the mixture and mix well. The grated apple will not discolour as the lemon juice prevents this.

Spread the runny lemon mixture over the base of the baked blind pastry case. Level the surface with the back of a spoon and arrange the apples slices overlapping around the edge. Sprinkle on the demerara sugar.

Carefully transfer the tart to the preheated oven and bake for about 30 minutes until cooked – the centre should feel firm to the touch and the apples around the edge will be tinged brown.

# 4

I truly believe that any success I have had in my career is down to the Domestic Science mistress, Miss Date. She was a small lady and you wouldn't have noticed her in the street except for her smile, which was warm and ever-present, but a lovelier, more inspiring teacher I can't imagine. She was more like a friend than a schoolteacher and we all adored her. Miss Bolton recalls coming to admire the new Domestic Science department and while she was talking to Miss Date at the front of the room I apparently came over to them and said, 'You two go on talking and don't turn round until I say so.' Can you imagine me daring to say that to the likes of Miss Blackburn? Evidently the pair of them humoured me, and when I finally gave them permission to turn around they discovered that I had rolled out a long thin sausage of pastry that I had formed into the words 'I love you Miss Date'.

After I spoke in a recent interview about my fondness for Miss Date – or 'Datie' as we called her – I was deluged with letters from other former pupils keen to share their memories. One recalled that Datie, a keen gardener and nature lover, had a tame owl called Flick that used to fly in through her spare bedroom window to retrieve the bits of meat she'd left out for it. Another remembers Miss Date bringing home a pet chameleon after a trip to Africa and all the pupils taking turns to hold it against their jumpers to see if it would change colour. She really was a wonderful character.

And so for the first time I found myself in the unusual

position of being desperate to get to school in the morning so I could get started on our latest Domestic Science project. It wasn't just the process of cooking that I found so enjoyable, it was seeing other people's appreciation of the end product and, to this day, one of the main reasons I love cooking is the 'oohs' and 'aahs' that a wonderful plate of food can inspire. To be able to put a smile on a loved one's face with something you've created from scratch is incredibly rewarding – especially for someone like me, who had been a total disappointment in all other areas of my schooling. One day I brought home a treacle sponge pudding I had made, excited (and a little nervous) at the prospect of serving it at supper that evening. While my parents and brothers waited around the table I reheated the sponge, turned it out of the bowl and poured the golden syrup over the top so it oozed down the sides as I brought it to the table. I remember watching Dad out of the corner of my eye as he took a bite, anxious to see his reaction. To my delight, his eyes lit up. 'Gosh, this is good,' he said. 'Just as good as Mum's.' Well, as you can imagine I was bursting with pride. My brothers were equally enthusiastic, and I was left with a real sense of achievement, a feeling that I had managed to do something well. Not only that, but my father started to take an interest in what I was doing at school.

I think it is very sad that nowadays – and I do hope this is changing – Home Economics is more about the science of food and the theory of nutrition rather than learning how to cook. I strongly believe that every child should leave school understanding basic food preparation techniques and having actually cooked some healthy meals, to know how to make gravy or mashed potatoes or custard, so that when they leave home they will be able to prepare food themselves rather than rely on takeaways and ready meals. Learning to cook is far more useful and important than a lot of other subjects that you never use again once you leave school. It's all very well saying that life is fast and there isn't time to cook, but it can really be very quick to create a meal, even from scratch. Besides, it's much more expensive to buy convenience food and if you prepare it yourself you know exactly what goes into it, whether that's beef in lasagne instead of horsemeat or worse. Most food-related health scares – salmonella, E. coli and the rest – come from buying cheap food; if you get ingredients that are unprocessed and from a reliable source there shouldn't be any problem. I would far rather buy a bunch of carrots with the tops on, still covered in mud, from a farm shop, than a few pristine individuals in a supermarket pack. I know that money is short, but I think it's far better to always buy the best you can afford and just eat meat less frequently. When it comes to buying ingredients for my cooking, I believe that good husbandry – knowing how the animal has been treated – is far more important than paying a premium for organic. I'm actually rather wary of organic products, especially from abroad, after talking to a vegetable importer who told me the story of a supplier he had gone to see in Italy who, when asked if he could provide organic tinned tomatoes, said, 'Of course, that's easy, it just means a different label.'

In 1952, at the age of seventeen, I left Bath High School. Although marriage and motherhood were still widely regarded as the epitome of feminine achievement at this time, most young, single women still went into employment after leaving school, at least until having their first child. There was never any question that I would not have a career as I had to earn my

keep. I wouldn't have expected my parents to support me –
and, even if I had, they certainly wouldn't have been prepared
to do so! But I had failed every subject at School Cert, passing
only Domestic Science and (to my surprise, as I wasn't very
good at it) Needlework, and with the bare minimum of qualifications my future looked extremely uncertain.

Vindicated in her long-held belief that I would never
amount to much, Miss Blackburn said to me, 'There isn't any
career that I can recommend for you as you haven't passed
enough exams to do anything.' Then, when my parents went
to see the headmistress to discuss the hopelessness of my
case, Miss Blackburn dourly told them that my only possible
option was to get a job looking after children. To which my
father apparently replied, 'Well, I pity the children.'

For my part, I was keen to build on my success in Miss
Date's Domestic Science classes. I would have loved to
become a teacher, but teacher training required five passes at
School Cert and I only had two, so I applied to Bath College
of Domestic Science to study Institutional Management. To
my delight I was offered a place, but even that was condi-
tional on three passes. I began to wish I had applied myself
a little more diligently at school. With his daughter's options
becomingly worryingly limited, my father took matters into
his own hands and wrote to the college saying something
along the lines of: 'My daughter is not very good at passing
exams, but she is a very good cook. Please take her!' Thankfully, the school also agreed to send a supporting letter, which
read: 'For a long time Mary has said she would like to be a
catering manager. She's read much concerning this and has,
for a schoolgirl, a surprising fund of knowledge.' To everyone's relief, the college were persuaded to accept me.

At seventeen I was too young to start the course that September so I had to defer for a year, but if I had hoped I was going to spend the next twelve months mucking around at home with my friends then my father had other plans. The city of Bath had an exchange programme with the French town of Pau (pronounced 'Po') on the edge of the Pyrenees, where my father secured me a place on a three-month course at a school for housewifery, the idea being that I would develop some useful skills while also improving my very average French. The previous year I'd had a French exchange (which had not been entirely successful) with a girl called Anna de Bastard who lived in a small village called Castelnau-Magnoac, an hour and a half's drive outside Pau, so it was decided that I would attend the school in the week, lodging with a local family, then at weekends I would go to stay with the de Bastard family. Although I would never have complained, everyone else seemed rather more enthusiastic about this plan than I was.

I arrived in Pau just after my eighteenth birthday to discover that the family with whom I would be staying during the week had ten children; the house was so full that my appearance barely caused a ripple. As I sat down to supper on the first night, surrounded by a dozen strangers who were either ignoring me or glancing at me warily, I felt close to tears. Although I had learnt the basics of French at school I didn't have a competent enough grasp of the language to be able to adapt it to my new environment, and I had no idea what was going on when the family suddenly broke into song at the table – a sung grace that would be repeated at every subsequent meal. I can still remember the words today, even if I still have no idea what they mean!

Supper on that first night was a stew; the meat was rather tough and had an unfamiliar flavour. Aware that I should at least try to strike up a conversation with my hostess, I asked Madame what it was we were eating. '*Cheval*,' she answered.

Unfortunately, that was one of the few French words that I knew. Horse. On the drive through Pau earlier that day I had noticed that there were horses' heads outside butchers' shops and I had thought to myself, 'I really don't like the look of that,' as I was already missing Kerry Lass. But to see it in front of me on the plate and to know what I had just eaten . . . oh, it was awful. There's absolutely nothing wrong with horsemeat – half of Europe eats it after all – but as a pony-mad teenager I was horrified. I still wouldn't touch it today, although my dislike is grounded in nothing but senti-mentality. I couldn't bear the thought of finishing the stew on my plate, but I didn't want to be rude. I can remember sobbing the whole way through the meal.

My relationship with the family barely improved over the following three months. I had never been away from home before and was horribly homesick. The children had their own friends and weren't very welcoming – although I'm sure my attitude also didn't help endear me to them – and while the mother was kind, with ten offspring she obviously had far too much going on to worry about me.

Fortunately, I was made to feel much more welcome at the school. The course I was taking was designed to prepare girls to become housewives: we were taught how to sweep floors, how to iron and mend clothes, how to clean windows inside and out with wet newspaper – all the useful skills you needed for running a home. There was a little bit of cookery and some instruction on etiquette, but it certainly wasn't a finish-ing school; it was far more practical than that. Although I was the only English girl there, all the staff and students were very friendly and kind. They were a great crowd, mostly girls taking a gap year before going to university, and we had a lot of fun together. I was at the school on the day of the Queen's Coronation on 2nd June 1953 – a momentous occasion that saw three million people line the streets of London – and they must have realized how disappointed I was not to be at home for the national celebrations, as they made me a special cake to mark the occasion. When they presented it to me I burst into tears of gratitude and homesickness; I thought it was such a lovely thing to do.

Every weekend, as arranged, I went to stay with Anna de Bastard in Castelnau-Magnoac. As I have mentioned, Anna had already been to stay with me in Bath, although we had certainly not become great mates. She was a nice enough girl, but we had nothing in common. Now fully recovered from the polio, I was very sporty and loved being outside, whereas Anna didn't play sport of any kind and preferred reading books. I was a bit of a tomboy, while she was always dressing herself up and was terribly concerned about what she looked like. Weekends were really quite boring – we spent an awful lot of time just hanging around the house and nobody ever thought of going for a walk or on a picnic.

Anna's mother was a baroness (her father was dead) and the family lived in an enormous manor house that had clearly once been extremely grand, with vast halls and soaring pillared ceilings, but had now fallen into decrepitude. It was the sort of place one could imagine finding Miss Havisham, sitting under a magnificent chandelier veiled in cobwebs and dust. I never ventured downstairs after dark because you could see rats running across the hall floor, their eyes flashing in the moonlight and – terrified as I am of rats and mice – I lived in fear that one night they would decide to bring their game upstairs. After dinner every evening Anna's two brothers would tie up the bottoms of their trousers with string and go out into the enclosed courtyard to shoot the rats. This was what passed for entertainment amongst the de Bastard boys: rat-shooting, and doing other horrible things like wringing the necks of chickens and then putting them on the ground so the poor creatures ran flapping around the yard, literally on their last legs, until they finally dropped dead.

Anna's mother was a very grand lady who was very dressed up. One of the things I remember most clearly is that the local minister was always dropping by to visit her; even back then this struck me as a little bit odd, especially as Madame didn't appear to be particularly religious, although I wouldn't have dared query it. But whatever was going on, I'm quite sure it was common knowledge in the village – everyone in Castelnau-Magnoac knew everyone else's business. It was a strange place, run by a very self-important mayor, and it seemed to be trapped in a time warp: you never saw any cars, only Vespas, and by nightfall on Friday, which was payday, the main street would be full of drunks and stray dogs.

Although the servants who no doubt had once run the household were now long gone, the de Bastard family still had a rather fat cook in their employ who produced the most wonderful classic French dishes. I have particularly wonderful memories of breakfast: the freshly baked croissants, yogurt and fruit. Wine was drunk with all the meals, although it was watered down for us young people. It was the first time I had tried wine and I can remember feeling terribly grown-up. I only once went into the kitchen during the whole time I was there, and that was when I offered to make the family my mother's Bread and Butter Pudding, which as I mentioned earlier went down extremely well. I put on a lot of weight during that trip because I was bored and eating so much; I must have been a good stone heavier when I went home. All in all, those three months in France were not a happy time for me, and I was hugely relieved when it was time to return to Britain.

By this time my parents were living at Charlcombe Farm, a beautiful property they had bought when I was around fifteen and which would remain their home until my father's death. He recalls that: 'After a year of bargaining we bought it for £5,700 with about two acres of land.'

After I arrived back home I had just a few weeks' grace before I started at the Bath College of Domestic Science, which was situated in nearby Brougham Hayes in a large building that in wartime had been taken over by the Admiralty. A local newspaper article published around the time I went to the college gives some insight into its history: 'The College owes its existence to a decision taken by Miss M H Lawrie in 1893. She was then conducting classes in cookery and sewing for a small number of ladies at 19 Green Park. They attended the classes merely to be more efficient in the supervision of their domestic staff, but in 1893 they were joined by a woman who had another purpose in mind – to qualify as a teacher of domestic subjects. And so in this accidental way the college changed its course and, raising its standards, started to cater for people who wished to become teachers.'

My exam results having not been good enough for the college's teacher training course, I was studying for the two-year Institutional Management certificate. This was a full-time course, five days a week, designed to prepare students for a career in catering, but its syllabus was extremely broad. As well as cooking, it covered everything one would ever need to know about running a home, from needlework to nutrition, table-laying to bed-making and even basic electrical skills, such as how to change a plug. It was all extremely useful – and good fun, too. Miss Nielsen, the college principal, took us for some of our lessons including one on the art of loo cleaning, and to this day I can still remember her rallying cry of 'Flush, Brush, Flush!' We all used to have a good giggle about that. It is thanks to Miss Nielsen that I am now an excellent loo cleaner and all-round super-scrubber.

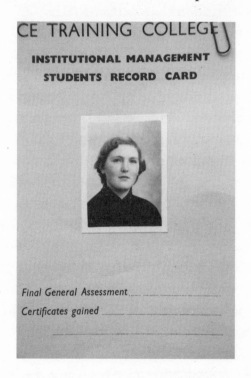

Nowadays most mainstream household cleaning products have become so mild you could probably drink them, so I'm always on a lookout to find the most powerful product you can buy. I discovered a brilliant extra-powerful loo cleaner online that I now order in bulk, twelve at a time, to hand out to my children, and when I came across a really good table-polishing product in Devon I bought every bottle they had in the shop.

We had laundry lessons with Miss Sutherland, who taught us all about the care of clothes, including hand-washing, ironing, folding and how to use a washing machine (only about a third of the population had one in those days). On one occasion we had to bring in a woollen item from home to machine-wash in class; I chose a V-necked fine-knit sweater, but I put it in the washing machine at far too high a temperature and when I took it out to my horror it had shrunk to child size. Rather than own up to my mistake I dried it, ironed it with a damp cloth and then folded it up as carefully as I could, and when Miss Sutherland came round to check on my work she said, 'You've done that just beautifully,' and gave me extra marks for presentation. She had absolutely no idea how big the sweater had been to start with! Of course I just smiled while the other girls were absolutely roaring with laughter because I had got away with it.

Since our course was in catering we were taught to cook for large numbers, usually twelve people and upwards, and to this day I find it very easy to feed masses of people, yet would have difficulty preparing soup for four; in fact I usually end up making far more than I need and freezing the rest. All the food that we cooked in class went down to be served for the college lunches and we prepared everything from scratch. Our cookery teacher, Mrs Varley, taught us the basics, but also more complicated techniques such as making filo pastry. I think I shocked a few people by recently admitting that I never make my own filo these days because it takes so much time and skill to get it as wafer-thin as it needs to be, but we had a lot of fun learning how to make it at college. You really need to work the gluten, so we would slap the dough on the table and bang it about, trying to muffle our giggles as we pulled it across the room when Mrs Varley wasn't looking. She was a kind woman but had very exacting standards, and you were careful not to make a mistake in her class. Thankfully we girls had a wonderful friend in the very lovely lady who helped with our washing-up, who would conspire with us to hide the evidence from Mrs Varley if we had burned something or messed up a recipe.

As much as I had hated school, I had a wonderful time at college. It was such a relief to be treated like an adult, because of course we were no longer schoolgirls, and because I had now chosen my vocation I was doing something that I hoped to make a career of, so wanted to do it to the best of my ability. I was with a crowd of people who enjoyed doing the same things as me and we were lucky enough to be taught by some wonderful, inspirational teachers.

I was a competent and diligent student, but nowhere near one of the best. However, despite not coming top in any of the subjects, I was very ambitious and wanted to make the most of my education; therefore during the holidays I arranged work experience. I worked at a bakery, a butcher, in the catering department at London Airport and at a fishmonger, where I learnt useful skills like how to bone a fish and skin a Dover sole. I didn't get paid for the work, but each position helped me to grow in competence and confidence – and I think the chaps I was working with were happy to have a nineteen-year-old girl around!

I also worked in the kitchens of the Gloucester Hotel, now no more, on the Isle of Wight over Cowes Week. The head chef was an absolute tyrant: he shouted at everybody in the kitchen and always had a pint of beer in his hand, which would slop into the pan when he was making omelettes. I was doing puddings, so largely managed to keep out of his way, but I hated the atmosphere of fear and bullying. I was there for three weeks and it's the only time I ever rang home to complain to Dad. 'I really hate it,' I told him. 'Just try and stick it out,' he said – and so I did, but I dreaded going in every day. Perhaps the memory of this experience is the reason I don't like watching things like Gordon Ramsay's *Hell's Kitchen*. I don't think shouting and swearing makes a good programme – and I certainly don't think a kitchen should be hell.

At this stage I had little idea exactly what I wanted to do for my career, although I most enjoyed the teaching elements of the course: we had to give demonstrations to each other and I loved sharing techniques and ideas. But I knew almost from day one that I had no wish to go into catering. In those days, a position in catering required that you work all hours of the day including weekends. I'm very happy to put everything into a job five days a week, but I really liked my weekends off. People who were in catering were working hardest when everybody else was at play – and that didn't appeal to me in the slightest.

Although I was living at home, I spent a lot of time at the college with my mates because everybody else was boarding. There were lots of college dances and parties and boyfriends, although I'm not going to get into any of that business because most of the people involved are still alive!

When I was eighteen I went on my first friends' holiday abroad with three girlfriends: Sally Rear, Jane Harvey and Pip Aubrey. We planned to drive to France and spend a month touring around on a total budget of just twenty pounds each. All the parents were really worried about us going off on our own – even more so after we pulled out of the driveway at Charlcombe Farm in Pip's mother's beautiful Sunbeam Talbot, loaded up with all our suitcases, and knocked straight into somebody's bumper! But that was the only accident we had, and after that slight hiccup we set off feeling terribly excited and grown-up. I will never forget the sandwiches that Pip's mum made us for the first part of our journey: they were veal with stuffing, a combination I'd never tried in a sandwich before, and were absolutely delicious.

We all took turns driving and got down as far as Arcachon on the south-west coast of France, stopping at pensions along the way where we'd ask for two double rooms and lay bolsters down the middle of the beds to turn them into two singles. There were lots of decisions to be made – maps to be read and routes to plan – but we loved every bit of it.

As there were four of us together, we encouraged each other to do all sorts of things we probably wouldn't have made the effort to do if we had only been two, such as having a fire on the beach and cooking the local fish. One morning, we all decided to get up at five o'clock to go to Chartres Cathedral in time to watch the sun come up and see those first morning rays pouring through the famous blue stained-glass windows. It was the most wonderful holiday. Given our limited funds we were extremely careful with money – we used to stop at a *boulangerie* for a bit of bread and cheese for lunch, then have breakfast and supper at our pension – but it's amazing how far our money stretched. We even came home with change!

# STEAMED SYRUP PUDDING

Most people love the comfort of a nursery style pudding – especially in winter. This one is always popular, even with people who would not normally eat puddings. To vary it I often add two chopped dessert apples to the syrup.

*Serves 4–6*

- 5 generous tablespoons golden syrup
- 100g (4 oz) soft butter
- 100g (4 oz) caster sugar
- 100g (4 oz) self-raising flour
- 1 level teaspoon baking powder
- 2 large eggs
- 2 tablespoons milk

Generously butter a 1 litre (2 pint) pudding basin and cut a square of foil to fit neatly into the base. Spoon the golden syrup into the base of the basin on to the foil square.

Measure the remaining ingredients into a bowl and whisk with an electric hand whisk until blended. Spoon the mixture into the prepared basin on top of the syrup and smooth the surface. There will be extra space above the mixture if you use a 2 pint basin.

Cut generous squares of both greaseproof paper and foil (large enough to overhang the top of the basin) and fold a pleat in the centre (this allows for the sponge to rise). Lay the paper first and then the foil on top and tightly twist around the edges to seal or tie with a piece of string.

Sit a pastry cutter in the base of a steamer or large saucepan and lower the basin and sit it on top of the cutter (this protects the base of the sponge from overcooking). Pour simmering water up to half way around the basin. Cover with a lid and steam over a low heat for about 1½ hours (keep checking if the water needs topping up).

Remove the paper and foil and turn the pudding out, then remove the base square of foil if it's attached to the syrupy sponge!

Serve hot with custard and cream. If you can find an excuse, serve with extra warmed golden syrup too – just heat some in a pan.

## 5

It was only a few weeks after leaving college that I saw an advert for a job with the South Western Electricity Board that sounded right up my street. Thanks to the improvements that the government had made to the national grid in the late forties, it had become possible for ordinary households to install electric cookers, which were seen as a cleaner, more efficient alternative to gas stoves, and there had been a nationwide boom as demand grew for the cutting-edge appliances. Since the technology was still fairly new, when you purchased an electric cooker you received a complimentary visit from a 'Home Service Advisor' from your local Electricity Board who would demonstrate to you exactly how it worked – and this was the position that was being advertised.

The job appealed to me for a number of reasons. It was based in Bath, so I could continue to live with my parents at Charlcombe Farm, plus it required expertise in both cooking and giving demonstrations, which were the activities I had most enjoyed on my college course. Despite my disastrous School Cert results, I had the right qualifications for the position and I must have performed reasonably well at the interview (even though I'm sure I was almost mute with nerves) as – to my absolute delight – I got the job.

From the very start I loved the work. Each home visit lasted for about an hour, during which time I would show the customer how to use all the different elements of their new cooker. To demonstrate how accurate and easy to control the temperature was I would whip up a quiche or Victoria sandwich in front of them and while it was cooking I would talk to the customer about the oven's other functions – the grill, boiling plate and so forth – then we could enjoy a slice of cake at the end of it. People would always make sure their kitchens were nice and tidy for me, and it was a pleasure to visit them and see their delight at learning what their new purchase could do. When glass oven doors first came in they proved to be a huge success because you could make a soufflé and actually watch it rising. It's difficult to imagine what an amazing innovation this was considered back then, but at the time the effect was magical: people just couldn't believe it!

As the job involved a great deal of travel, all employees were given a black Ford Popular; I had learnt to drive when I was eighteen (and had passed my test first time) but this was my very first car. Even though I didn't actually own it myself, I felt like quite the high-flyer. The car had no heater and the windscreen wiper hardly worked, so it could be pretty hairy when you were rattling around the countryside on cold and rainy nights, but it was all huge fun because you were out and about rather than stuck in an office. Sitting behind a desk all day just wouldn't have appealed to my spirit of adventure.

Having been thoroughly lacking in ambition at school I now worked as hard as I could, never turning down offers of overtime. In the evenings I would do demonstrations to Women's Institute meetings in village halls all around the area. An engineer would set up an oven and a table for me, and I would arrive and bake a Victoria sandwich for the ladies. There I was, visiting all these villages in the dark, zooming around in my little Ford Popular with all the equipment and ingredients for my demonstrations loaded in the back. I felt as brave as brave!

Despite my reluctance to work at weekends while I was at college, I would also do occasional demonstrations on Saturday mornings in the Electricity Board showroom. There was a particular reason why I enjoyed these sessions. On our home visits the customers were nearly always women, but at weekends you would often get the husbands and a few young single men coming in as well, so I would always look forward to Saturday mornings because I might get a few glamorous chaps through the doors.

I can't tell you how proud I was to be finally earning my own money. I've never taken money for granted and, much as I didn't like Miss Blackburn, something she had once told us in a school assembly stayed with me: 'Remember that money is a representation of somebody's work. It may be your parents' work, it may have been given to you, but at some point somebody has worked for it, so respect it.' I've been a saver ever since. Nevertheless, when I got my first pay cheque I was keen to buy myself something to mark this milestone and so I went to Mallory Jewellers in Bath and got a sapphire-and-pearl brooch, ever after referred to as my 'overtime brooch'. I also bought my mother an electric kettle: times were moving on!

Yet although my career seemed to be taking off, at the back of my mind I was concerned that my qualifications weren't quite up to scratch – not having been able to study for the full IMA (Institutional Management Association) qualification at college. The fact that I had a lesser qualification didn't seem to concern my new employers, nevertheless with an eye on my future career I was still keen to develop my teaching skills and so I signed up for evening classes at Bath

Technical College. In order to be eligible for the City and Guilds teaching qualification, however, I discovered that I would have to go right back to the beginning and start from scratch with a course in Domestic Cookery, followed by one in Advanced Cookery. And so that's what I did: I worked for the Electricity Board during the day and studied at Bath Tech in the evening.

My cookery teacher at Bath Tech, Miss Simkins, was a wonderful woman who not only taught me valuable new skills, she also helped me to refine the bulk-catering techniques I had learnt at college and adjust my existing recipes so I could prepare things in smaller quantities and to the higher standard required by City and Guilds. I still have the handwritten menu that I devised for my final Advanced Cookery exam, which reads as follows:

June 1957

Melon Ball Cocktail

Chaud-froid of Salmon

Veal and Ham Raised Pie

Mayonnaise of Potatoes

Dressed Tomatoes

Britannia Strawberry Flan

Cream

And then, at the top, I have written with a flourish: *'Bon Appetit!'*

I don't recall how I performed in the exam, but I must have passed because I then went on to take the Practical Teaching course – or City and Guilds 151 as it was called. This wasn't specific to cookery or any other subject; it was purely focused

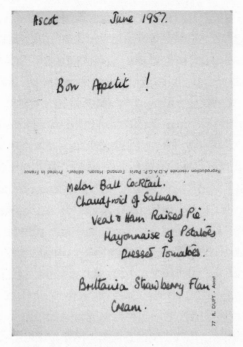

Ascot        June 1957.


Bon Appetit !

Melon Ball Cocktail.
Chaudfroid of Salmon.
Veal & Ham Raised Pie.
Mayonnaise of Potatoes
Dressed Tomatoes.

Brittania Strawberry Flan
Cream.

77 R. DUFY - Ascot

The menu for my City and Guilds exam.

on the skill of teaching. Since this particular course wasn't on the syllabus at Bath Tech I had to ask permission from the Electricity Board to go on day release to Bristol College once a week, which fortunately they granted.

One part of the practical section of the course involved me having to teach a class myself one night a week, which I did back at Bath Tech – you can see why I was so pleased to have my own car! I started out with seventeen students on my 'Entertaining at Home' course and was thrilled when I still had all seventeen by the end of it. These were all busy working people, yet I didn't have a single dropout over the year. I was immensely proud that I had managed to enthuse the students sufficiently to keep them coming back each week. In each class I would demonstrate how to cook a main course and a pudding and then everyone else would have a go. I chose recipes that I thought would appeal to busy people and that could be prepared in the two and a half hours we had for the class. I remember doing chocolate éclairs one day, which went down very well. Standing up in front of my lovely group of students, showing them how to make something really delicious to take home and seeing their pleasure when they managed to do it for themselves, I really felt I'd found my forte. I remember having a nasty case of 'flu one day and still struggling into college to teach, determined not to let the students down. My enthusiasm for both my job at the Electricity Board and my newfound skill for teaching must have been obvious: my father wrote in his memoirs that I 'suddenly blossomed' during this period. Even today, the one thing that motivates everything I do in my career is my desire to share my passion for cooking. I love showing people how to make something really well, be that a chocolate cake or a fish pie, so that they can get the same thrill out of making it as I do. My aim is for everyone to have the same success and pleasure; it's what keeps me wanting to work at a time when most of my contemporaries have retired!

As you can imagine I didn't have much spare time during this period, but my social life has always been very important to me. A group of friends and I started the 49 Club (so called because there were forty-nine of us), which would meet every Friday night at the Lansdown Grove Hotel. We arranged all sorts of different social activities: motor rallies, ice-skating, picnics, speakers and dances. They were a terrific gang and we had a lot of fun. If I wasn't working on Saturday morning, the first thing I would do was to find out who was about and then arrange to meet up for coffee. Most of my girlfriends still lived and worked in Bath and although the chaps had mainly moved to London for work they would usually come back at weekends. In the afternoon we might go to Jeff's – the pub to go to in the centre of Bath – for a drink or to watch a rugby match, and this would be where Saturday night was planned. I wasn't a huge rugger fan, but you'd have to go in order to get Saturday night's date fixed! You would never dream of asking a boy out – you'd always wait to be asked. In the evenings we often went to dinner dances at the Pump Room, an elegant Georgian building housing a restaurant that is still a Bath institution today. I would have the occasional gin and orange, or gin and tonic, but I wasn't a big drinker – and after spluttering over that cigarette in the goat shed when I was a young girl I didn't smoke – so I was pretty well-behaved. The boys would get quite drunk when they were watching the rugger, but on the whole the girls wouldn't. It just wasn't something you did in those days.

While I was working at the Electricity Board I only had a fortnight's holiday allowance a year, but I'd go on long week-ends to Devon or other coastal spots with friends. I had become great mates with one of the other Home Service Advisors from Bristol, a wonderful girl called Mavis Patterson who is still a close friend today, and we once went to the Peacock Vane Hotel on the Isle of Wight – where I remember that they had a whole corridor wallpapered with old Christmas cards, which I thought was very clever indeed.

I had been with the Electricity Board for three years when I was summoned to attend a course in Bristol, run by a Mrs Powell-Hills, to demonstrate the latest developments in electric ovens. As much as I enjoyed my work, I was desperate to move to London and had been scanning the newspapers for a job that would take me there since turning twenty-one, the magical age that my father had decreed was when I would be old enough to go to the capital. We don't have that sort of control over our children nowadays! But while there were always plenty of jobs advertised for secretaries or typists – the most popular career choice for women at this time – I wanted to build on the skills I had developed during my spell at the Electricity Board and Bath Tech, and opportunities in domestic science were rare. So it was with more than a little excitement that on the bus ride to Bristol one morning I spotted an advertisement in the *Telegraph* that sounded like it could be a perfect next step for me. The Dutch Dairy Bureau who were looking for a Home Economist to develop and demonstrate recipes using Dutch butter and cheeses. (In an ideal world I'd have loved it to be for English produce, but beggars can't be choosers.) Not only that, the job was in London. But while I had the right qualifications, the advertisement specified a woman aged between thirty and forty. At twenty-two, I was eight years too young.

Nevertheless, that evening I went home and told my parents I was planning to apply for the job. My father's reaction was typically blunt. 'I told her not to be so stupid,' he recalled in his memoirs, 'but Mary was determined to try for it.' And so I replied to the advertisement in my very best handwriting, sent off the letter and then a few weeks later to my absolute delight I was invited for an interview at the Dutch Dairy Bureau's offices in central London, just off Southampton Row in Bloomsbury.

As the date approached, my excitement turned to nerves and then, on the morning itself, terror. Apart from occasional trips to the theatre in the West End with friends, I hadn't been to London that often, and certainly never by myself. To try and boost my confidence – and my age by a few years – I dressed in my very best: dress, coat, heels and a little felt pillbox hat (probably the first and last time I ever wore a hat to work) all in navy blue. I was rather obsessed with navy. A few years later I bought an MGA car for five hundred pounds and the first thing I did was pay another twenty-five pounds (quite a lot of money at the time) to get it sprayed navy blue, as the dealer had only stocked them in light blue. My brothers thought I was mad.

The interview was with the Bureau's manager Mr Sevink, a jovial Dutchman who must have been about my father's age. I was too nervous to say very much; I think Mr Sevink did most of the talking. He explained that the successful candidate would be based at the London office, where there was a test kitchen in which to develop recipes, but would also have to travel around the country visiting schools and exhibitions to promote Dutch dairy products. It sounded like the ideal next step in my career, and I was thrilled to bits when Mr Sevink offered me the job – even more so when he told me that the salary was a thousand a year. A thousand pounds! It seemed too good to be true – I had started on about half that at the Electricity Board. In the provinces, that sort of salary meant you'd arrived.

I can remember getting home after the interview, walking through the front door, registering my parents' expectant faces, and saying casually, 'Well, I got the job.'

Dad looked shocked. 'Really? What are they going to pay you?'

'A thousand pounds a year,' I said, as nonchalantly as I could.

There was a stunned silence. Bear in mind that the average British annual salary was just a few hundred pounds in those days.

'A thousand pounds a year?' said Dad eventually. 'For you?'
I nodded.

'Who interviewed you?'

'A charming man called Mr Sevink. Dutch.'

'Right,' said Dad. And he was on the first train to London the next morning to check out Mr Sevink. I wouldn't have dreamt of trying to stop him. I suppose I could've said, 'Don't you trust me?' but I'd hardly have dared. In those days, your father was always right.

For his part, I think Mr Sevink found it admirable that my father was so concerned about me. 'Have you come especially to talk about your daughter?' he asked, when Dad met him. 'Well, I have five, so I shall never be off British Rail . . .'

I was waiting at home with bated breath when my father returned home later that afternoon.

'You're quite right,' he said. 'It sounds just the job for you.'

I was thrilled and couldn't wait to get started, but first of all I needed to find somewhere to live. My friend Pip was already working in London as a medical secretary but was staying in temporary digs, so we decided to get a flat together. After a few fruitless days trekking around London we were getting desperate. It turned out that my impressive new salary wasn't at all impressive for London. Everything was so expensive; we couldn't even afford a flat in Hampstead, which in those days was nowhere near as smart as it is today. It was beginning to look as though we wouldn't be able to afford anywhere suitable, so Pip's mother came up to help our search – and together we eventually found a top-floor two-bedroom flat in South Kensington.

Number 31 Thurloe Street was a grey-brick building with a white porticoed entrance and black railings running along the front. Despite its smart exterior, the flat was extremely scruffy and very cramped, as we couldn't afford the rent on our own and had to get two more friends to move in with us, but I thought it was absolutely lovely. It was sparsely furnished and I don't remember much in the way of heating: I think there was a gas fire and that was about it! We had an old-fashioned gas geyser to heat the water and agreed on the house rule that nobody was allowed to take deep baths because it was too expensive.

Our flat was right opposite South Kensington tube station and from our vantage point on the fourth floor you could lean out of the window and watch visitors making their way from the tube to our house. There was a very posh carpet shop at the corner of the station, which offered to clean your rugs for a vast amount of money, and from our flat we could look down on the roof and see people armed with squeegee, soap and buckets scrubbing away at these rugs. Customers were paying through the nose for someone to clean their prize rug with a yard brush! It did make us laugh. Next to the carpet shop was a greengrocer, where we'd often pick up our supper. Each week the four of us girls would put a pound in the kitty and that would be enough to pay for four nights of meals. We would take it in turns to cook on our little Baby Belling stove, doing things that were quick to prepare like chops, sausage and mash, stuffed marrows or rice pilaff, and there would always be eggs because someone's parents would give us some from their chickens. I used to make Nasi Goreng, an Indonesian fried rice dish – the recipe for which came from the Dutch Dairy Bureau thanks to Holland's close links with Indonesia. I remember getting avocados from our greengrocer when they first came in. They were considered terribly exotic at the time and people didn't know what to do with them; we just cut them in half and filled them with salad dressing. We all did our fair share of cooking and learnt from each other: Pip used to put lemon juice and mustard in her white sauce, which was new to me, but is something that I've done ever since.

My new job involved travel so I needed to buy myself a car (my Ford Popular had been taken back by the Electricity Board) and my brother, who was working in Devon at the time, mentioned that the baker in Kingsbridge – a town close to where Roger worked – was selling his green Morris Minor Traveller. It was reliable, roomy and suited my needs perfectly. I parked it right outside our flat (these were the days you could still park on Thurloe Street) feeling really rather proud. I had my own car, a smart new job and a flat in Kensington: I had arrived!

A few days later I was in the flat when there was a knock at the door and I went downstairs to find a policeman standing on the doorstep.

'Good evening, Miss, I'm from Chelsea Police Station. I'm enquiring about the car parked outside. Do you know the owner?'

'Yes,' I said, with a hint of pride. 'It's mine.'

'Well, I have reason to believe it may have been stolen,' said the policeman.

I was horrified, but as I launched into the stammered explanation of how I had just bought it from a baker in south Devon it became clear that the whole thing was a misunderstanding. By coincidence, the policeman was engaged to the daughter of the baker in Kingsbridge and had recognized his future father-in-law's car – not realizing that it had been sold!

We actually became quite good pals with that policeman and his fellow officers. In those days you'd always see a policeman about, which of course you don't now, and they were such a lovely bunch. They would keep an eye on us girls and often drop in to have coffee with us, keeping us entertained with tales from the beat. I remember they once told us that most major crimes in Chelsea were committed before three o'clock in the morning, because after that time the streets were so quiet that you'd instantly be noticed. I'm not sure why, but that has stayed with me to this day!

Meanwhile, I was thoroughly enjoying my work at the Dutch Dairy Bureau. It helped that I was passionate about the product: I became a total convert to unsalted butter, having it on my toast and using it in cooking to this day. My days were spent either in my little test kitchen at the Bureau's offices in Bloomsbury, developing recipes for magazines and writing information leaflets, or travelling all over the country to show people how to cook with Dutch butter and cheese. I would set off in my Morris Minor Traveller, stopping off at hotels or B&Bs on the way (quite a treat for me, as I had never really stayed much in hotels as a child) with my samples of Edam and Gouda in the back. During this time I often carried a carful of cheese, which brought problems of its own. On my first trip to Scotland I remember driving down Argyle Street in Glasgow when out of the corner of my eye I spotted something moving in the footwell of the passenger seat. I glanced over to get a better look and to my horror saw a mouse. I can cope with most things, but I can't stand mice and dead birds. Without even thinking, I slammed on the brakes and jumped out of the car in the middle of Argyle Street, blocking a lane of traffic. I was just standing there, wondering what on earth I could do (and worrying what state my cheese would be in, as I was on my way to give a talk in a school) when a policeman materialized.

'Is there a problem, young lady?'

'I'm terribly sorry,' I said, 'but I've got a mouse in my car, and I can't get back in because I really don't like mice.'

The policeman just smiled. 'I completely understand. Go and stand on the pavement.'

So that kind policeman got in my car and drove it over to the side of the road, then emptied out all the cheese and shook out the mats.

'I'm sure the animal has gone now,' he said, after reloading the car.

Sure enough, I didn't see the mouse again and, when I got to the school, I was relieved to discover that most of my samples had survived intact, and I just trimmed the gnawed bits of those that had not. (Apropos of that story, just the other day we had people over for lunch and I did a lovely cheeseboard with grapes and half figs – it really looked very pretty – but when I walked out of the kitchen for a moment I came back to find that Poppy, my twin granddaughters' spaniel, had the whole piece of cheddar on the floor. Rather than throw it all away, I just cut off the bit with the teeth-marks and put it back. The floor was reasonably clean!)

It was during this trip to Scotland, my first ever, that I was able to visit the place where my mother had grown up. Mum used to tell me that she had been 'born on the banks of Loch Lomond', which had always tickled me, so while I was in the area I took a detour to look for her childhood home, Dal-monach House. My grandfather had been in charge of the cotton mill at Alexandria, but then came the advent of synthetic fabrics, the mill closed and the family had to leave that part of the world. They moved to Sale, near Manchester, so he could find work, while my mother was sent away to Harrogate College for schooling. Still, she had very fond memories of Dalmonach House, where her family had lived from when she was aged two to eighteen, and she would often talk to me about her very happy childhood home. 'The mill managers lived in some style,' she remembered. 'The houses they were given needed maids, gardeners and so on. We had a lodge at Dalmonach with huge entrance gates that were closed and locked at night. Our house had a billiard room, tennis court and beautiful gardens run by the lodge keeper, and also several conservatories.'

Although I wouldn't have asked to look around the house itself, I'd been hoping I might be able to ask the current owners for permission to walk around those 'beautiful' gardens, but when I got there I was terribly disappointed to discover that the house had been pulled down. As I stood at the huge entrance gates by the lodge (which was still standing), staring at the spot where the house had once stood and thinking about all my mother's happy memories of the place, I felt really quite teary. There was a consolation, however, because when I arrived at my hotel, The Buchanan Arms, later that afternoon I found that the carpet throughout was in the pattern of Buchanan tartan. My cousins were Buchanans, so to find their tartan all the way up the stairs was a lovely reminder of them.

As well as travelling around Britain, I visited Holland to see how the dairy business was run and took groups of journalists on press trips to meet the farmers and see the cheese being made. I became quite an expert on Dutch cuisine; one of my favourite recipes was Boterkoek, which is like a very buttery sort of shortbread. My mastery of the Dutch language wasn't quite as proficient, however – in fact the only phrase I can now recall is '*Oop der plaats*', which is what you say to dogs to get them to sit in the corner!

I loved my job but I was often quite lonely on these trips.

When I was working at exhibitions they would sometimes employ girls to dress in Dutch costume and hand out samples of cheese, but most of the time I was on my own – and I'm not at all good at being on my own away from home. I'm a very social person, so having dinner by myself or sitting in a hotel room reading is just not my scene, but it was part of the job so I just got on with it. Besides, my increasingly busy social life made up for the occasionally solitary times during work hours . . .

# VICTORIA SANDWICH

A Victoria Sandwich sponge is a great British classic, and is the cake I used to make to demonstrate ovens for the Electricity Board. Using the all-in-one method, it is one of the simplest cakes to make. Vary the jam as you wish. I have given a choice of butter or baking spread: baking spread will give an excellent result, but make sure you use high-fat spread (over 69%) and not a spread with a low fat content.

*Serves 6*

- 225g (8 oz) butter, softened or baking spread
- 225g (8 oz) caster sugar
- 4 large eggs
- 225g (8 oz) self-raising flour
- 2 level teaspoons baking powder

**for the filling and topping**
- about 4 tablespoons strawberry or raspberry jam
- a little caster sugar

Preheat the oven to 180°C/Fan 160°C/Gas 4. Lightly grease two deep 20cm (8 inch) loose-bottomed sandwich tins and line each base with a circle of non-stick baking parchment.

Measure the butter or spread, sugar, eggs, flour and baking powder into a large bowl and beat for about 2 minutes until just blended. An electric mixer is best for this, but of course you can also beat it by hand with a wooden spoon. Divide the mixture evenly between the two tins and level it out with the back of a spoon or plastic spatula.

Bake in the preheated oven for about 25 minutes, or until well risen and golden. The tops of the cakes should spring back when pressed lightly with a finger. Leave the cakes to cool in the tins for a few moments then run a blunt knife around the edge of the tins to free the sides of the cakes. Turn the cakes out, peel off the paper and leave to cool completely on a wire rack.

Choose the cake with the best top, then put the other cake top downwards on to a serving plate. Spread with the jam, put the first cake on top (top upwards) and sprinkle with caster sugar.

Cut into wedges and serve.

# 6

It was the dawn of the sixties, but London wasn't swinging just yet: the miniskirts and white patent boots would come a few years later – although I wouldn't ever have the guts to wear them! At the time, the really glamorous places to go in the evening were the new nightclubs in Soho or for dinner at the Ritz or Savoy, but for us Thurloe Street girls with limited finances and hectic careers, our social lives revolved around going to friends' flats or inviting people back to ours. There would often be bottle parties, where you'd take a bottle of wine to someone's flat and a group of you would drink and chat, just like you'd do at a pub these days. We were friends with a group of boys who lived at 5 Sydney Place, a few minutes' walk away, so we would sometimes pop over there for tea; they could usually just about rustle up a bit of bread and jam!

One of those chaps, Tony Bull, became my boyfriend for a time. I was immensely fond of him; he was a very good sportsman, playing hockey for the county, and was in London training to be a doctor. We remained great friends and when Tony later became an Ear, Nose and Throat surgeon, one of the youngest on Harley Street, it was he who removed my husband Paul's tonsils. As Paul was wheeled down to theatre I can remember him saying, 'Now don't forget, Tony, it's my tonsils you're removing!' Tony married the lovely Jilly, who was a nurse, and I am godmother to the Bulls' first child, Amanda, who is just as special to me as her parents are.

While we were living at Thurloe Street, more often than not we'd all go back to our parents' houses at weekends, but if we did happen to stay in London for the weekend, then our dinner dates would be to restaurants like Fiddlers Three on Beauchamp Place or The Stockpot on the Kings Road, which is still there today. The boys would sometimes go to Ronnie Scott's to listen to jazz, but that wasn't really our scene. We preferred The Stable, just off the Cromwell Road, which was a small club where you could have dinner and dance. It wasn't posh like Annabel's (where I have been only once or twice) but we thought it was fabulous. I would always dance at the clubs – the classics, such as the Foxtrot and the Waltz, along with the Twist. I was a hopeless dancer and never took it seriously, but I love music with a rhythm; we always had Radio Luxembourg on in the flat, and I particularly enjoyed listening to songs by The Beatles and The Seekers.

Mostly, however, our weekends were spent back in Bath. I would come up the driveway on Friday night and Dad would be at the door waiting with a gin and tonic and I'd know I was home. I usually drove straight up the A4 from London, but if the traffic was bad I would occasionally take a detour through Melksham, about twelve miles outside Bath. On one such occasion I was belting through the village when a police car suddenly overtook me, lights flashing and siren wailing, and signalled for me to pull over. As the policeman walked back to my car I sat frozen in my seat, trying to calm my nerves: I had absolutely no idea how fast I had been going.

The policeman bent down at my window. 'Good evening, Miss. Do you know you were speeding?'

'Oh I'm so sorry, I had no idea,' I said, feeling extremely flustered because I was convinced I was about to get a ticket. Despite that, I couldn't help but notice that the young officer was terribly handsome. 'I'll make sure I keep an eye on my speed in future.'

Well, we chatted for a while; he was ever so nice and, to my relief, let me off with just a caution before sending me on my way. However, when I got home the following weekend there was a letter waiting for me on Avon and Somerset Constabulary headed stationery. 'Oh no,' I thought. 'I must have been given a speeding ticket after all.' When I opened the letter up I discovered that it was actually from that smashing young policeman inviting me to accompany him to the upcoming police ball. I was immensely flattered and if I'd known anyone else who had been going I would have accepted, but I was far too nervous to go alone. I showed the letter to my father, who said, 'That chap will either be chucked out of the force at a very early age or he'll make chief of police.'

By this time I had sold my second-hand Morris Traveller and had bought a sporty little MGA. Although hire purchase was just coming in at the time, I wasn't one for buying anything that way, so I put aside a portion of my Dutch Dairy Bureau earnings every month until I had saved up enough. I remember going to Bath Garages with my father and feeling as proud as anything when I announced to the salesman, 'I would like to buy an MGA.' At that time number plates consisted of three letters, denoting the licensing authority town, followed by a number. I had noticed that 'NGL 1' was coming up and quite fancied it for my cherished new car. The garage told me that as long as Bath's police chief or mayor didn't want it, I could have it; eight weeks later, to my delight, my number plate arrived – and I've put 'NGL 1' on every car I've owned since. I didn't have to pay anything for it but, of course, it's really quite valuable now. Over the years I've been stopped in the street many times and offered vast sums of money for my number plate, but I would never sell. All my friends recognize it instantly, so I can be anywhere from Scotland to St Tropez and get a note on my windscreen saying: 'What are you doing here?' It's just lovely.

I had always enjoyed driving, but now that I was the proud owner of a sports car I decided it was time to take my Advanced Driving Test. I passed first time, and when I went home to tell my brothers they couldn't believe it.

'An advanced motorist?' they spat. 'You?'

I nodded, smiling. But they were still unconvinced, so I showed them the badge on my car and explained that as an advanced motorist I was now entitled to ten per cent off my car insurance. Well, within a month both my brothers and father had taken the test – but I never let them forget that I was the one who got there first!

These were good times: none of my friends were out of work and although money was tight we had enough to have fun. We'd sometimes go to Carnaby Street at weekends and everything would be so alive; you never knew who you were going to bump into. It was while living at Thurloe Street that I went on my first skiing trip along with my dear friend Jilly Clements, who was one of our flatmates at the time. I hadn't a clue what to pack, never having been skiing before, and I ended up taking the most enormous bag stuffed full of things that I would never use – I think I even took a small iron! In contrast, Jilly had this little red suitcase that was terribly small and neat. We must have been quite a sight as we made our way along the platform: me – rather short, barely able to lift my large suitcase – and Jilly, who was very tall and strong, striding along with her tiny red bag. In the end Jilly very kindly insisted that we swap bags and she carried mine instead.

We travelled to Austria by rail on the 'Snow Sports Special', which was basically a party train full of young people. It was a lot of fun: it even had a carriage in which you could dance. When Jilly and I joined the train in London we found ourselves sitting opposite three girls who looked like they were about the same age as us, but any similarity ended there. While we were bundled up in bulky borrowed clothes, they were decked out in sleek designer skiwear with matching luggage. I can remember glancing over at the glossy-haired trio and whispering to Jilly, 'Anyone would think they went to Roedean.' For those who don't know, Roedean is a girls' boarding school that was considered terribly posh in my day.

Well, it was a long journey and we did end up chatting to the girls, and it turned out that I was right – all three of them had been to Roedean! Jilly and I thought they were awfully snobby and hoped that they weren't going to the same place as us, but when the train stopped for Lech they followed us off. Not only that, it turned out that we were all staying at the same hotel. As we trudged through the snow, the three of them seemed to be frightfully amused that Jilly was carrying my great big suitcase for me. In fact, that seemed to break the ice and we ended up becoming very friendly with them. Their names were Penny, Jill and Julia, and while we didn't see much of them during the day because all three of them were such beautiful skiers and Jilly and I were still in ski school, we got together every evening and had a wonderful time. The higher up the mountain you went the better your tan, so when it was time to go home the Roedean girls were brown as berries while Jilly and I were still as pale as pale! We parted vowing to stay in touch, and when one of our flatmates moved out of Thurloe Street soon after we returned home we offered the space to Penny Block. At the time she was working as a high-flying secretary, having attended a top secretarial college. Penny was very pretty and elegant, extremely clever and a brilliant sportswoman: she not only skied beautifully, she hunted and was a good tennis player. All quite annoying really! Anyway, she accepted our invitation and came to live with us at Thurloe Street – and has been my best friend ever since.

As much as I enjoyed my job at the Dutch Dairy Bureau I viewed it as a stepping stone. By 1960, soon after I turned twenty-five, I was already thinking about my next move. I was getting to know journalists on magazines and newspapers and had ideas about moving on, but first I wanted to make sure I gave myself the best possible chance of climbing the career ladder. I had heard that Le Cordon Bleu in Paris was the best cookery school in the world and I knew that if I could go and study there it would look good on my CV, but the month-long course was extremely expensive and there was no way I would be able to afford to pay for it myself. I had to find someone else who could.

My boss, Mr Sevink, had quite an eye for the ladies, but I knew how to play him. After I had worked on a particularly successful exhibition I went to his office to see him; as expected, he was thrilled with my efforts and full of compliments.

'You know, I think it would be really useful if I went on a course to develop my skills,' I said carefully. 'Perhaps to the Cordon Bleu in Paris? I would obviously arrange my accommodation, but I wonder if you would give me a month's leave to study there – and perhaps pay for my tuition . . . ?'

Mr Sevink didn't even hesitate. 'A wonderful idea!' he said enthusiastically, agreeing that it would definitely benefit my work. In fact, he seemed to believe that I was being extremely fair in offering to pay for the accommodation.

My flatmates thought that I was terribly lucky, off to Paris for a month, but I was feeling very nervous and unsure about how I'd get on by myself. I had booked myself into a shared room in a dirt-cheap student hostel that was quite a long way from the Cordon Bleu, so on the first morning of the course I set off almost when it was still dark to make sure I could find it. Money was tight so I had to walk. I had assumed that the world-renowned Cordon Bleu would be housed in some magnificent marble-floored building, but when I arrived at the address that I'd been given – 129 Rue du Faubourg Saint-Honoré – I found myself standing outside what looked like a backstreet bakery. Convinced I must be at the wrong place, I knocked on the door and a tiny bird-like woman appeared, whom I would later discover was the school's director, the famously formidable Madame Brassart. She would run the school until 1984, when she retired at the age of eighty-seven.

'*Bonjour Madame,*' I said in my shaky French. '*Le Cordon Bleu, s'il vous plaît?*'

Madame Brassart regarded me for a moment with her piercing blue eyes, then gestured to a flight of stairs that led to the basement.

'*Le Cordon Bleu est en bas,*' she said imperiously.

I found myself in a dark and gloomy room with sawdust on the stone floor and rows of long wooden tables but no stools. It wasn't one bit what I had expected. Could the world's most prestigious cookery school really be here in this . . . cellar? It was really rather depressing. I later discovered that there was a definite hierarchy at the Cordon Bleu: the 'regular' students, most of whom were rich Americans who only seemed to be taking the course so they could learn the odd recipe to give to their cooks, studied in the airy, well-lit room upstairs, while the cheaper 'professional' course was taught '*en bas*' – down in the dingy cellar.

I was quite frightened of our instructor, a fiery chef who was very noisy and shouted a lot. All of the teaching was done in French, which was rather stupid because most of the students were non-French speakers and the chef spoke perfectly good English.

In the morning we would be given typed sheets with recipes that we would prepare under the beady eye of Chef, who gave you marks for your dish, and we would then eat whatever we had cooked for lunch. French food was held in such high regard at this time that I had been expecting to learn how to prepare some amazing dishes, but although we did a few classics, most of what we prepared on the course was fairly unexciting and unmemorable. The first dish we made was a version of Croque Monsieur: a bread case filled with a sort of souped-up scrambled egg (not at all authentic, and not particularly tasty, either). Despite the school's astronomical course fees there was a definite air of penny-pinching about the whole operation – something that was also picked up by the American cook Julia Child, who had studied at the Cordon Bleu ten years before me, and who said of Madame Brassart: 'It seemed to me that the school's director should have paid less attention to centimes, and more attention to her students.' The ingredients we were given to cook with were obviously inexpensive: cheaper cuts of meat and dairy products that had been hanging around a bit too long. The cream smelled slightly of cow; it wasn't like the lovely fresh cream we got in England. (I should note that when I went back to visit the modern Cordon Bleu in Paris last year it was wonderful, absolutely top class, and exactly the sort of place my twenty-five-year-old self had been expecting! It was interesting to glance through their visitors' book: noteworthy names included Elizabeth David, Katie Stewart (cookery editor of *The Times*) and Rosemary Hume, who founded the first English Cordon Bleu school in London along with Constance Spry.)

After lunch, we would go upstairs where the chefs would demonstrate how to prepare dishes in front of an audience, including the rich American students and any members of the public who wanted to attend. It was always a relief to see daylight when we emerged from our dungeon. It was at these afternoon demonstrations that the chefs would focus on the more elaborate dishes and use expensive ingredients, for their bigger audience.

Although I have no regrets about going to the Cordon Bleu as it undoubtedly looked good on my CV, I'm afraid I don't really have any fond memories of my time there. After the course had finished each afternoon I would go straight back to the hostel, as I didn't have any spending money for visiting galleries or museums. I shared the tiniest room imaginable with a nice French girl, but she was out every night so I would just sit in the room reading a book and nibbling a baguette. The American students were staying in five-star hotels and dining out at the top restaurants, so I certainly couldn't have socialized with them. All in all, I spent my month in Paris feeling rather lonely.

The one thing I did enjoy while I was there was looking around the street markets. There would be all these wonderful ingredients that I had never seen in England: different varieties of fruits, wild mushrooms and huge bunches of fresh herbs – at the time all you could get in London were dried herbs. I was introduced to thyme, flat-leaf parsley and basil, still with the soil-dusted roots attached to help them keep longer. Wandering around the stalls, sampling the produce and enjoying the smells and sights, I was at least able to experience some of the excitement that I had expected to gain on the course. I returned home to England after four long weeks with my Cordon Bleu certificate and – thanks to those wonderful markets – a reinvigorated sense of excitement about the potential of food.

Soon after I returned from Paris, I handed in my notice at the Dutch Dairy Bureau. I had applied for a job I had seen advertised in the newspaper, for a Senior Home Economist to test and develop recipes at a public relations company that specialized in food. The role would be a step up in responsibility and status, with a monthly salary of £128 – plus the company's clients were largely British, and I was keen to be promoting home-grown products – so I was very excited when I got the job. Considering that Mr Sevink had just paid for me to 'improve my skills' at Le Cordon Bleu, yet would reap none of the benefits, he accepted my resignation with surprisingly good grace.

It worked out that I had a few months off before I started my new job at Benson's Public Relations and by coincidence my friend Penny had recently left her secretarial position, so we decided to take advantage of our mutual temporary unemployment and rent a chalet for the ski season. We managed to get a loan from the bank, with which we were able to secure a three-month lease on a chalet in the village of Saanen in the Swiss resort of Gstaad. We then sent out a letter to all our friends and well-liked acquaintances inviting them to come and stay with us for a fortnight. We proposed the following arrangement to potential guests: we would provide accommodation, catering and basic housekeeping, and in return all they had to do was get themselves to Gstaad and pay us twenty-two pounds for the two weeks. To our surprise, we had no problem filling the chalet for the whole three-month period.

Setting off from Penny's parents' house at Little Gaddesden, we loaded up her little green Mini with everything but the kitchen sink – although I probably would have taken that too if it hadn't been plumbed in. As well as my new Head skis from Harrods and ski kit from C&A, I packed all my spices and seasonings, mountains of butter that I had been given as a parting gift by the Dutch Dairy Bureau, even a turkey. I think I must have imagined that there would be no shops in Switzerland; honestly, I don't know what we didn't take. Soon the Mini was so full that it was impossible to see out of the back and we still hadn't got everything in, so we persuaded Penny's younger brother Tim to fit a roof rack on to the car for us. Being a chap, we had assumed that he would know all about such things; he certainly seemed confident enough.

Feeling thoroughly excited about our adventure ahead, we set off in Penny's jam-packed car, but we hadn't even reached Hemel Hempstead when suddenly the whole roof rack slid off, flinging bags and boxes and skis all over the road. Amazingly, we managed to retrieve all our belongings before they (or we) were run over, and then went and found a phone box to ring Tim, who came and fitted the roof rack back on again – securely, this time. We've never let him forget it.

When we finally made it to Saanen we were delighted to find a picture-perfect Swiss village. One of the first things I remember doing on our arrival at the chalet was putting the turkey in a snowdrift to keep it cold because it wouldn't fit in the fridge. I put the butter inside the bird, packed the gaps with snow and made a little igloo out of it.

We had expected our three months as chalet girls to be pretty hard work, but really they were a doddle. We were very lucky in that all our guests were our friends, so everyone helped with the washing-up after meals. Penny and I did clean the main rooms downstairs and the bathrooms, but when it came to the bedrooms we told our guests, 'If you tidy your room we will clean it, but if it's not tidy we're not cleaning it.' So we never had to clean any of the bedrooms!

Everyone was always starving hungry and we had to provide plenty of food. Penny and I would get up early every morning to bake a cake for tea and prepare breakfast; we would then ski all day, before returning to the chalet in time to serve our guests the cake and hot chocolate. We always did a nice dinner, repeating the menu every fortnight when our guests changed over. Fish and liver were the cheapest options, so I would make things like fish pie or casseroles – the sort of dishes I could prepare ahead – followed by proper puddings such as fruit pies. And then, while our friends helped clear up after dinner, Penny and I would prepare everyone's packed lunches for the next day's skiing.

On the whole people would stay in during the evenings to chat and play cards. Wine was quite inexpensive so we always had masses of bottles and I made great vats of Glühwein, which always went down very well. Our guests would usually take us out on their last night before they left and on several occasions we went to the nightclub at the Palace, Gstaad's famous five-star hotel that is still going strong today. It was right at the top of the mountain, accessed by cable car if I remember correctly, and was frightfully glamorous. Penny and I had what we called our 'Palace kit', which consisted of our smartest clothes – a silk shirt over a very thin polo neck, velvet evening trousers and little suede boots – but I think

Me skiing in Gstaad.

we still looked pretty scruffy. We didn't eat in the restaurant, but we drank and danced and had a fabulous time.

When each new batch of guests arrived, we would take them to ski school to get signed in and, because we were supplying the school with all these students, Penny and I got free skiing and generous discounts all over Gstaad, meaning that we not only covered all our expenses for our stay, we returned home in profit. As I've mentioned before, Penny was a really excellent skier and I was not, but I muddled along, improving slowly, and by the end of the season I had joined her in the top group of the ski school. We were the only two in the class and so had the instructor, the very glamorous and extremely handsome Adolf, all to ourselves. Since Gstaad isn't at that high altitude, for our final weeks of skiing in March there was very little snow left on the slopes and I remember the clatter of pebbles on my skis as I zipped down the Wasserngrat. Terrible for the skis, but great fun! It was on one of these late spring days after all our guests had gone home that Penny and I found ourselves sharing a lift with the Hollywood actor David Niven. We ended up skiing with him for the day and he was just as handsome and charming as you would expect, a complete gentleman and an excellent skier as well. Ski gear was far heavier and much more unwieldy in those days – and the boots took ages to put on, as you had to lace them up – but one of the great things about being a girl was that the chaps had to help out, so I can proudly declare that David Niven carried my skis around for a day!

Finally it was time to return home and Penny's father, Pa Block, drove out to accompany us on the journey back to England. He took us in convoy on a four-day wine tour of Germany, stopping off at all the different vineyards; he spoilt us rotten and I think we were permanently tipsy. We went out for some wonderful restaurant meals, which was a real treat after three months of mass catering.

Our time in Switzerland had been such fun – all very jolly hockey sticks! – and I think our guests enjoyed themselves tremendously. It was a wonderful experience for carefree young girls like us, but there was a terrible tragedy in the middle of it that gave me my first taste of the fleeting preciousness of life. We had been in Gstaad for about a month when our flatmate Jilly Clements (she of the tiny red suitcase) arranged to come out to see us. While most people took the train to Switzerland, Jilly had decided to fly to Innsbruck and make her way from there. On the day of her arrival we were so busy greeting the other new guests that when Jilly didn't appear at the time she said she would we just assumed that her flight had been delayed and got on with supper; a few hours later and still with no sign of her we tried ringing the airport, but the line was constantly busy. We finally got through, to be told

Penny, a brilliant skier. I'm always far behind her.

to our horror that there had been a plane crash in Austria: Jilly's plane had hit a mountain on the descent into Innsbruck and all seventy-five passengers and eight crew members had died.

It was devastating, but we had made a commitment to the chalet and had to soldier on. As soon as we got back home we went to see Jilly's parents, but they were so upset they couldn't speak to us. I noticed there were no photos of her in the house; it was as if they had just switched off. A few years later I saw Mr and Mrs Clements again at Pip Aubrey's wedding and they were still unable to talk to me about Jilly. It was very sad, because I had some really lovely things to say about her, but I was clearly a vivid reminder of their daughter, and that was just too painful for them.

# ICED LEMON FLUMMERY

This is a wonderfully refreshing, sophisticated dessert.

*Serves about 12*

- 300ml (½ pint) double cream
- finely grated rind and juice of 2 lemons
- 350g (12 oz) caster sugar
- 600ml (1 pint) milk

**to serve**
- a little whipped cream
- sprigs of fresh mint or a sliced strawberry

Pour the cream into a bowl and whisk until it forms soft peaks. Stir in the lemon rind, juice, sugar and milk and mix well until thoroughly blended.

Pour into a 1½ litre (2½ pint) shallow plastic container, cover with a lid and freeze for at least 8 hours – or preferably overnight – until firm.

Remove from the freezer, cut into chunks and process in a processor until smooth and creamy. Pour into 12 small ramekins, cover with cling film and return to the freezer until required.

To serve, remove from the freezer about 15 minutes ahead. Spoon or pipe a blob of whipped cream on top of each ramekin and decorate with a sprig of mint or slices of strawberry.

## 7

I started work at Bensons Public Relations in 1962 when the workplace was still very much male dominated, certainly at a more senior level; I remember taking the tube to work in the morning and being a rare flash of colour amidst a sea of black bowler hats. Although all my friends had gone into careers after school, it was still quite unusual for women to continue working once they were married. Bensons, however, was an all-woman company – apart from a few men working in finance and managerial roles. My boss was a wonderful woman called Olwen Francis, who would become one of my most important mentors. As well as her role at Bensons, when I joined the team she was also editor of an educational magazine called *Home Economics*, so her knowledge and experience were extremely broad. She was a big, handsome woman – Australian originally, I think – and, although I was rather in awe of her, she was always very encouraging and her faith in me greatly increased my own self-confidence.

Bensons had something like sixteen different clients, all of them in the food industry, including the Butter Information Council, Flour Advisory Bureau, Colmans, the Herring Board, Stork Margarine . . . I could go on! Working under Mrs Francis were four account executives who ran these different accounts. As home economist, my role was to develop recipes using our clients' products for magazines and newspapers; for instance, the account executive for the

Egg Marketing Board might come to me and say they were doing a Christmas feature for the *Daily Telegraph*, so I would develop a number of Christmas recipes that used English eggs and the account executive would pay my department three pounds for each of them. For the first time in my career I had my own assistant, a lovely girl called Jenny Reekie, and together we would cook the recipes in the morning and photograph them in the afternoon, so the newspaper would have pictures to go with the words. It was easier to come up with ideas for some clients than it was for others: the Flour Advisory Bureau was obviously a doddle, but the Herring Advisory Board proved more of a challenge. I did things like Rollmops and Stargazy Pie (a traditional dish of herrings, eggs and potatoes, named for the fact that the fish heads poke out of the pastry crust as if gazing skyward – horrible!)

My time at Bensons proved to be a fantastic learning curve for me as I was working with so many food companies, popping into magazine offices and dealing with all sorts of different people. Just down the road at Bensons Advertising there was a wonderful cook who used to prepare the directors' lunches and I would often visit her to borrow something or just to see what she was cooking that day. One day when I arrived she was making a pâté of liver and various meats and, as we were talking, she took a little bit of the raw mixture and tasted it. I remember being horrified and wondering if I was less of a cook because I wouldn't have been able to do the same. The thought of eating raw meat turned my stomach – and yet how else could you check it for seasoning before cooking? So I came up with the idea of taking a little of the raw mixture, putting it in boiling stock for a moment until it was cooked through and then tasting it.

One of the things you realize as you grow older is that you never stop learning, whatever level you reach in your career. Even today, working on *The Great British Bake Off*, I still come across new things. One of the Showstopper challenges last year was to create a 'Hidden Design' cake, which is when you cut into it to discover a secret pattern or shape inside. It was something I had never made before, and I was hugely impressed by the contestants' efforts.

When I started work at Bensons one of my first tasks in the role was to set up the test kitchen at the firm's HQ at Windsor House in Holborn. To my delight, I was given free rein to kit it out and decorate it in whatever style I liked. I chose everything from the flooring to the pots and pans, all in a colour scheme of white and navy blue (still my favourite colour). That was tremendous fun: just like getting married, without the bother of a husband! Although I was in my late twenties and most of my friends had already walked down the aisle this really wasn't a burning ambition of mine at the time. Since moving to London I'd had a succession of boyfriends, most of them very lovely, none particularly serious. My parents never asked me why I wasn't settling down, and I had a career I loved and a fulfilling social life, so I felt – and I suppose that this was quite a modern way of thinking – that marriage and motherhood could wait.

My friend and flatmate Pip was getting married though, so I bid a fond farewell both to her and the flat at Thurloe Road and moved a mile up the road to a mansion block at 124 Knightsbridge. It was another top-floor two-bedroom flat, but we now had a little bit more room and a rather more fashionable address, just a few moments from Harrods. Our building was opposite the Knightsbridge Sporting Club casino and backed on to Hyde Park, although the interior had seen better days. The marble-floored entrance hall seemed bleak and unwelcoming (an impression hardly helped by the grumpy old porter manning the front desk) and the whole place smelled of oil from the ancient heating system. At least our flat on the fifth floor had its own front door, which felt very smart and grown-up after the communal entrance at Thurloe Street.

As well as Penny (who was five years younger than me and still happily single), I was now sharing with our friend Molly Berwick – although she wasn't there that often because she worked as an air stewardess for British Airways. These days all the glamour has gone out of the career, but back then you had to have a particular shape to become an air stewardess, just as you had to be a particular height to join the police, and 'Molly the Dolly' (as we called her) was certainly very shapely. The remaining place in the flat was filled by whichever of our friends needed somewhere to live at the time.

From our building you could walk to Harrods down a side road, on which there was a gallery and a dear little shop that sold nothing but miniature animal figurines, but we rarely shopped locally as everything was so expensive. Although our salaries were going up, there was little extra for spending money – especially for those of us with cars, as any spare went on petrol and garage bills. I would do my grocery shopping near where I worked, at the Sainsbury's on Drury Lane, and everything else I would get in Bath, as I was still going home to my parents' house most weekends.

I had been in my job at Bensons for a few years when Olwen Francis came up to the test kitchen to speak to me one day. I didn't realize at the time, but this meeting would turn out to be one of the more important of my life. As I went about preparing the recipes for that day's shoot, she explained that she'd just had a call from a friend of hers, who was the editor of *Housewife* magazine.

'Apparently her cookery editor has gone on a press trip to Spain with Seville Oranges without giving in her copy for the next issue,' said Mrs Francis. 'The poor woman's stuck without anyone to write the feature – and so I've told her that you'll do it for her.'

I froze in the middle of whatever I was doing. I knew I was good at my job, but developing recipes was a very different matter to actually writing an article for a magazine. I was a home economist, not a journalist.

'Mrs Francis, I'm terribly sorry but I can't do it,' I told her, terrified of letting her down, but convinced by my lack of skill. 'I failed English at school. I don't know how to write.'

'Well, you often tell me what to cook for supper and how to prepare it – just write as you talk.'

Her manner suggested that the subject was not open for further debate and so, reluctantly, I agreed to the assignment. That afternoon I sat down to write my first ever magazine feature: 'Mary Berry's Dinner Party for Four'. The starter was Scandinavian Herrings (which conveniently gave me an opportunity to include one of Bensons' clients – the Herring Board), then a main course of Roast Stuffed Veal, the recipe for which was given to me by my friend Shirley Nightingale, and Rum Dessert Cake for pudding.

Mrs Francis' suggestion – just write as you talk – proved to be the most useful piece of advice that I've ever been given; to this day when I sit down to write anything I keep it in mind. I like to think that I'm there, holding my readers' hands while they cook my recipes. Here's an extract from that very first article:

The blushing bride and groom. Paul and I on our wedding day at
Charlcombe Church.

A photo shoot at our Farmer Street home for *Housewife*. I'm having tea with Paul (above) and making some very 1960s-style curtains (below).

My kitchen in Farmer Street at a photo shoot in the 60s during my time as Cookery Editor.

One of my early cookery demonstrations.

Paul and I with Thomas and William holidaying in Salcombe.

Our golden boys.

A photo shoot for one of my first cookbooks with my two helpers, Annabel and William.

A day's sailing with Captain Tom.

Tom, William and Annabel showing off their Christmas jumpers.

A Saturday morning demo for the Electricity Board.

At a photo shoot for a book cover – believe it or not, the food was very modern for the time!

My first experience as a judge, on 'Junior Cook of the Year'. Great practice for *Bake Off*, some forty years later!

Filming at the Red House with Annabel, a very proud baker.

The secret of carefree entertaining is meticulous advance planning. Start by taking stock of what you have in the store cupboard, then make a shopping list. Consider the drinks – or see that your husband does. A claret or burgundy goes well with the roast veal. Be sure there is plenty of room in the refrigerator, and that it has been defrosted recently. Check the linen, clean the silver and, of course, do not forget to have sharp knives for carving.

The day before, arrange your flowers and your table decoration. Lay the table early in the afternoon of the party day, not forgetting to make mustard and fill the pepper mills and salt cellars . . . Lastly, brief the children, if they will still be up when the guests arrive – get them to help hand round the drinks and appetizers. But make sure that they have a good supper first, so that, their mission accomplished, they go off happily to bed with a minimum of protest.

To my astonishment and considerable relief, the editor of *Housewife* seemed pleased with my article, so much so that she offered me the job of Cookery Editor when the then incumbent was sacked soon after her return from Spain (employers were able to do that in those days).

As flattered as I was, my immediate reaction was that I should turn it down. I loved my job at Bensons too much to give it up; besides, what would happen if I went to work at *Housewife* only for the editor to realize that I couldn't actually write after all? Yet again it was Olwen Francis who found me a way out of my dilemma. She suggested that I stay at Bensons on a full-time salary, but offered to give me leave on Mondays and Fridays to work at *Housewife*, which was based at IPC (International Publishing Corporation), just five minutes' walk away, so I could always nip between the two offices if necessary. It was an incredibly generous offer, although I have no doubt that Mrs Francis had recognized that it would be advantageous if the cookery editor of *Housewife* magazine could promote Bensons' clients in her articles and recipes. Unable to believe my luck, I agreed to the proposal at once.

Landing the job of Cookery Editor on a magazine like *Housewife* was an unbelievable dream for me. It is easy to forget, but the media of the early sixties was a completely different world to what it is today. There was no internet, of course, but television was still really in its infancy too, meaning that magazines and newspapers were far more important and influential as a source of information, instruction and entertainment: back then *Woman's Own* had a circulation of something like three million, compared to 200,000 today. Over the previous few years I had got to know most of the key players in the women's magazines and read all of them religiously, but I would never have imagined that I might end up as a journalist myself. If only Miss Blackburn could have seen me!

*Housewife* was a monthly magazine, a bit like *Good House-*

*keeping* today, and its target audience was, as the cover strapline put it, 'For Go-Ahead Young Wives'. The working environment was far from glamorous – the offices were poky and rather scruffy and the budgets extremely tight – but none of this mattered to me; I was just determined to do the job really well and help to build the readership. I had sixteen pages to fill every month, which included about thirty of my own original recipes. From the very start it was vitally important to me to get these right, as I wanted the readers to be able to recreate them at home without a hitch, so I was a stickler for accuracy and clarity, and would spend many hours in the test kitchen trying the recipes out and getting my colleagues to taste them until they were perfect. I started a new monthly feature in the magazine in which I chose a particular recipe and explained how to make it in great detail: a full step-by-step guide with pictures. One of the most popular of these was the Fuller's Walnut Cake, which was my recreation of the speciality served at Fuller's, a nationwide chain of tearooms that could be considered the Starbucks of the time. People still ask me for that recipe today.

With Olwen Francis' advice to 'write as I talk' ringing in my ears, I then wrote everything out longhand and gave it to a secretary to type it up. This worked brilliantly for the recipes; later, when I started to interview people for the magazine, I just wrote down exactly what they said and then sent it to the Subs department to be smartened up. Despite my initial concerns about my writing, I never remember being in agonies over anything I wrote. I certainly didn't have the vocabulary of an English scholar – and I would always envy food writers like Jane Grigson and Elizabeth David, who had such wonderful command of the language – but I didn't ever fuss about it too much. Although my spelling was pretty dreadful, I could tell when something looked incorrect and would just look it up in the dictionary. Anyway, I knew the basics: I could spell 'recipe' right, at least! And to my surprise I could actually remember a few things I had learnt at school, such as 'I before E except after C', so despite my disastrous exam results something obviously went in.

On magazines these days a journalist will write the words and then someone else will be responsible for the photography, but back then I had to do everything myself. I would oversee the shoot and make sure the food was looking as appealing as possible, a job that today is the responsibility of a food stylist. There were various tricks that people would use to make sure that the photographs looked appetizing, such as using scoops of mashed potato instead of ice cream (in the days before freezers), but while I might put a bit of oil on the top of something to give it a sheen I never used anything phony.

For one issue we did a step-by-step feature on creative children's birthday cakes. I'm not great at icing, but I sort of made it up as I went along and after slaving away for hours in the studio – with the photographer taking shots at each stage – I managed to create a fairly respectable centipede, a 'gold rush' cake decorated with chocolate coins, and a castle complete with toy soldiers and marzipan brick walls. When we had finally finished the shoot it seemed a shame to throw the cakes away, so I took them in a taxi to the nearby Moorfields Eye Hospital and gave them to the matron, who was delighted to serve the cakes for the children's tea that day. The following morning I got a phone call from the photographer: there had been a problem with the camera and none of the photos had come out. I had to make and decorate those cakes all over again.

When I started out food photography was very precise, with the aim of showing an idealized vision of the recipe, but gradually the more informal style that we see in books and magazines today began to appear, pioneered by top photographers like Anthony Blake. Rather than a pristine jar of jam, he wanted to see a drip oozing temptingly down the side. I always enjoyed doing shoots at Anthony's studio in Richmond: I would get there early to start on the cooking for the photographs, but then at one o'clock everyone would down tools and someone else would come in to cook lunch for us! There would be steak and wine; Anthony always made lunchtime a real event.

If we were doing a feature on dinner parties and needed people to be in the shot I would just round up my friends to take part: Pip, Jilly Bull and Molly the Dolly all appeared in various editions of *Housewife*. For a feature entitled 'Mary Berry tells you how to cook a Chinese Meal' I not only roped in my friend Shirley Nightingale and her husband James for the shoot, but we shot it in their house and all the Chinese plates, spoons and dishes were theirs. James was an airline pilot and Shirl was an air hostess – they were very well travelled and had a great selection of authentic Chinese bits and bobs. I had absolutely no idea how to cook a Chinese meal and so the recipes were theirs too.

Despite my best intentions, juggling two full-time jobs on my own proved to be rather too much and I was very grateful when *Housewife* agreed that I could have an assistant. While working at Bensons I had met a talented girl called Sue Hosier, who was then a junior at *Good Housekeeping*, and I poached her as my right-hand woman. We are still in contact today and I'm very grateful to Sue for sharing her memories of this time.

*Sue:*

I started working for Mary at the end of 1965 when I was twenty. I had been the junior at *Good Housekeeping* for two years, after taking a Cordon Bleu diploma at the school in Marylebone Lane, but I wanted more experience – and more money – so I applied for the job with Mary.

*Good Housekeeping* had these wonderful offices on the tenth floor of a very pleasant office block on Vauxhall Bridge Road with a lovely view out over the river and it was all very lady-like and genteel, so I had quite a shock when I moved over to the hard-nosed environment of *Housewife*. At that time IPC was a 'closed shop', which meant it only employed union members, so everyone had to belong to a union. It was very strict – we all had to pay our dues and attend union meetings – and the offices themselves had clearly seen better days.

Mary was quite unlike anyone I had met before; I think I was actually quite in awe of her. She was always delightful to work for, but I wouldn't have messed around with her! She was far more ambitious and single-minded than anyone I'd met, much more like career women of today, but also extremely kind and compassionate. She has wonderful taste in a very traditional way and I learnt a great deal from her – not just about cooking, but how to make the home a really attractive, lovely place.

Because Mary was only in the office for about two and a half days a week, I would hold the fort while she worked at Bensons. There had been a team of us in the department at *Good Housekeeping*, but here there was just Mary, part-time, and me aged twenty! I would run the office, answer the phone and reply to readers' letters on an old-fashioned sit-up-and-beg typewriter – with only Tippex for mistakes, as of course there were no computers. You can't imagine how different it was in those days: all the layouts were done on drawing boards, and if a photo needed cropping you would have to stick bits of paper down the side. It seems like something out of the ark! I was amazed how much work we got through.

Accuracy was very important. Mary would give me the recipes as a rough draft and I would go to the test kitchen upstairs a day or two a week and, having shopped for all the ingredients, test them out to make sure they absolutely worked. A lot of our features seemed to involve cakes: christening cakes, Simnel cakes, Christmas cakes, birthday cakes . . . There was far less variation in the food pages those days, because there wasn't such an interest in international cooking or the choice of ingredients we have now. I remember Mary doing Paella in one article: that would have been considered to be frightfully exotic!

On the photo shoots Mary was the creative person on the set, while I produced stuff out the back. Mary's talked about the tight budgets she was on, something I wasn't really aware of as her assistant, but everything did have to be done on a shoestring.

Work was very pressurized, but we always laughed a lot. We sometimes worked on location and on one occasion we zoomed off in Mary's little sports car, chatting away for the whole drive, and when we got there we could smell burning. 'My goodness,' said Mary, 'I think I had the handbrake on all the way here!' But we managed to get home safely. Another time we had to go to Longleat to see Lord Bath's Spanish cook and Mary made a day out of it. She took me to see her mum at Charlcombe Farm because that was nearby, and then she said to me, 'Have you ever been to Bath?' And when I told her that I hadn't, Mary said, 'Well, you can't come to

Bath and not have a Bath Bun,' and so she trotted me off to the famous Sally Lunn tearoom and we sat down to have tea.

I think we were quite an efficient team. I still look back over the vast numbers of cuttings I have from this time and wonder how we managed to produce them all. I think it was probably down to Mary's enormous capacity for work.

I left my job in June 1969 as my husband's job was taking us to Southampton, and in a way I felt I left Mary in the lurch because she was pregnant, but she was very gracious about it. I spent three and a half years with Mary – and have some very happy memories of our time together.

My career was going swimmingly and, around this time, my personal life took an interesting turn as well. I was at a party back in Bath one weekend when my brother made a beeline for me with a tanned, dark-haired chap in tow, whom he introduced to me as Paul Hunnings, one of his rugby friends. We talked for a while and Paul, who was from Enfield in north London, told me he worked for Harveys of Bristol, selling booze on export, although until recently he had been working for a shipping supply company in Singapore – hence the tan. He was very nice and polite and, I remember thinking, really rather handsome. I later found out that after our chat Paul had told my brother that he quite liked me, to which my brother apparently said, 'Well, you'd better get stuck in there then,' or something equally rude!

Our first date was dinner at The Stable and I can remember very little about it apart from the fact that I had smoked mackerel pâté. I don't recall being particularly taken by Paul at the very start; I was still sharing a flat with the girls and we were out with all sorts of chaps at this time. I certainly didn't come back from that first date thinking I'd met the man I was going to marry. Good god, no!

Paul stuck around, though, and began asking me to do things with him. We would go for dinner at Fiddlers Three or the Soup Kitchen; I never cooked a meal for us while we were courting, as I was too busy at work. Besides, food wasn't at all important to him – it never has been really. Typical man, he just liked the things his mother used to give him: Sunday roasts and mince. Although we didn't share the same interests at all, I always looked forward to our dates; he was so well travelled, so interesting, and he made me laugh, which I think is very important. And while Paul was very supportive of my career, he always wanted me to hurry back when I had been away on a press trip.

When we met, Paul was living in an upstairs flat in Muswell Hill with his school friend Tony Guest. I'm afraid I wasn't very keen on Muswell Hill – it was awfully busy, not a bit like Knightsbridge – and their flat was very male, with clothes strewn everywhere and lots of washing-up stacked on the side. The first time Paul took me there I noticed a string of pearls on his bedside table. 'Those are my aunt's,' he told me, as quick as I flash. 'Oh yes?' I said, raising an eyebrow. We never discussed it again!

Paul is a brilliant sportsman; he played rugger for Singapore, was a squash champion and enjoys tennis. Sport has always been more important to him that anything else: he has no tolerance for anybody who can't chuck a ball, so I can only assume I must have slipped through the net! There were always lots of rowdy rugger parties at his Muswell Hill flat and people coming and going at all hours. The landlady lived downstairs and one day, after yet another noisy night, she summoned Paul to see her.

'Mr Hunnings,' she said. 'I've lived here all through the war, all through the Blitz, but that was nothing to what I'm going through now. I'm afraid you'll have to go.'

And so Paul and Tony were looking for somewhere else to live.

Paul did a lot of travelling for his job and it so happened that he was away for my birthday a few months after we started courting. I had hoped he might send me something, but my birthday came and went with nothing having arrived and I remember thinking, 'Well, that's it then.' I assumed he had lost interest, so I was rather surprised to get a phone call from him as soon as he got back. 'Did you get the flowers?' he asked. 'No I didn't,' I said, still rather miffed. It turned out that he had ordered a bouquet from the florist Moyses Stevens, which was just round the corner from his office, and had been expecting something really special to be delivered, but it never arrived – possibly because no one was in our flat that day. He even went to get a note from them to prove to me that he did actually do as he said!

I'm not sure how long we had known each other when Paul first proposed, but it was in a restaurant one evening after he'd spent the afternoon playing rugby and drinking with his friends, so I just assumed he was a bit drunk and didn't say yes or no but told him I'd think about it. Anyway, he kept on asking me to marry him, but it only ever seemed to be after he'd been out drinking and so I always gave the same answer: 'I'll think about it.' This went on for quite a while and eventually I decided that if he'd got enough courage to ask my father's permission – because my father was pretty frightening – then that would prove he was serious. So the next time Paul proposed I said, 'Well, why don't you go and ask Dad?'

The very next weekend Paul drove up to Bath in his battered old Riley to speak to my father. I'll always remember that car because it leaked on the passenger side: whenever you drove through puddles, the water would splash through the floor and soak your feet, so Paul put a layer of plastic on the floor. And I always felt very guilty because he sold that car to a trainee vicar and when I asked if he'd come clean about the leak, Paul said, 'Well, it wasn't on the driver's side.'

Anyway, Paul was obviously very nervous about asking my father for my hand and as he came up the driveway to Charlcombe Farm he must have been distracted because when he pulled up outside the house he ran over one of Dad's prized white doves. A moment later Dad flew out of the door, shouting, 'You stupid boy!'

I called Paul later that evening, having stayed behind in London. 'So,' I said, 'did you ask him?'

There was a pause. 'Actually no, I didn't, because I killed one of his doves, but I will come back next week.'

True to his word he did just that, this time wisely taking a case of rather nice wine along with him so Dad greeted him with open arms. From what I've been told, the conversation went something like this.

Paul: 'I'd like to ask your permission to marry Mary.'

Dad: 'She's very difficult. You do realize what you're taking on?'

Paul: 'Well, yes . . .'

Dad: 'And she may never have children.' (I hadn't yet discussed this with Paul, but doctors had told me I might have trouble conceiving.)

Paul: 'Well I love her, so that doesn't matter.'

And so the following week Paul and I went for a walk in Hyde Park, near my flat in Knightsbridge, and he went down on one knee and asked me to marry him, and this time I said yes.

After he proposed, Paul explained that he wasn't yet able to afford to buy me a ring. 'The thing is, I don't actually have any money,' he said. I told him that I already knew that, and it didn't matter.

I would have been happy to wait for the ring, but I knew that Paul wanted to do things properly and so he went to ask his mother for help and she gave him a matchbox with a pair of diamond earrings rattling around inside. We went to Mallory Jewellers in Bath and had them made into a very pretty engagement ring, which I am still wearing to this day and wouldn't change for anything.

# SMOKED HADDOCK BOUILLABAISSE

A substantial soup can be a meal in itself on a cold winter's day or when out fishing.

*Serves 4–6*

- 50g (2 oz) butter
- 1 leek, washed and thinly sliced
- 1 medium carrot, peeled and chopped into 1cm (½ inch) cubes
- 250g (9 oz) old potatoes, peeled and cut into 1cm (½ inch) cubes
- 40g (1½ oz) plain flour
- 600ml (1 pint) hot fish or vegetable stock
- salt and freshly ground black pepper
- 500g (1 lb) undyed smoked haddock, skinned and cut into bite-sized pieces
- 600ml (1 pint) full-fat milk
- a small bunch of fresh dill, chopped

Heat the butter in a large pan. Add the leek and carrot and fry over a high heat. Cook for a minute or two then add the potatoes and stir the pieces around with the leeks and carrot.

Sprinkle over the flour, stir and cook for a few moments, then pour in the stock, slowly at first, stirring over the heat to blend it in, and allow the soup base to thicken. Season with the pepper (no salt at this stage). Bring to the boil, cover and simmer for about 10 minutes until the vegetables are tender.

Put the haddock pieces into the pan and add the milk, then simmer gently for about 5 minutes until the fish is just cooked. Check the seasoning, add the dill then pour into bowls to serve.

## 8

I was thirty-one when I got married, which was considered pretty ancient in those days. Apart from Penny, I was the last of my friends to walk down the aisle. Paul likes to joke that he rescued me from the shelf.

After we got engaged my father told us he was intending to give us two thousand pounds for a wedding present, which was a great deal of money in those days.

'You can either spend that all on your wedding or put it towards a deposit for your house,' he told us. And so Paul and I ended up having a very frugal wedding, because we needed somewhere to live.

When I think about the huge productions that weddings have become (my own children's included) involving so much time, effort and money, it astonishes me. In my day there just wasn't the faff there is now. Both my daughter Annabel and Sarah, my wonderful daughter-in-law, put so much energy into their wedding days, thinking about even the tiniest detail. For them it was an absolute dream and they were truly wonderful occasions, but in comparison, my own wedding day – 22nd October 1966 – looks positively spartan.

Choosing my wedding dress, which today seems to have become a momentous occasion involving multiple friends and glasses of champagne, was rather more of a box-ticking exercise for me. I knew that I needed a white dress to get married in and so I went out and bought one: it was as simple as that. I hadn't got a clue where I should look, so I asked the fashion editor at *Housewife* and she suggested I try a place called Susan Small in Camden Town, which was having its annual sample sale of the dresses models had worn in fashion shows. The idea appealed to my innate thriftiness, so I got the bus out to their factory in Camden, had a quick look through the rails of samples and found a classic, creamy-white dress with a bit of a tail at the back in my size. And it was only five pounds! I slipped it on and it fitted like a glove. 'Oh, that will do very nicely,' I thought to myself.

I took the dress to my parents' house and carefully packed it away, assuming I wouldn't see it again until my wedding day, but a few weeks beforehand my sister-in-law Margaret (who was married to my brother Roger) asked if she might have a quick look. I had been telling her all about this wonderful dress, which fitted so perfectly and had only cost five pounds, and so was very happy to oblige. However, when I tried it on in front of her it was immediately obvious to both of us that the dress was in need of drastic alteration. It had clearly been made for a model with a huge bosom and the front stuck out terribly. I must have been in such a hurry when I tried it on that I hadn't even noticed! Thankfully Margaret, who taught needlework, was able to alter it for me in time for the wedding – she ended up having to take literally feet off the bust to make it fit. Otherwise I would have needed a great deal of padding!

I had very little to do with organizing my wedding day: I was more than happy to let my mother make all the important decisions, so my only job was to turn up, although I did make the wedding cake. It was a simple, two-tier fruit cake with plain royal icing. I've never been the sort to spend hours icing a cake, because it vanishes in minutes and I always feel I could be doing lots of other useful things with my time, so with the help of my friend Shirley Nightingale I simply decorated it with bright blue gentians; I do love the look of fresh flowers on a cake.

Our wedding day in 1966. Oh, how it rained!

The night before, I drove up to my parents' house, Charl-combe Farm, with the cake, while Penny accompanied Paul to keep an eye on him and stop him spending too long in the pub with his best man – and former flatmate – Tony Guest. Penny was my bridesmaid and was to wear a beautiful gentian-blue gown that she already had in her wardrobe with a matching lace bolero that she had made to go over the top, so she didn't have bare arms in church. My two smaller bridesmaids were my godchildren, Mary Cavender, now Godwin-Austen, and Amanda Bull, now Tapp, and the page-boy was my godson William Patterson.

Our wedding day dawned dull and damp. The ceremony was at two o'clock in tiny Charlcombe Church, just down the road from Charlcombe Farm. A family friend, Barry Harris, had a Rolls Royce and he drove us up to the Church and back, all of five hundred yards! I wore my mother's veil and carried lily of the valley, just like Mum had at her own wedding. All girls want to be like their mother, don't they? Well, I did at least.

Charlcombe Parish Church is the oldest in Bath diocese, dating back over a thousand years, and is so tiny it can only hold sixty people, so the guests who couldn't fit inside had to stand outside in the drizzle while we were married. It was very lovely but I didn't cry during the ceremony; I think I was far more emotional at my children's weddings than I was at my own! Afterwards we held the reception in a tent in the garden but all I remember about the wedding tea is that we had raspberries and cream. Then Paul and I got in the MG and left for our honeymoon. It was absolutely pouring with rain as we drove away and I remember thinking, 'I wish I'd stayed for the party . . .' But there was no party. The whole thing was over by six o'clock.

Paul had booked an inn in the Cotswolds called The Shaven Crown for our honeymoon. Because I was working I could only take three days off – and it rained for every single one of them. My husband decided he wanted to take up fishing, so we spent a great deal of our honeymoon shivering on a rainy riverbank. There I was, the loyal little wife encouraging my husband while he tried – and failed – to catch a fish. I'm still waiting for my really hot, luxurious honeymoon!

It was lovely though, because we'd had such a busy time and it was wonderful to spend a few days alone together. During our time in the Cotswolds we went to a hotel called The Lamb for dinner and they had a circular rosewood table for sale, which became our dining-room table and has now been passed on to our daughter, Annabel. Every time we sit down to eat at that table it brings back happy memories of my rainy Cotswolds honeymoon.

I had assumed that we would buy a flat to live in after we were married, but Paul very wisely said that we should look for a house. During the time we were looking for a property I went to interview the novelist Charlotte Bingham, the author of a bestselling novel called *Coronet Amongst the Weeds*, for *Housewife*. She lived in the Hillgate Village part of Notting Hill and, enchanted by the area, I told Paul about this lovely collection of workmen's cottages I'd seen, all painted in different ice-cream colours and which would have looked more at home in Cornwall. That weekend we went to have a look at the area together and although we agreed it would be a wonderful place to live, with the atmosphere of a village yet moments from the tube station and a short hop from central London, we felt it was far too expensive for us. Nevertheless, we went to speak to the estate agent and were delighted to discover that they did have one property for sale that just fell within our price range: a pretty three-bedroom cottage with its own back garden, just two minutes from the tube. At first we couldn't understand why it was so much cheaper than neighbouring properties. It was only when we went to view the property – number 6 Farmer Street – that we realized the problem: it was next door to a fish and chip shop. Nobody wanted to buy it because they were worried about the smell of fried food.

The little cottage had been languishing on the estate agent's books for some time, but it seemed like such a bargain that we thought it was worth further investigation, and so the following weekend my father came down from Bath to carry out a survey for us. After a thorough look around, both inside and out, he came to the happy conclusion that the property would be completely unaffected by the smell, because the fish shop's chimneys were so tall that the fumes would be piped about eight houses down the road, missing its next-door neighbour entirely!

We bought the house on Farmer Street for nine thousand pounds, spending pretty much all of the money Dad had given us for our wedding present on the deposit, and moved in straight after we got back from our honeymoon. It had been freshly decorated and we had new curtains (my mother used to say that as long as you have good curtains and carpets, you can wait for the rest) but we hardly had any furniture. There was our honeymoon dining table, of course, a few bits and bobs from Charlcombe Farm and the four-foot-six bed from

Paul's flat – plus our wedding presents and all the cookware I could ever need, courtesy of my job – but that was it. Our plan was to acquire everything else gradually from junk shops and antique fairs. When we first moved in we didn't even have a cooker, so for a good few weeks I just balanced a pan on the two-bar electric fire in our bedroom and boiled and fried on that – highly dangerous, as you can imagine! Paul and I had a great hoo-hah about what colour we were going to paint the outside of the house, which was still the original brick facade when we moved in. We changed our minds about the colour virtually every weekend: we thought about navy, then ochre – even black. In the end I seem to remember that we abandoned all our plans and just lived with the brickwork.

The back garden – well, yard – was absolutely tiny, just a little patch that was even smaller than my kitchen today. I knew nothing about gardening and bought a lot of plants that didn't really take because it was so shady, but I enjoyed trying to make it look pretty. We could just fit a small table in there and it was really lovely to get home after work in the summer and be able to sit outside and have a glass of wine.

Notting Hill was an amazing place to live at the time. Next door we had a dear old lady who would take in parcels for us when we were away and would stop to pass the time of day on the doorstep. She never expected us to come in for lengthy chats, though – the perfect neighbour! She was ever so sweet, and when I had my first baby she welcomed me back from the hospital with an array of lovely little knitted things. On the other side, of course, there was the fish and chip shop, Geales, which was actually more of a restaurant than a chippy and is still there today. We would often get something for supper from Geales, although on special occasions such as

birthdays and anniversaries we would go to the Italian restaurant just up the road. In the late sixties, Italian restaurants
were springing up all over London: they still felt rather exotic,
but were a cheap and fun way to eat – and Italians do make
such wonderful restaurateurs, always smiling and so welcoming. At the end of our road was a narrow alleyway that cut
through to Notting Hill Gate, coming out just by the Classic
Cinema, and on the corner was a little bric-a-brac shop selling small items of furniture and ornaments, where every
morning the lady who owned it would set up a display of all
her goods outside like a market stall. We bought a lot of stuff
for our house from here, including a ceramic 'Sitting Hen',
slightly chipped but full of character, which became my first
in a collection that's still expanding today.

Sitting by the steps down to the tube station there was often
an old man with the most enormous basket of violets for sale.
Not long after we married, Paul came home from work one
evening bearing two huge bunches. I thought that was such a
thoughtful thing for a newly-wed husband to do, as he knew
how much I loved spring flowers, but when I looked at them
more closely I realized the violets were almost dead. Paul must
have seen my face. 'I know. They don't look very well, do they?'
he said. 'I mentioned exactly the same thing to the chap at the
barrow, and he said to me, "Well, sir, what did you expect for a
tanner [sixpence]?"' We've laughed about it ever since.

I think the only other time Paul ever bought me flowers
was when the children were born, because he thought he
should; he's never been one for grand romantic gestures, but
he's always very kind and sincere, which are far more important qualities.

This was a lovely time of my life, being newly married. I
enjoyed it a great deal. During the week we would always sit

down for breakfast together (Paul would have cornflakes and I'd have toast – nothing has changed over the years!) and then we would catch the tube into town. Paul would get out at Bond Street, where he was then working at the drinks company Hiram Walker, and I would stay on a few more stops to Holborn. We would usually get back at around the same time and I would either cook something for supper or, if I'd been testing recipes at work, we'd eat whatever dish I'd brought home.

I was working very hard and would often have to do a bit of work in the evening because I was still holding down two jobs, but we did do a lot of entertaining, usually on a Friday or Saturday night. Our social life at the time revolved around having dinner parties or going to other newly-wed couples' houses for supper. If we had people coming to us I would cook something like Coq au Vin or Steak and Kidney Pie. There was really no such thing as convenience food at this time; you couldn't even buy packs of chicken joints – if you wanted drumsticks or breast portions you would have to get a whole chicken and joint it yourself.

We did still go out to clubs sometimes, although less often now we were married. One night after a party Paul took me to a casino, because I'd never been to one and was intrigued to find out what it was like. Well, as soon as we got in there I couldn't wait to get out again! I felt completely uncomfortable. There were a lot of older men with young girls, focusing intently on the games, and although there was the possibility that you could win a great deal you could lose so much too. To me, it seemed like such a waste of what you worked hard to earn. Paul and I put a few pounds on and once they were gone I wanted to leave. It wasn't my scene at all.

At weekends we often used to go to Penny Block's parents' house for Sunday lunch, rather than to my parents in

Bath, as they lived in Hertfordshire and were nearer London.
Paul was still playing a lot of sports in those days, and many
weekends were spent at his Old Boys' cricket matches where
I would join the other wives and help with the teas.

It suited me very well, being married. I'm often asked what
the secret is to a happy marriage; Paul would probably joke
that it's always saying, 'Yes, dear,' but I think it's down to hard
work and compromise. I was taught that marriage is for life –
do people still believe that now? I just don't know. What I do
think is that nowadays many people go into marriage with a
naively starry-eyed view of what it will be like. Marriages are
made: they take a tremendous amount of work and sacrifice,
and it often seems like people aren't prepared to put in that
effort.

Some people argue all the way through their marriage and
it's still immensely happy, but I'm not like that; Paul and I
never argue, because it upsets me too much. There will always
be tough times in a marriage and occasions when you don't
agree, but if you can elaborate on the good things in your
relationship, accept the bad and work through problems
together, then you can survive the rough patches. We've had
ups and downs like any couple, but I can honestly say I love
Paul more each day.

I never considered giving up work after we got married.
Some of my friends did, as their husbands expected them to,
but we had a mortgage to pay. Even if I had wanted to stop
working – which I didn't – it just wasn't an option. Nevertheless, one of the things I had been most looking forward to
after getting married was changing my name. Mrs Mary
Hunnings – I thought that was wonderful! But once again,
Olwen Francis gave me a sound piece of advice. 'Everyone's

got to know your name,' she said to me. 'Why bother changing it to a different one?' At the time, this was a very modern way of thinking, but I could see the sense in it; I kept Mary Berry for work and Paul didn't mind one bit.

As I grew in confidence in my role at *Housewife*, I started to come up with different ideas to fill the pages to keep things fresh and interesting, including a new monthly feature in which I invited a celebrity to prepare a meal and then interviewed them about their interest in food and cookery. Of course all magazines are celebrity-oriented nowadays, but back then the idea of involving personalities was quite innovative. The feature was, on the whole, a great success, with stars of the day such as TV presenters, models, athletes and designers preparing their signature dishes in their own kitchens. I would approach people for the feature if they were known to be keen cooks; for instance, if I read in the newspaper that so-and-so was a great party giver, or had taken a picnic to Ascot, then I could be pretty sure that they had an interest in food. As there weren't the agents back then I would usually write to the celebrity directly with my request and then follow it up with a phone call. Most people, even famous ones, weren't ex-directory, so I could just get their details from the phone book, and they were almost always pleased to take part because they liked the publicity.

There were a few hiccups along the way, of course. After interviewing the TV and film actor Ian Carmichael, I received an irate letter from him when the article was published because I had written that he lived in suburbia. His home was in Totteridge in north London, which to me was most definitely the suburbs, but he was adamant that he lived in the country! And I did get very nervous about some of the interviews, especially with the bigger personalities, worrying about what we would talk about and how accommodating they would be. I can remember driving to the home of Eammon Andrews, at the time very famous as the presenter of *This is Your Life*, and arriving in front of this grand house with enormous, intimidating gates. Terrifying! In the event, however, Eammon was perfectly pleasant and cooked a very nice Dover Sole with Almonds for me in his kitchen.

One of my favourites was the feature I did with the fashion designer Mary Quant, a very keen cook who even started an Italian restaurant beneath her first shop. On the day of the interview, I arrived at her flat in Chelsea to be shown into this rather minimalist dining room that contained a stark white table and little else. I particularly remember the rather unusual window blinds, which looked like they were made of foil. There was no sign of Mary – and no sign at all of any food. I glanced in the kitchen, but nothing was going on in there either. Anyway, eventually Mary arrived, looking as wonderful and glamorous as ever, and she started talking to me about the recipe she wanted to do, which was some sort of rice dish with crispy sausages and almonds, and all the time I was just thinking, 'Well, where's the food and when are we going to start cooking?' Time was ticking on, and I thought there was no way we would be finished in time. And then suddenly the front door opened and in came this wooden bowl filled with sausages and rice and tomatoes, the most beautiful-looking dish, and Mary gave it a bit of a tweak, laid the table with green napkins and flowers, and suddenly the whole room came alive. She'd had it made at the restaurant around the corner!

It was a very exciting time to be working in magazines; we really were spoilt rotten. Public relations companies would take you out for these fabulous lunches at the Ritz or the

A photo shoot with the wonderful Mary Quant.

Savoy (although I never drank any wine, because I thought I might be persuaded to do something I didn't want to!) and if there was anything you needed, from ingredients to equipment, you just contacted the relevant company and it was sent straight over. It was a grand life. At *Housewife* I was writing about cookware as well as food and one of the companies that stood out even then was Lakeland, which had only recently appeared but was already well ahead of its time. They were just so friendly and on the ball, sending gadgets down to London overnight for me to try out for the magazine and even now, forty years later, they still have their great family values and always have a helpful voice at the end of the phone.

With the advent of cheaper air travel and package holidays people were able to travel abroad more easily – and foreign ingredients were becoming more readily available in the UK – so, to take advantage of this growing interest, food companies would take groups of journalists on promotional trips around the world. During my time on magazines I went on numerous press trips and we always had a whale of a time.

There would usually be a party of about twenty of us and, because the magazine world was fairly close-knit, we all tended to know each other; there was Katie Stewart from *Woman's Journal*, Audrey Hundy from *Woman* magazine and a young writer called Delia Smith, who would later become a good friend. We travelled in enormous comfort, stayed in posh hotels, were terribly spoiled and felt very important. These trips were always huge fun – and it felt like such a privilege to be invited to tour these different countries. I went all around Europe, to America with Uncle Ben's Rice, where we had a fascinating day in the cotton fields, and to Israel with avocados. The latter was particularly interesting, as along with learning about the cuisine we visited all the religious sites. I remember being quite disappointed with Bethlehem because I had expected it to be quite a humble place, but we went to the stable and it was so overdressed and gilded that it detracted from the real meaning of the city. At the time my daughter Annabel was just a few months old and when we went to visit the Sea of Galilee I took an empty wine bottle and filled it with seawater to bring home for Annabel's christening, so she could be baptized with holy water. By the time the water had travelled home with me and sat around for a few months it was starting to look rather green and murky, and when the vicar came to open the bottle at the font the cork shot out with the most almighty pop like it was champagne! But Annabel had a very special baptism.

Mum and I at Annabel's baptism.

During my six years on *Housewife*, the readership steadily grew until it was selling 200,000 copies an issue, a healthy sales figure for a monthly magazine, but our budgets were still being slashed. To save money, photographs were increasingly being bought in from other magazines, rather than being styled and shot in-house. In my early days at *Housewife* I would come up with the recipes myself and then shoot the pictures to illustrate them, but now I was being given a set of pictures and asked to come up with a recipe to match. This was fine if it was a photo of something simple like roast chicken or a prawn cocktail, but more often than not the pictures would be from *Elle* magazine in France and, while the photographs were always beautifully shot and very creative, the food was not at all to my taste. For example, on one occasion I was presented with a photo of a meringue pudding that was a lurid green colour. I wrote a recipe for a gooseberry and hazelnut meringue and – with a heavy heart, as I'm not keen on colourings – suggested readers add 'a few drops of green food colouring' into the cream. Another time I was given a photo of a moulded rice pudding absolutely covered in maraschino cherries. I would always use dark cherries in a recipe, but I had to stick to what was in the picture – and you would have needed to use about eight jars of maraschino cherries to recreate it!

As IPC's cost-cutting drive continued apace, in 1968 *Housewife* was merged with its sister magazine, *Ideal Home*. The first thing any of us knew about the merger was when one of the senior managers came into our office and announced that this was to be the last ever issue of *Housewife*. It was handled terribly badly. Without notice, every single person was made redundant; the only ones to keep their jobs were my assistant Sue Hosier and myself. I was to become Cookery Editor of *Ideal Home*, shifting the current incumbent into the position of Homes Editor. She was a difficult woman, who clearly resented being made to move jobs, and she made a point of telling the magazine's editor that it was necessary for her to oversee everything I did because she had been in the job before. I didn't realize at the time, but this would later get me in rather a lot of trouble.

# LEMON DRIZZLE TRAYBAKE

Traybakes are the easiest cakes to make and this one has a wonderful crunchy lemon topping. It is important to spoon the icing on to the warm cake so the lemon juice soaks into the sponge.

*Cuts into about 24 pieces*

- 175g (6 oz) soft butter
- 225g (8 oz) caster sugar
- 225g (8 oz) self-raising flour
- 2 level teaspoons baking powder
- 3 large eggs
- 6 tablespoons milk
- grated rind of 2 lemons

**for the icing**
- juice of 2 lemons
- 175g (6 oz) granulated sugar

Preheat the oven to 180°C/Fan 160°C/Gas 4.

Grease and line the base of a 30 x 23 x 4cm (12 x 9 x 1½ inch) traybake tin or roasting tin with non-stick baking parchment. Measure all the ingredients into a large bowl and beat well for about 2 minutes until well blended. Turn the mixture into the prepared tin and level the top.

Bake in the preheated oven for 30 minutes until golden.

To make the icing, mix together the lemon juice and sugar to give a runny consistency. Spread out evenly over the warm cake and leave to set.

# 9

Paul and I had been married for two years when sadly I suffered a miscarriage. I had stayed up late one night to work on a tablecloth that I was making to fit the rosewood dining table that we had bought on our honeymoon, and around two o'clock in the morning I was just finishing the final stitches when I started to lose the baby. I'm thankful that it was an early miscarriage, but it was still very distressing. Paul was hugely sympathetic and did his best to cheer me up – taking me out to restaurants when we couldn't really afford it – but of course he was terribly upset too. For weeks he wouldn't let me do anything remotely strenuous; I'd come home from the office and he would send me straight up to bed. I went back to work almost immediately and I remember everyone at Bensons being really kind. 'At least this means that everything works,' they would reassure me. 'Just give it some time.'

All our friends were having children at the time and we were very keen to start a family ourselves, but as I have mentioned we knew that it might not be as straightforward for us as it was for most couples. When I was younger I had been diagnosed with a bicornuate uterus, which means that I have two wombs: a fairly unusual condition that can make it difficult to conceive and carry a baby. I'm not the sort of person to fret endlessly over problems – I tend to just assume that everything is going to work out all right in the end – and so I didn't particularly worry about it, but after suffering another couple of miscarriages it seemed sensible to go and see a specialist.

My consultant was George Pinker, the esteemed Harley Street obstetrician who went on to deliver Princes William and Harry as well as many other royal babies. The first time I went to see him he was wonderfully reassuring, telling me, 'Don't worry, you will have children, I'm going to make sure of it.' Although my condition was quite rare, at the time Mr Pinker had three other patients with a bicornuate uterus – one in Scotland and two more in London (by coincidence both of whom I knew!) One of those girls was Shirley Nightingale, a special friend of mine who lived just down the road. Both Shirley and I adored Mr Pinker. He was slightly older than us, but tall, handsome and utterly charming; we thought he was perfect. We were both trying to conceive at the same time and would always compare notes after appointments: 'So how did you get on with the gorgeous Mr Pinker?' I remember one day Shirley came to see me straight after her consultation with the most enormous fur hat on and, in fits of giggles, explained to me how she had taken all her clothes off ready for her examination but had forgotten to remove this colossal hat. It wasn't until afterwards, when she was getting dressed and caught sight of her reflection in the mirror, that she had realized. She said to Mr Pinker, 'Well, you might have told me I'd still got my hat on!' From then on we always teased Shirley about the correct occasions to wear a fur hat.

To my delight I soon fell pregnant again and this time, with the help of Mr Pinker, things progressed normally. Thankfully it was an easy pregnancy, although I do remember battling morning sickness up until about the four-month mark and constantly drinking Coca-Cola and nibbling Marmite on toast to try and combat the nausea. My assistant, Sue

Hosier, remembers me struggling: 'When Mary was pregnant she would come in on the tube from Notting Hill Gate, throw up in the ladies loo, get herself sorted, put her face on and then come into the office and start work.'

There were times when I would be at a studio photographing food and feel so ghastly that the photographer and assistants had to help me prepare the dishes, because I felt too sick to continue. On a few occasions I even had to go home, but I'd be back there the next day. Another thing I really struggled with was the fatigue. Having been used to having fairly boundless energy, I was suddenly finding myself getting home from the magazine at six o'clock and putting myself to bed. I do remember feeling very tired indeed.

Of course, one of the aspects of pregnancy that was very different in those days was maternity wear. Today most people want to wear things as tight and clingy as possible so that everybody knows they are pregnant, but I don't think it becomes anybody – and it must be frightfully uncomfortable. In my day we all wore tents. We wore them with tights and sensible shoes, but they were beautifully tailored and always looked extremely elegant – nonetheless, they were tents. Despite my questionable needlework skills, one of my favourite maternity dresses was one that I made myself: a long, gently A-line evening gown in deep pink quilted fabric with gold braid around the neck and long, drop sleeves. It looked a bit 'We Three Kings', if you can imagine what I mean, but it covered everything beautifully. My daughter Annabel wore it while she was pregnant, although the rest of the time she was in the same stuff as everyone else. Perhaps I'm just rather old-fashioned about this, but I just don't understand why people want to have an enormous tummy on display. I was lucky enough to meet the Duchess of

Cambridge earlier this year and she was dressed so beautifully in a simple, loose dress that just skimmed over her bump. I do hope her example inspires other expectant mothers to dress a bit more elegantly.

Paul and I had a lovely time getting the nursery ready for the new arrival. We found a beautiful Victorian brass cot on the Kings Road, which has ended up being terrific value as all

Meeting Kate at a charity event. William says she uses all my recipes!

my children – and most of my grandchildren – have slept in it over the years. I think babies must have been bigger in Victorian times, because the bars were so wide apart that our children could easily fit between them, but I made a cot liner out of blue quilted material and that prevented any accidents. Of course, when they were really tiny the children started out sleeping in a Moses basket and, as this was in the days before children's car seats, whenever we drove anywhere we just wedged the basket behind the car's front seats, not tied in or secured in any way! How times have changed . . .

I was in the office on the morning of 12th March 1968, a few days before my due date, when at around eleven o'clock I began to realize that I felt rather odd. Things must be starting to happen, I thought happily. I didn't want to disturb my husband at work, so I phoned Shirley Nightingale's husband James, the pilot, as I knew he was at home that day, and he picked me up from the office and took me straight to St Mary's Hospital, where I was given my own room (one of the perks of the private health insurance that my husband's company had provided). Shirley and I had gone to antenatal classes in Weymouth Street in central London with Mrs Parsons, who at that time was the lady to go to for learning how to huff and puff, so I had a good idea what to expect from labour and made sure I got an epidural as quickly as possible. My husband arrived a few hours later and was at my bedside when our son Thomas arrived at six o'clock that evening – although, as Paul says, he 'wasn't at the sharp end'. What a wonderful moment, to finally meet my new baby! Of course, Paul was thrilled to have a son, so while the baby was being cleaned up and I gave him his first feed, Paul went to the pub across the road from St Mary's for a celebratory drink. Bursting with pride, he went to the bar and announced, 'I've just had a

son!' However, the barman clearly had no time for such senti-
mentality – or perhaps he was just weary of congratulating new
fathers – and simply replied, 'Was that a half or a pint, sir?'

Paul with son and heir Thomas – what a joy.

In those days new mothers remained in hospital for quite
some time after giving birth. I stayed for ten days, with Thomas kept in a nursery with all the other babies at night where
I would feed him and then go back to bed. This was such a
blissful time; I had masses of visitors and so many flowers
that we ran out of space on the window sills and ended up
having to sit vases of flowers in each of the drawers of my
bedside chest. I have always associated Thomas's birthday
with the arrival of the first daffodils – although when I picked
a bunch for his first birthday and sat them next to him in a
vase, the little monkey threw away the daffodils and drank
the water!

Paul came to visit me at St Mary's most days, and while I was in hospital his mother moved into Farmer Street to look after him. My parents came down from Bath and Dad presented me with an envelope, inside which was a letter that read: 'I hope in the long run with all its ups and downs Thomas will be as much pleasure to you both as you children are to us. As one gets older it is one's immortality through one's children which assumes the most importance ... Enclosed is £50 to help launch the Good Ship Thomas. Much love to the three of you. Pa.'

He did the same after the birth of my next son William and daughter Annabel. Dad was usually a very unemotional man, but I remember after Annabel's birth he said to me, 'I'm delighted you've had a third child, as you never know what's going to happen.' I'm sure it was just intended as a comment on the unpredictability of family life, but his words would go on to have particular resonance for me in later years.

Because of all the assistance I had been receiving in hospital it was rather a shock when Thomas and I arrived home. Now I was in charge – or rather, Thomas was – and like most new mothers it took me a little while to find my feet. After our first night at home, Mr Pinker phoned to see how I was managing and I was immensely grateful to hear from him because Thomas's poor lips were covered in blisters and I had no idea what to do. It turned out that I was feeding him from a brand new bottle and – whereas the teats in hospital were well used and very soft – this one was too hard for his tiny lips.

Mr Pinker – who later became Sir George – went on to deliver all three of my children, and I will be forever grateful to him for helping to make my pregnancies and births such easy experiences. In later years he developed Alzheimer's; this is always a terrible disease, but almost more wicked in his case because he had been such a brilliant man. Mr Pinker died a few years ago and Shirley and I were fortunate to go to his memorial service in London. It was a very moving occasion and a fitting tribute to an incredible life.

Five weeks after giving birth to Thomas I went back to work. This was partly out of necessity but also I never really felt that I wished to give up work and become a full-time mother. I loved my job, and wanted to do well and progress in my career – and I really have Paul to thank for encouraging me to continue working, and supporting my decision. I did feel guilty about going back to work so quickly, because it really wasn't the done thing at the time – most of my girl-friends gave up work after their first baby and then took it up again once their children were at school – but the problem was that I was really awfully nervous that if took too much time off I wouldn't have a job to come back to. In those days there was no such thing as maternity leave; you were expected to leave and then never come back. I knew that lots of people would want to be cookery editor of a national magazine and would do it very well indeed – and I'm quite sure that one of them would have taken my place if I hadn't made a swift return to my desk. My one concession to motherhood was that I resigned from my job at Bensons, so I was now work-ing part-time, only three days a week.

On the days when I was at *Ideal Home* I had a nanny to look after Thomas, who was joined eighteen months later by my gorgeous second son William. Shirley Nightingale had given birth to her son David (soon to be joined by baby Jason) and was also going back to work part-time, so on the two days that I didn't need our nanny, Jill, she went to work for Shirley, and if it ever happened that both of us needed her help on the same day she would happily have all four boys heaped up in the pram together.

I put on twenty-one pounds while I was pregnant with

Thomas and would go on to gain the same amount with both my subsequent pregnancies, although strangely I put it all on in the first few months and then didn't seem to gain a pound after the six-month mark. With my return to work I was very keen to lose the extra weight and get back into my normal clothes and I'm sure I went on all sorts of faddy diets, although nowadays I firmly believe that if you have a good, varied diet and not too much of the things you shouldn't then you'll stay at a healthy weight. It also helped that I was very active – but then I've always been the sort of person who rushes about a lot. If we all just walked more we wouldn't have so many problems with obesity in this country.

As our family expanded, the little house on Farmer Street began to feel rather cramped. Paul was concerned that the boys wouldn't have room to play growing up with our pocket-handkerchief of a yard and, as we couldn't afford a house in London with a decent-sized garden, he suggested that we move to the country. I was not at all keen on this idea because I was perfectly happy in Notting Hill: I knew all the shops, had my friends nearby and I could get from home to the office, door to door, in about twenty minutes. However, although I was happy to stay put, I could see the sense in what Paul was saying – I certainly didn't want the boys to feel cooped up – and, after a little procrastination, I agreed to the move.

We started our property search to the west of London, so we would be in easy reach of my parents in Bath, and almost immediately found a perfect place in Iver, near Uxbridge, called Love Farm, which was situated on Love Lane. 'That would just do for us!' I thought. But then we discovered that there were plans for an arterial road coming very close by the property – now the M25 motorway – and so it was back to the drawing board. As the months went by, our search gradually took us

further out of London until just before Christmas we were
sent the details of a property called the Red Cottage in the
pretty Buckinghamshire village of Penn that looked quite
promising. Paul was working very hard at that time and he certainly wouldn't have been able to take time off during the week
to go house-hunting, so as we were driving to Bath on Christmas Eve we took a little detour to look at it – just from the
outside, though, because we wouldn't have dared turn up and
knock at the door unannounced. We hung over the big metal
five-bar gate at the bottom of the driveway to get as good a
view as possible and from the outside at least it seemed to be a
spacious family house with a good-sized garden. It was on the
market for twenty-five thousand pounds, which seemed like an
awful lot of money, but we'd just sold our London house for
eighteen thousand and that was tiny in comparison, so in that
respect it was quite good value. Paul and I both agreed that it
seemed lovely, and well worth further investigation.

After Christmas I arranged to go and see the Red Cottage
with my father, while Paul was busy at work, and the owner,
Susan Allen, showed us around. From the moment I stepped
through the door I knew it was perfect for us. It was a period
property, dating from the 1870s, and was a little higgledy-
piggledy but with bags of character. There were lovely
fireplaces, high ceilings and lots of cupboards and alcoves,
which I thought would be great for games of hide and seek!
The kitchen was tiny, but we could easily make it bigger when
we had enough money. Upstairs the rooms were arranged in
such a way that there was a real heart to the house, with three
bedrooms grouped together that would be perfect for the
children and us, then a corridor leading off into a maze of
other bedrooms and cupboards, so if we had guests to stay
they wouldn't be disturbed.

While my father jumped about on the floorboards and checked for dry rot, I went out into the garden with Susan. As we wandered around, I could almost see the children running about, playing and kicking a ball. There was a great expanse of lawn (you don't want flower beds with little children) and lots of trees to climb and places to hide, and then through an arch was a vegetable garden, which looked like another great play area. I could already imagine us living here.

'So what do you think?' asked Susan as we walked back towards the house.

'Actually, we would like to buy it,' I replied.

'What about your husband?'

'Don't worry,' I told her. 'I know my husband's going to like it.'

As we were saying our goodbyes, I told my father that I had spoken to Susan and agreed to buy the house. He didn't say anything – although I do remember him giving me a rather pointed look – but when we were in the car he turned to me and said sternly, 'Mary, this is not how you go about buying houses at all. What about the survey?'

I was convinced that I had found our new home: not only did it have loads of room and a lovely garden, it just felt right, so I said to Dad, 'I like it, Paul's going to like it and Susan says that we can buy it, so it's fine.' And it was.

For me, the only thing that I didn't like about the Red Cottage was its name. Not only was the property far too big to be described as a cottage, but I also much preferred 'Red House', which was the name of my dear friend Penny's family home. Soon after we bought it I went to see the postmaster at the local post office and asked if it would be possible to change the name to the Red House. 'I just deliver the letters,' he said. 'You can call it whatever you like!'

The Red House, our first home in Penn.

Luckily the house didn't really need redecorating. Some of the decor wasn't quite to our tastes – the dining room had the most amazing wallpaper that was brightly coloured and covered with birds – but we got used to it and ended up rather liking it. Ever mindful of my mother's advice on the subject, we did get new curtains and carpets, though. I decided to go with brown carpet throughout, because I thought it would be a good colour to have with little children running around, but although it did give a sort of spacious feel to the place it was really very boring and it showed every white mark. Learn from my mistake and never get a white kitten or a white dog if you have brown floor coverings!

Since the house was so much bigger than Farmer Street we didn't have quite enough furniture, but around the time we moved in Paul's firm Hiram Walker had a fire at their Brook Street offices and they got rid of any furniture that was even slightly damaged. We took two large sofas, which had the odd hole in them and smelled of smoke but we had them re-covered and they were just fine; in fact, we've still got them in our home today.

The one thing we did buy new was an Aga. I had first tried cooking on one a few years previously when I had done some catering work for Penny's parents at their Red House in Little Gaddesden, Hertfordshire. Mrs Block – or Ma Block as I knew her – 'ought to do a lot of entertaining', as she would say with a roll of her eyes, so I went to stay with them for a fortnight and helped cook for a succession of dinner parties. I greatly enjoyed cooking on their Aga – I liked that it was always on, so you didn't have to remember to turn it on to preheat – but I also loved the way that it turned the kitchen into the heart of the home, the warmest and very best place to be. When we lived in London our tiny kitchen heated up as soon as you switched the oven on or put on a pan to boil, but our new cold, solid house in the country needed the warmth of an Aga. My husband certainly wasn't going to let me put the heating on willy-nilly! It was turned off like clock-work on the first day of April, and didn't come on again until October. So Paul agreed to the Aga, even though he thought it terribly extravagant, and since then I've always preferred to cook with an Aga instead of a conventional oven.

We moved to Penn in 1970, when Thomas was a year and a half and William was still in his Moses basket. To help with the childcare, we found a wonderful nanny, Margaret, who came to live with us, and without whom I could never have continued to work.

The boys loved having so much space and as they got older were always outside: climbing trees, kicking a ball, getting into trouble – they never stopped. A few months after we moved to the Red House I was delighted to find myself pregnant once again and I remember saying to Margaret, 'If it's a boy we're going to call him James.' And she just gave me a look and said, 'We're not having any boys. No more!' And she was right.

When Annabel arrived it was a huge joy. To have another perfect child is the main thing, but to have a daughter after two wonderful boys – well, suffice to say we felt extremely blessed. Annabel was the first girl in the Hunnings family in over one hundred years, and when Mr Pinker announced the baby's sex Paul was so surprised he asked him to double-check!

In addition to the help I was getting from Margaret, when Annabel was born I had a maternity nanny called Webby for the month after I came home from hospital. It might seem like an extravagance, but with two small boys and a new baby the extra pair of hands was invaluable. During the night, Webby had Annabel with her in her bedroom, which was at the other end of the house to ours, and so I hardly saw Annabel until after Webby left. I know it's quite an old-fashioned idea, but when Annabel and my daughter-in-law Sarah had their first children my gift to them was a maternity nanny for the first month, because I think it is a tremendous help at a time of great upheaval and adjustment.

As the children got bigger, I would get young students to come and help out over the school holidays; it was great fun for my three to have a temporary 'big sister' who would play outside with them and invent games. One of these was a girl called Sally Harwood, who was the daughter of the headmistress of the lovely local primary school in Beaconsfield, New Gregory's, where Thomas, William and Annabel all started their education. Sally had a fairly battered old Morris Minor and the children used to love going off with her on picnics, piled up in the back with the roof down. My lot could be quite a handful, but although she was young Sally knew exactly how to handle them. One day Thomas was bragging, saying, 'My grandfather was Mayor of Bath.' And Sally just smiled sweetly and said, 'My grandfather was Prime Minister. His name was Clement Atlee.' Well, that put Thomas in his place! I still see Sally today, and she's tremendous fun.

Despite my reservations about moving out of London, I was very happy in our new rural surroundings and cherished the sense of community in the village. There was a wonderful family-run grocer's shop that made its own bread and sold absolutely everything you could think of. (Although I did once suggest to the owner's son, Brian, that he should stock avocados and he said, 'There's no call for them here,' so I left it at that.) It was always a pleasure going shopping, as the service was wonderfully old-fashioned and attentive: the grandfather would dole out sweets to the children and Brian would always insist on carrying the shopping bags back over the road for me.

We had a little red grocery book and every day I would write in there what we needed – bread, two tins of baked beans or whatever – and our nanny Margaret would go across to the shop with the children hanging on to her to pick everything up. Margaret's daily visits must have made quite an impression on Brian, as a few years later he asked her to marry him – and now they have two married sons of their own!

Just past the village shop was Kings' the butcher, which was run by Harry and Ken. They were lovely chaps, and very friendly; in fact they were the first people I showed Annabel to when I came home with her from hospital. If I was at home during the week I would often mow the lawn to help Paul and, if I was struggling to get our rather temperamental mower started, Harry or Ken would usually hear me yanking at the cord and walk over to get it going for me.

Our move to Penn coincided with what I would later view as a turning point in my career. A new concept to appear at this time was cookery cards, sets of individual recipes on laminated wipe-clean cards that were presented in a little box. Originated by the American food writer and restaurateur Robert Carrier, these were a huge success, and when I was approached to create a set by the publishers Hamlyn (prompted, I presume, by the popularity of my magazine recipes) I was happy to oblige. It seemed like a natural extension of my work on magazines, and I've always been keen to diversify in my career.

The cookery cards did well and I really thought no more of it, but then a few months later I received a phone call from Hamlyn. They wanted to use my recipes from the cards in a new cookbook and asked if I would edit the book, too. I was immediately interested – even more so when they explained to me that this book would be something of an innovation. Cookery books at this time were largely in black and white with few, if any, illustrations, but Hamlyn's revolutionary new idea was that each recipe in the book would be accompanied by its own colour photo of the finished dish, so you could see exactly how it was supposed to turn out.

I thought it was a brilliant concept, as from my experience on the magazine I knew that people were longing for pictures to accompany a recipe in order to get a clear idea of what they were supposed to be making. So when I accepted their offer I was pretty confident that the *Hamlyn All Colour Cookbook* would do well. But I don't think any of us could have imagined quite what a success it would turn out to be.

# EASTER SIMNEL CAKE

A Simnel has become the traditional Easter cake, but originally servant girls would give one to their mothers when they went home on Mothering Sunday. This is a lighter version of the usual recipe.

*Serves about 8–10*

- 175g (6 oz) light muscavado sugar
- 175g (6 oz) butter, softened
- 175g (6 oz) self-raising flour
- 3 large eggs
- 25g (1 oz) ground almonds
- 2 tablespoons milk
- 100g (4 oz) sultanas
- 100g (4 oz) glacé cherries, quartered, washed and dried
- 100g (4 oz) dried apricots, snipped into small pieces
- 100g (4 oz) stem ginger, finely chopped
- 1 teaspoon mixed spice
- 2 teaspoons ground ginger

**to cover and fill the cake**
- 450g (1 lb) golden marzipan
- 3 tablespoons apricot jam
- 1 large egg, beaten

### to decorate

- primroses, narcissi or violets
- egg white
- caster sugar

Preheat the oven to 160°C/Fan 140°C/Gas 3.

Grease and line the base and sides of a 20cm (8 inch) deep round cake tin with non-stick baking parchment.

Measure all the cake ingredients into a large mixing bowl and beat well by hand until thoroughly blended. Place half the mixture into the prepared tin and level the surface.

Take one third of the marzipan and roll it into a circle the same size as the cake tin, then place the circle on top of the cake mixture. Spoon the remaining mixture on top of the marzipan and level the surface.

Bake in the preheated oven for about 1¾–2 hours or until golden brown and firm in the middle. If towards the end of the cooking time the cake is getting too brown, loosely cover with a piece of foil. Allow the cake to cool in the tin before turning out on to a cooling rack.

When the cake is cool, brush the top with a little warmed apricot jam. Roll out half the remaining marzipan to the size of the cake and sit it on the top. Crimp the edges and make a lattice pattern in the centre of the marzipan using a sharp knife. Roll the remaining marzipan into 11 even-sized balls and arrange them around the edge.

Brush the marzipan top with beaten egg and glaze under a hot grill for about 5 minutes, turning the cake round to heat it evenly, so the marzipan is tinged brown all over. (You can also do this with a blow torch if preferred.)

To crystallize the primroses, narcissi or violets, arrange the fresh flowers on a cooling rack. Lightly whisk the egg white in a bowl, then carefully brush over the flower petals with the egg white. Sprinkle on caster sugar so the sugar sticks to the egg white. Leave to harden, in a warm place such as a shelf above a radiator or in an airing cupboard, until dry and firm. Carefully remove from the rack and arrange in the centre of the cake.

Hamlyn asked me to contribute a hundred recipes for the first of three sections in the book (the other two sections were to be written by fellow food writers Ann Body and Audrey Ellis) and edit the entire thing. I didn't have an agent at this time and had no idea how to handle the negotiations myself, so when I was offered a flat fee of something like £128 per 50,000 copies sold – a pretty rum deal! – I accepted immediately.

Celebrating one million copies sold of the *Hamlyn All Colour Cookbook*.

Broadly speaking, the recipes in the book were all classic family dishes done in a simple way, things like Irish Stew and Chilled Lemon Flan. In fact, over eighty books (and counting) later, this is still pretty much how I would describe my style of cooking: simple classics with a twist. Although the recipes in the book are fairly straightforward, I tried to make up appealing names to tempt people to make them. If you call something 'Poachers' Pie', 'Gleneagles Pâté' or 'Swiss Steak', even if it doesn't actually mean anything, it makes it sound more interesting. People might skip past a recipe for Fish Pie, but Trawlers' Pie – well, that sounds far more appetizing!

Back then and still today, when I'm devising recipes I bear in mind a few loose guidelines. To start with, I don't use too many different ingredients or things that people will struggle to get hold of. All sorts of interesting ingredients are now much more readily available than they were even just five years ago, so when I see that you can buy something in most places I'll start to include it in my recipes. For instance, I would have never have dreamt of using fennel in recipes in 1966 as you couldn't buy it anywhere. Paul and I were out for dinner last week and the first course was a little piece of trout with samphire. This pretty sea-side plant is still quite expensive, but you can get it at many of the supermarkets these days and a little mountain of it makes a rather original accompaniment to fish instead of just serving the usual green leaves. You could dress it with a lemon dressing and that would be a nice and quite unusual dish.

I don't ever create recipes that are going to take awfully long to make, because people have other things to do with their time, so if I can make something easier or include a shortcut I will. I prefer to use my time doing something I enjoy – gardening, for instance, or playing tennis – rather than slaving away making something that is really no better than a ready-made version you can buy. Just as I wouldn't dream of making my own filo pastry, neither would I make puff pastry, which you can buy in an excellent ready-made butter version.

I'm all for taking shortcuts and making life easy for yourself, and I'll admit that stock cubes are an essential in my kitchen. If I'm making a chicken stock and I haven't got enough bones, I'll just add a little stock powder; it actually really helps to bring out the flavour.

Most importantly, we always test new recipes repeatedly – and I say 'we', because I have a wonderful team working for me now, although when I started out it was just me on my own. Testing is quite a lengthy process, as the recipe must be so perfect that everyone who tries it is successful. I always tell my readers, make the recipe as I suggest it the first time round, then feel free to make your own additions or changes after that.

Because my family and I usually end up living on the recipes that I'm testing, I've never been tempted to write a book on, say, rice, or sauces, as I don't want to have to eat these for weeks on end. When I was approached by a publisher to write a book on puddings in the nineties I happily did so, since at that time of my life my family ate a lot of puds, but I don't think that I would do one now.

I'm constantly on the lookout for inspiration for my recipes, be that on television, in magazines or when I'm shopping or eating out – I'm always having to come up with something new. I keep a notebook in my handbag to jot down ideas, thoughts and interesting combinations of ingredients if inspiration strikes while I'm out and about. Before I write a new book or start a television series I'll always wander round my local supermarkets and nip into Harrods and Selfridges food halls to have a look at what's on the shelves. On a recent visit to Selfridges I noticed that the tabbouleh at the Lebanese food counter was wonderfully green, with masses and masses of parsley compared to very little bulgur wheat.

People are liable to put in just a sprinkle, so I made a note that next time I make tabbouleh I should put in far more parsley and less bulgur wheat. I'll also have a nose in people's shopping baskets, but I have to admit I'm always rather shocked at what I see! All too often they are full of micro-wave ready-meals and processed convenience foods, and it makes me think, 'What on earth are you buying that for?'

Looking back through the *Hamlyn All Colour Cookbook*, I can remember every photograph almost as if it was yesterday. I think we prepared and shot eight of the recipes a day, which was an exceedingly tight schedule. If you go on a shoot now there will be a whole roomful of people, including home economists, food stylists and vast numbers of assistants, but back then it was just me and the photographer. I was on a budget, so all the bowls and serving dishes in the photos were either from my own kitchen or borrowed from friends; I got the cups for the Chocolate Pots on my honeymoon! I think that's a good thing though, as the reader might think, 'Oh, I've got that dish at home – I'll give the recipe a try.'

Compared to the lavishly beautiful food photography of today, where the dish is made to look as appetizing as possible, there's nothing at all stylish about the presentation in the book. It's really very functional, with no arty close-ups or atmospheric lighting, just a straightforward photograph of the finished recipe. But while the photographs do look very dated, I think they tell the right story: they give the impression that here is something straightforward and easy to make. Most of the recipes in the book have stood the test of time and I actually still make quite a few of them myself, including among others the Chocolate Rum Torte, the Coffee Ice Cream and a variation of the Lasagne.

The *Hamlyn All Colour Cookbook* was published in 1970 and

became the bestselling book in Britain at the time – and remained the most successful cookbook for many years. When sales reached the two million mark I was presented with a leather-bound copy of the book and two thousand pounds, and obviously I was thrilled to bits with that.

The relationship with publishers is very important. My first BBC commissioning editor was Heather Holden Brown, who is a gem; the phone would ring at six o'clock in the evening and I knew it would be Heather, calling for a chat and catch up. It is very special when we meet up at foodie events now that she is an agent for other writers. I am not contracted to just one publisher so have had the pleasure of getting to know many different people. Mary-Clare Jerram at Dorling Kindersley is just a joy to work with and for many years now she has looked after us and produced some very special books – including the *Complete Cookbook*, which has now sold over a million copies worldwide. Mary-Clare has built up a wonderful friendship with Lucy and me, and for that we are so lucky. Muna Reyal, our commissioning editor at BBC Books at Ebury, has been a great support to us and the *Baking Bible* we published with her is one of the books Lucy and I are most proud of. Headline have produced some stunning books for us too – Jo Roberts Miller is our editor there and friend, and it always feels that she is on our side, just like one of the family. Headline was the first publisher to give prepare ahead, freezing, conventional and Aga timings in our books, which were great advances.

As I've said, the success of the *Hamlyn All Colour Cookbook* was a turning point in my career, primarily for the opportunities the book opened up for me. The year after it was published I was approached to appear on *Collector's World*, an antiques programme on BBC Two presented by Hugh

Scully and Arthur Negus. The episode I was to appear on was being filmed at The Georgian House Museum in Bristol, an eighteenth-century townhouse that had been restored to its original glory, and my job was to recreate an authentic dinner party from the time. When I was sent the menu by the researchers and scanned a list of ingredients that included ox eyes, udders and sparrows, I began to wonder if I had made a terrible mistake in agreeing to take part. I ask you, how on earth do you cook an udder?

Since the programme was being filmed in Bristol I arranged for all the ingredients to be sent to my parents at Charlcombe Farm, because Bath was so much nearer than London, and I did all the preparation and cooking in Mum's kitchen. The Georgians ate a lot of freshwater fish, so the first dish was pike, which was fine. I roasted it in the oven and, because there were so many tiny bones, removed the flesh and made a pâté. It tasted rather muddy, but it was interesting enough. Then the udder arrived looking unappetizingly flabby and pink, like a deflated balloon. I snipped off one of the teats and put it through my brother Roger's letterbox, which was a very naughty thing to do! They wanted me to make Udder Pie, so I chopped it up and cooked it for hours and hours in stock, but by the end it was still tough as old boots and tasted like wet nowt. I put it in a heavily seasoned fricassee sauce and then into a pastry case and kept my fingers crossed.

The udder wasn't the worst of the ingredients, however; that honour went to the sparrows. Post office workers were striking at the time, so BBC Bristol persuaded the chaps who were on strike to go out and catch the little birds. A plastic bag arrived at Charlcombe Farm containing about thirty dead sparrows, feathers and all. I couldn't even touch them; I'm terrified of dead birds, from when my brothers used to

chase me round with them stuck on a stick, so I had to tell
the researchers, 'I'm sorry, I will roast them, but you'll have
to take the feathers off for me first.'

When the sparrows were returned to me, thankfully now
plucked, I cleaned, seasoned and then roasted them, in the
same way the French cook songbirds. They were so tiny they
only took about ten minutes in the oven and yielded no more
than a single mouthful, but they tasted all right – rather like
chicken, from what I remember!

There were other dishes, too: Mincemeat Tarts, which
were of course made authentically from minced meat rather
than fruit, and a classic Syllabub using cream and wine. Despite some rather dubious ingredients I spent a lot of time
working on the presentation so the finished dishes looked
quite appealing, and at least everything was fresh: in Georgian times they would have added lots of spices because the
meat probably wouldn't have been in the first bloom of
youth.

To say that I was nervous on the day of filming was something of an understatement. Watching the programme back
I seemed awfully prissy, but that's only because I was terrified. My role was to serve the banquet to guests including
the programme's presenters and various historians and join
in the discussion about what we were eating. As well as more
general nerves about how I should conduct myself on television, I was scared stiff about the prospect of discussing the
food with all these eminent experts, as I didn't have a clue
about the subject. The researchers had done all the work –
I'd just cooked what I had been told.

When I recently saw a clip of this, my very first television
appearance, I was in fits of laughter at the sound of my voice.
Just like Margaret Thatcher and Queen Elizabeth, my voice

has naturally lowered a little since I've got older, but back in those days we all sounded frightfully proper! Society has changed so much, and with it the way we speak. Nowadays my friends and I sound far more ordinary.

Despite my nerves, the series' producers were happy enough with my contribution to ask me back on the programme and I went on to appear on several more episodes of *Collector's World*, each time recreating and discussing food from a different era. On the Christmas programme, I cooked a traditional five-bird roast, made up of a turkey stuffed with a duck, stuffed with a chicken and then a couple of game birds, which was an absolute bore to make as you can imagine.

One of the episodes was filmed at Saltram House in Devon, a magnificent mansion dating from the early 1800s that had the most incredible kitchen equipped with over four hundred pieces of beautiful antique copper cookware, in which I was lucky enough to be allowed to cook. I love to see things that have been used down the ages and have always collected vintage kitchen paraphernalia as I appreciate how beautifully such objects are made. My collection is now framed on my kitchen wall and includes vegetable and herb choppers, whisks, sugar nippers and bottle openers. One of my favourite items is a nineteenth-century tin opener, used to open cans of bully beef, that has a bull's head with a spike on the top. I'm always in and out of junk shops, adding to my collection. Anyway, when I arrived in this glorious kitchen at Saltram House a woman in a white coat, who was obviously in charge of the copper collection, bustled over and said, 'You're not going to cook in them, are you?'

'Well that's what I'm here for,' I replied. She glared at me for the rest of the afternoon, but I had a wonderful time making all sorts of jellies in those wonderful copper moulds.

Another dish I made for this particular episode was a raised pie with lots of hard-boiled eggs inside it. I remember removing it from the tin on camera and was delighted when it came out looking burnished and glorious. The presenter, Arthur Negus, picked up a knife to cut it, but I said to him, 'Oh no you don't,' because I'd taken the trouble to mark the pastry to remind me where the eggs were positioned inside, and I wanted to cut one in half so that when the slice was lifted out the viewers saw a perfect circle of sunshine-yellow yolk. So I was in charge of the cutting – and it did look magnificent.

I learned a great deal from my handful of appearances on *Collector's World*, which was something of a crash-course in television broadcasting for me, and have fond memories of the experience. Arthur Negus was an enchanting man, with great warmth and a lovely West Country accent you could listen to for hours, which was fortunate because he could talk the hind leg off a donkey! He did have an eye for the girls – you could see him giving all the pretty young researchers the glad eye – and he was always very charming to me. After filming had finished one day, he had already starting driving away but turned around and came back because he'd forgotten to say goodbye to me. I was very touched by that.

Whenever I've been on an exciting trip or worked on a particularly enjoyable project I do like to bring something home to remember the experience by; for example, when I went on a walking holiday from Siena to Florence I bought a set of twenty tablemats made out of Italian lace, so that every time I laid the table I would be reminded of the holiday. On the day of my last appearance on *Collector's World* I was in the props room when I spotted a little antique figurine of the cricketer W. G. Grace. My immediate thought was how much Paul would love it, as he was such a keen cricketer, so I asked if it was possible to buy it. 'Well, nobody else is going to want it,' the props man said. 'The poor chap's only got one leg – you're welcome to him.' I took W. G. Grace home with me, had him restored to his former two-legged glory and presented the figurine to my delighted husband that Christmas. He still sits on the side in our dining room today, a cherished reminder of my first intriguing taste of television – and the rather less appetizing taste of Udder Pie.

As the saying goes, when one door closes another opens; while I was taking my first, faltering steps in my television career, my time at *Ideal Home* came to an abrupt end. The magazine's former cookery editor clearly hadn't got over her resentment at being made to move jobs after the merger, and was still doing her best to make my life as difficult as possible, telling the magazine's editor that I wasn't getting the copy in on time and generally making trouble. This went on for some time and eventually in 1973 she managed to get me sacked – and for the first time I saw the benefit of working in a closed shop, as the unions immediately and volubly stuck up for me. A meeting was called at which many of my colleagues spoke out against the decision, insisting that I was doing an excellent job and that there was absolutely no reason for me to be sacked. By this time, however, I'd had quite enough of the whole nonsense and told them, 'I'm going anyway.'

*Ideal Home* was to be my last staff job; since then I have always been freelance. Although I was glad to leave what had become a difficult working environment, I was very nervous about stepping out on my own and was in constant fear of being out of work. I loved the commitment of a permanent job and the security of knowing you'd get a cheque at the end of every month; as a freelancer you never know what's around the corner, so you take whatever you're offered because you're worried you might not get any work the following week. These days I have no such worries, and I am all too aware of what I can do and what I can't, but then that's one of the joys of getting older: I have experienced most things by now and know exactly what I am prepared to do – and not do – again! But back then, although I knew I was good at my job and doing my best, I never felt confident.

I started my freelance career writing articles for magazines such as *Family Circle*, and in 1975 was taken on as a consultant at *Home and Freezer Digest*, a tiny magazine that told you how to use your freezer. It is worth remembering that freezers only started to become widely available in the late sixties. I got my first chest freezer in 1966, when we moved to Farmer Street. As the technology was fairly new, consumers were still quite nervous of it, so they would buy books and magazines for guidance on how to use their new freezer. There was a real demand for information; I wrote several books on the subject, including *Popular Freezer Cookery* and *The Complete Book of Freezer Cooking*, and they sold like hot cakes. In the magazine we would give advice on what to freeze and how long you could freeze it for, discuss the importance of wrapping food properly, so it didn't deteriorate, and recommend people keep a list of their freezer contents – so much more organized than we are today! In those days we used to get freezer bags from Lakeland that were different colours, so you'd have fish in blue bags, vegetables in green and meat in red, then use waterproof pens to label everything.

Rewind another forty years and apparently there was the same confusion around refrigeration, with people wondering which shelf they should use and so forth. We take these things for granted now, but so many kitchen innovations have appeared over my lifetime. I remember sitting in one of the monthly editorial meetings we had at *Home and Freezer Digest*, where we would decide what was to go in the next issue of the magazine, and the editor, Jill Churchill, said, 'Look what I've got from America!' It was a sheet of aluminium foil. We passed it around the table like it was some rare archaeological artefact, marvelling at this new innovation. 'Do you use it shiny side up?' we wondered. 'What happens when you put it in the freezer? Do you wash it and use it again?' And a few years later we went through the same thing all over again when cling film came out!

I've never had a career plan at all other than saying 'yes' to those things that interested me, and so it was with my next move. I had been freelance for a few years when I was contacted by the team from ITV's daytime programme, *Good Afternoon*. Hosted by a different presenter each weekday, *Good Afternoon* (which changed its name to *Afternoon Plus* in 1979) was the forerunner for the popular magazine programmes of today such as *This Morning* and *Daybreak*, although its average viewing figure of over four million was considerably more than double those of its contemporary equivalents. Like a televisual version of Radio 4's *Woman's Hour*, *Good Afternoon* covered a blend of serious topics (including interviews with the likes of Margaret Thatcher) and more light-hearted material, with features on celebrities, fashion and cookery – which is where I came in. The programme's producer, Diana Potter, had apparently picked up a book I wrote for Marks & Spencer on freezing and had told her team: 'I understand what this girl is talking about – why don't you get her in and see if she's worth having on the programme?'

After a bit of back and forth, I was booked to appear on *Good Afternoon* to discuss the principles of freezing. During my appearance on the programme I was interviewed by the presenter, Judith Chalmers, about why freezing was the best way to preserve food – because you don't get the deterioration of other methods of preservation – and offered tips and suggestions for making the most of one's freezer. It seems obvious today, but back then people hadn't really thought of making double the amount of a casserole and then freezing half for another time; this was groundbreaking stuff! While I talked, Judith would chip in with layman's questions about the sorts of things you could freeze, and whether you had to cook food first before freezing, and she was so wonderfully relaxed and professional that I managed to forget about my stage fright and found the whole experience rather enjoyable.

At the time, Judith – or Judy as I came to know her – was a very well-known face on television, presenting shows including *Come Dancing* and *Wish You Were Here . . . ?*, and from our very first meeting I liked her enormously: she was so warm and welcoming, plus she was about my age and a working mother, so we had a lot in common. After we had finished filming I thanked her and told her how much I'd enjoyed the experience, and she suggested that I send Diana Potter ideas for more cookery features. 'We could have some fun,' she smiled.

'I'll do that,' I told her.

I don't remember what my suggestions were, probably something based around whatever ingredients were in season at the time, but I sent them in to Diana Potter and was thrilled when I was asked back on the programme again – and again the following month. I would go on to become a familiar face on daytime television for much of the next ten years.

# BAKED SALMON WITH PARMESAN AND PARSLEY CRUST

This is a perfect fish dish to prepare ahead and is one of my recipes that people always tell me they have enjoyed cooking

*Serves 6*

- 6 x 150g (5 oz) salmon fillets, skinned
- salt and freshly ground black pepper
- 75ml (⅛ pint) white wine
- 175g (6 oz) chestnut mushrooms, sliced
- 300ml (½ pint) double cream
- 25g (1 oz) fresh white breadcrumbs
- 25g (1 oz) Parmesan cheese, coarsely grated
- 2 tablespoons chopped fresh parsley, plus extra to garnish
- grated rind of ½ lemon
- a sprinkling of paprika

Preheat the oven to 200°C/Fan 180°C/Gas 6.

Season both sides of the salmon fillets with salt and pepper and place on a greased baking sheet or roasting tin.

Measure the wine and mushrooms into a wide-based pan, bring to the boil and cook for 1 minute. Lift out the mushrooms with a slotted spoon and reduce the wine to about 2 tablespoons. Add the cream, bring back to the boil, then reduce until reaching a sauce consistency. Season with salt and pepper and return the mushrooms to the sauce. Leave to cool completely to thicken.

Spoon about 1 teaspoon of the cold mushroom mixture on top of each salmon fillet but do not spread to the edge, saving the rest of the sauce to reheat and serve separately. Mix the breadcrumbs, Parmesan, parsley and lemon rind in a small bowl and season. Sprinkle the breadcrumb mixture over the mushroom sauce on the salmon and then sprinkle with paprika. Leave the prepared salmon fillets in the fridge up to 24 hours if not required immediately.

Bake for about 15 minutes in the preheated oven. To tell when the salmon is done, check that it has changed from translucent to a pink opaque. Serve immediately, garnished with chopped parsley.

Although I never had a contract, I became a regular contributor on *Good Afternoon*, appearing on a Monday once a month alongside Judy for a half-hour segment of her hour-long programme. I never prepared a script or rehearsed what I was going to say; I would decide on the recipes and bring everything in, then Judy would lead the chat. She would quiz me on things that the viewers might like to know, saying: 'Ooh, I've never used celeriac before – how does that grow? Where do I get it? Does it have a flavour like celery?' So we were something of a double-act.

The theme of my cookery segment on the programme would be dependent on the time of year. For instance, when the early rhubarb came in I would be doing rhubarb recipes; during a cold wintery spell it might be soups; at Easter it would be Simnel Cake. One of my first programmes was about lasagne, which at the time was still considered quite exotic. I had already included the recipe in the *Hamlyn All Colour Cookbook* and as a step-by-step guide in *Housewife* magazine, and it had proved very popular, so it seemed a logical choice for television. After the programme, Judy asked me to help her make lasagne for the guests at her house-warming party, as she had just moved into a new home with her husband, the sports reporter Neil Durden Smith, and their two children, Mark and Emma, which I was very happy to do. Now, of course, you can buy no-cook lasagne sheets, but when I first devised the recipe you had to cook the pasta sheets before you assembled it, which creates quite a lot of extra work if you're preparing the dish for large numbers. Making the lasagne for Judy's housewarming, I found that if I left the sauces a bit sloppy I could put the whole thing together and cook it in the oven without pre-cooking the pasta (particularly if I let the lasagne sit in the dish and soak before baking), and I tweaked my recipe accordingly. So much of cooking is experimentation.

Judith Chalmers, who taught me the value of smiling to camera.

Like the *Hamlyn All Colour Cookbook*, the recipes I devised for *Good Afternoon* were on the whole quite basic family meals, with the additional qualification that I needed to be able to make them within the half-hour of the programme. In time, Thames Television started to bring out cookery books to accompany each series of *Good Afternoon*, to capitalize on the interest in recipes such as Family Meat Loaf, Tuna Spaghetti Bake and Chocolate Brownies – although very often these weren't out until after the series was broadcast, which was most annoying.

*Good Afternoon* was filmed at the Thames Television studios, which were near Euston station in central London. On a filming day I used to arrive at the studio at about six thirty in the morning, long before any of the crew or production team were there, since I was coming in from Penn and was always worried the traffic might be bad. The only people around at this time of day would be the security chaps, who would help me carry all my bags and equipment in. I had to bring in every single thing I needed to prepare the recipe from home – every pan, utensil and tin – as there was nothing at the studio. I also had to bring in all the ingredients, plus the recipe pre-prepared at different stages. For example, if I was making a cake I would need to bring in a finished product so that I could demonstrate putting the icing on. During filming I would make up the mixture, put it in the oven and then – hey presto! – here's one I made earlier. If I thought they would suit the theme of the programme, I would also often bring in flowers from the garden; I might take in a vase of forsythia in early spring and chip in during my chat with Judy that if you pick the branches before they are in bloom and put them in a warm place the blossoms will come out earlier and last longer than in the garden.

So, laden down with all my stuff, I'd walk into this cavernous, cold studio where there would be a few tables with a pile of scripts from filming the news the night before but not much else (the whole set was built from scratch each month). At around eight o'clock everyone would start to arrive and the props chaps would start putting the kitchen together – well, more like the illusion of a kitchen. There was a clock on the wall and the sparks would wire in a cooker, but none of the drawers or doors opened, and there was no running water in the taps. If you needed water you moved your hand towards the tap and the props man would gesture to someone out the back who would then turn the hosepipe on. Neither was there any plumbing underneath the sink: instead, the water flowed down into a bucket and if you weren't careful it would flood. On one occasion the water started to overflow and Judy was there in her best shoes desperately trying to signal to me to turn the tap off.

While the props chaps were assembling the kitchen, I would be laying out all my stuff, rigorously double-checking that I had everything on my list of ingredients and making sure I had exactly the right utensils. As people arrived at the studio they would say hello to me, perhaps try to engage me in conversation, but I was so focused on what I was doing, determined that I wouldn't make any mistakes, that I would just mutter, 'Good Morning' and barely lift my head. After a few months of this, Judy took me to one side.

'All these people in the studio are here to help you,' she said. 'They just want to tell you that their mother's suet pudding is famous, and would you like the recipe, so perhaps you should stop what you're doing for a moment and listen to them.'

'But I've got to get ready,' I told her. 'I've got to check I have everything, and there's so much to remember . . .'

Judy just nodded and said, 'Yes, of course, but I think it would be a good idea if you remembered to smile. Not just at people in the studio, but when you're on the box. You love what you do, but you can be a little bit serious. If you don't look as if you're enjoying yourself, people will just change channels. Just try to remember to smile.'

Such a simple piece of advice, but one of the best I've

been given during my television career. Judy also advised me
to forget about the audience and imagine that I was talking
to just one person, who might be doing the ironing, and if I
wasn't fun or interesting enough to keep their attention they
would change channels. I think it's very important to maintain this illusion of intimacy when you're presenting.

Although I was enjoying this new challenge, I was still battling terrible nerves. My anxiety was largely centred around
the fact that I had no idea how to 'perform' on television: I
didn't have a clue where I should be looking, or whether I
should be talking to Judy or to the camera. It didn't help that
at school I had never been the one to read aloud in English,
as I was always hidden away at the back of the classroom,
and as a result I found it very difficult to speak to camera. To
make matters worse, around the same time as I started
appearing on *Good Afternoon* I developed a very irritating
cough, which was often so bad that it would interrupt filming. Concerned that I might have something seriously wrong
with me, I went to see my old boyfriend Tony Bull, the Ear,
Nose and Throat specialist, who referred me to one of his
colleagues, and after various tests they discovered that my
cough was purely the result of nerves. I eventually got over
it, but in the meantime it was a very great help to have Judy
by my side, because she was a brilliantly skilled presenter and
always chipped in when stage fright got the better of me and
I didn't know what I was going to say next.

We would pre-record *Good Afternoon* on a Monday morning
for transmission later that afternoon, so there wasn't much
time for retakes. We only had the studio until twelve thirty and
then the team came in to prepare for the news, which went out
live at one o'clock, so if mistakes were made while we were
filming more often than not we would just work around them.

As pressurized as this could be I suppose it was also a more realistic way of demonstrating cooking, as things don't always turn out perfectly in the kitchen. On one occasion I was making a quiche and when I baked the pastry case blind it came out of the oven with a huge great crack across the bottom of it. We were in the middle of recording so I said something like, 'Oh Judy, look what's happened. If this happens to you at home what you would do is push it together again, brush beaten egg over the crack and put it back in the oven until the egg sets, so the case won't leak.' After we finished the shot I asked the director, 'Would you mind if we did that again? I don't like showing a cracked one.' And he just said, 'If that can happen to people at home we should leave it in.'

At this stage of my career I was still trying to do lots of different projects and accept any offers of work that came my way, but as a working mother with three small children I also had to learn to prioritize. Family comes first – that has been, and always will be, my mantra – but they had to fit in with my other commitments as well. Although I did everything I could to be part of my children's school life, whether that was going to plays or helping at fetes, as many working mothers will know it just wasn't always possible. I had a career at a time when not many other mothers worked (you might say I was something of a trailblazing anomaly!) and there wasn't the childcare infrastructure there is today, so it was a challenge to juggle all my different responsibilities.

Shortly before the schools broke up for half-term one year I was still struggling to find someone to look after the children for the day we filmed *Good Afternoon*. I mentioned this to Judy, who said that she hadn't managed to find anyone to look after her lot either, so we went to Diana Potter and suggested that we do an item on cooking with children during the half-term break. Fortunately Diana thought this was a wonderful idea and gave permission for us to have all five of our children on the programme. Judy and I were relieved that our childcare problems were solved, but while it's bad enough being nervous for yourself when you're appearing on television, imagine what it's like to be nervous for your children. Terrifying!

All of the children were under ten, with Annabel the youngest at the age of five, but each of them made their own recipe with our help. Like my own mother, I had always involved my children in the kitchen, delegating simple tasks like grating cheese and stirring cakes, so they were fairly confident with basic recipes. We used to have a rocking horse in the kitchen at the Red House and Annabel in particular would love to sit on it, rocking happily, watching me prepare lunch. (I had rescued that rocking horse from the top of a bonfire in the village: I asked if I could have it and they told me I could if I brought back some more wood for the fire, which I did. We had it restored to its former glory with a real horsehair mane and tail and it was then beautifully repainted.) I sometimes organized pizza parties for the children and their friends, teaching them to knead the dough and choose their different toppings, which is a great way to get children interested in cooking. It helped that my lot enjoyed food and weren't fussy eaters; the only thing they didn't like was olives, with which they used to chase each other around the kitchen.

For the programme, Thomas made 'Thomas's Flan', a crumb crust case with a filling of condensed milk, cream and lemons, which he was very used to doing as he liked to make it at home. William made bread. I remember him kneading the dough, really bashing it about, and Judy asking, 'William, what is it you like about making bread?' to which he replied, 'Oh, the thumping!' He really treated it like Play-Doh, making it into little shapes and rolls. And Annabel, who as a small child was nicknamed 'Pudding' for her love of cakes, did something with chocolate – although she didn't achieve an awful lot. As she grew up she was always experimenting in the kitchen, making up her own recipes (and chasing her brothers around with a wooden spoon) but on this particular occasion she spent most of the half-hour programme licking the chocolate bowl. Thankfully nobody seemed to mind; in fact we got a lot of positive comments from viewers after the programme, and most of them were about how lovely Annabel was!

Looking back, I don't feel that I was the most brilliant mother. I was always very good at giving my children the right food – they had an impressively varied diet, because I was always trying out recipes at home – but it is one of my regrets in life that I didn't spend more time listening to them or playing with them. I felt guilty working, although I wanted to do it. It was usually Paul who read their bedtime stories, as I was busy trying to do five things at once. I was very fortunate in that a few years after we moved to Penn, my husband left Hiram Walker and bought a gallery in the village, turning what had been a hobby of his – collecting antique maps and prints – into a career, and so he was able to do the school drop-offs and pick-ups if I wasn't around. I had great friends nearby, too, which was important to me. Ann Usher had young children of the same age and frequently gathered my lot after school when I was held up or busy. I've always been a firm believer in what you give is what you get back: I often had other people's children round to play and for tea, so that when I was absolutely stuck they would be happy to have my lot. Yet despite my shortcomings as a mother, I look back on the years when our children were young as some of the happiest times of my life.

# MEXICAN SPICY LAMB

This dish is great when entertaining all the family for a get together. It's particularly delicious served with a tomato salad and chunky garlic bread.

*Serves 6*

- 1 kg (2 lb) lamb neck fillet or end-of-leg fillet
- 2 tablespoons sunflower oil
- 2 garlic cloves, crushed
- 1 large onion, sliced
- 2 level tablespoons flour
- 1 teaspoon ground cumin
- 1 teaspoon ground coriander
- 150ml (¼ pint) white wine
- 1 x 400g (14 oz) tin chopped tomatoes
- 2 level tablespoons tomato purée
- salt and freshly ground black pepper
- 1 x 400g (14 oz) tin black-eyed beans
- 1–2 tablespoons mango chutney
- 150g (5 oz) carton Greek yoghurt
- 2 teaspoons fresh coriander or mint, chopped, plus sprigs to garnish

Remove any excess fat from the lamb and cut into large cubes. Heat a large frying pan, add 1 tablespoon of the oil and fry the lamb cubes in batches, to brown. Remove the lamb with a slotted spoon on to a plate. Turn down the heat, then add the remaining oil, garlic and onion to the pan and allow to soften for a few minutes. Stir in the flour and spices and cook for 2 minutes.

Add the wine, tomatoes and tomato purée, and return the meat to the pan. Stir well and bring to the boil, then season, cover and cook over a low heat for about 1½ to 2 hours.

Drain and rinse the beans, then add them to the lamb about 10 minutes before the end of cooking, along with the mango chutney. Check the seasoning.

Garnish the dish with sprigs of coriander or mint. Season the Greek yoghurt with salt and pepper, and mix in the chopped coriander or mint. Serve the lamb with the flavoured yoghurt alongside.

We had a very outdoor life when the children were young. They were never the ones who'd be sitting in the corner with a book; they'd be outside playing sports or getting into trouble. Perhaps that's why none of my children ever had any difficulties sleeping. Chips off the old block, you might say! Thomas was particularly adventurous – and terribly naughty. One incident comes to mind: it was William's fifth birthday party and all of his friends from school were there with their mothers; we were having a lovely time in the garden at the Red House. The children were in the middle of a game of grandmother's footsteps on the lawn when suddenly I heard a gasp from one of the mothers. I glanced over and saw her looking back at the house with an expression of horror. There, balancing on the narrowest point of the roof, three stories up, was Thomas. He must have climbed through the little hatch from the attic on to the flat roof and then somehow clambered up, and was now making his way along the very top of the pitched roof like a six-year-old tightrope walker, no doubt hoping to grab back some of the limelight from his younger brother. By now all of the other mothers had noticed, but nobody said a word. They just looked at me and then in unspoken agreement we all returned our attention to the game on the lawn. I was absolutely terrified, of course, but the worst thing I could have done would have been to start yelling at Thomas, telling him to go back and get down, because he would have fallen. All I could do was ignore him, stay focused on William and his friends, and pray that he would be all right. Thankfully, when Thomas realized that nobody was paying him any attention he somehow got back inside and came downstairs. I hugged him hard, but had strong words with the little monster – and the next day there was a childproof bolt fixed on the attic door.

*Thomas:*
As a child I just remember being out in the garden the whole time, messing about, climbing trees and making camps: the things small boys like to do. When I was quite young a friend and I crawled under the hedge in the vegetable garden to make a den. We built a little campfire under there; then made it bigger and bigger, enjoying the blaze, until the hedge caught fire. As we scrambled out of the way I could hear the roaring sound of the holly crackling away and, as a little boy, you're terrified that the whole garden's going to go up. Mum was out at the time, so I remember running to tell Granny – and Granny not being that bothered! In the end I turned the hose on it and managed to put it out.

I never did anything really terrible, but I was a little monkey. I'd get bangers, put them inside windfall apples and lob them at passing cars. Another time we climbed on top of the wall with Annabel's vanity mirror and dazzled drivers as they came around the bend. I got in trouble for that.

I think the worst trouble I ever found myself in was when I got my penknife and cut all the way along the decorative beading on the seats of Grandpa's new camper van. As I was doing it I had an inkling that I was doing something bad, but I was enjoying myself. My grandfather – Mum's father – could be very stern and quite scary, and all I remember Mum saying to me when she discovered my handiwork was: 'Don't go anywhere near Grandpa.' I'm sure he would have given me a good old clout. Mum was certainly angry with me, but she was more afraid of the wrath of her father!

William was a little quieter than Thomas, the most lovely and loving boy who adored his elder brother. He was diligent and worked hard at school: out of the three of them, William was my little bright button – although he could be just as wild as Thomas. On one occasion I discovered that William had been at a friend's house playing 'it' with an air rifle, the rule being that whoever got hit by a pellet was 'it'. However, he was also a very considerate child; when Annabel first started at New Gregory's School at the age of three she would cry inconsolably after being dropped off, and so William used to go and sit with her in class until she was settled. I thought that was such a sweet, thoughtful thing to do.

The school were actually rather concerned about Annabel as she didn't talk at all when she joined the school. She would come out with a sort of gibberish, but she couldn't string sentences together. The school thought that Annabel should be referred to a psychologist, but I knew that there was nothing to worry about. She didn't have any need to talk because whenever anyone spoke to her, Thomas or William would just jump in and answer on her behalf. Neither did she walk until two and a half, as her brothers used to carry her or push her around in a wheelbarrow. Sure enough, at the grand old age of three and a half, Annabel pointed at my cup and said her first word, 'cockee', which was her attempt at 'coffee' – and she hasn't stopped talking since.

Although they all got on very well, my children tended to play with their own friends rather than with each other; they weren't a close-knit tribe – except when we went away on holiday. I look back on our summer holidays when the children were young as some of the happiest days of my life. Just like my own childhood, we never went to hotels; instead, we would usually go on farm stays or to B&Bs in Devon. We would drive down there in my dad's old blue VW camper van with navy leather seats, which he lent to my brothers and I so that we could have inexpensive family holidays. It had a fridge, and, if it was pouring with rain on a day out, you could all stay snug inside and play cards. On long journeys we would sing, 'We're all going on a summer holiday . . .' and my husband would tell stories as he was driving along to keep everyone quiet, usually about Mr McGregor, the gardener from *Peter Rabbit*, and all the adventures of the animals who dared to creep into his garden. Of course, the children weren't in seatbelts in those days, so they would be perched on top of the fridge or leaning over the front seats to listen, which was lovely.

Thomas, Annabel and William on one of many fishing trips.

One year I borrowed the camper van and drove all the way to the French resort of St Malo with my friend Hilly Turner and her children – Charles, Edward and Harriet – but without either of our husbands. As Annabel put it: 'No daddies, two mummies and six children!' We stayed in a tent, did all our cooking on a little camping stove and it was such glorious sunny weather that we were on the beach every single day. What a wonderful holiday, but we were exhausted, Hilly and I, with the effort of keeping six children under control! We were awfully glad not to have our husbands with us, though, because the children were so full on and very, very noisy. Although my children weren't fussy eaters, Annabel went through a stage of drowning all her meals in my home-made salad dressing, but I forgot to take any to St Malo and as a result she flatly refused to eat a thing. In the end I had to go out to buy the ingredients and make up a batch, which Annabel proceeded to drink straight from the bottle!

The first place we stayed in Devon as a family was a lovely farmhouse in the village of Great Aish, on the estuary of the River Dart, which was owned by Mary and Bill Slade. We came back here several years running. The children used to love all the animals: the boys would ride Smoky the pony, play with the dogs and feed the chickens. There were always a lot of jobs they could help with on the farm, whether that was picking the beans for supper with Mary or watching Bill do the milking. They still managed to get into mischief though: I remember on one occasion Thomas locked himself in the loo and, as there was no way we could get in, our friend John Pittman, who had joined us on holiday with his wife Hazel and family, had to climb up a ladder and break the window to get him out.

Just outside the front of the farmhouse was a monkey

puzzle tree where for some reason the farm's cockerel had made its home, and every morning it started crowing at the crack of dawn and woke us all up. All the other guests at the farm used to talk about how annoying this bird was, and at the end of our holiday I said to Mary, half-joking, 'I'd like to buy that cockerel and have it roasted so it doesn't wake us next year.' She laughed, but sure enough when we left it came home with us, plucked and ready for the oven.

We spent a lot of time in the kitchen at the Slade's farmhouse, where there was a big Aga and always plenty of delicious food. I used to love watching Mary Slade make these wonderful large Cornish pasties – often big enough to feed sixteen people – dicing the meat with a tiny little knife and mixing in potato and onion and plenty of pepper. I recreated her recipe in one of my later cookery books and christened it Slade's Pie in her honour. In the evenings, Bill Slade – who worked very hard – would often be in his chair by the Aga, and he'd have the very young Annabel on his knee while we talked.

Great Aish is on Dartmoor and, of course, the moors are very wet. In the morning Mary would come up to our bedroom with a cup of tea and she would draw the curtains and say, 'Raining again, my dears.' It did seem to rain an awful lot, but that doesn't matter at all if you're dressed for it. We would go for day trips to Dartmeet, where two major tributaries of the River Dart converge and the water flows particularly quickly, parking up the camper van and having a picnic lunch while the children entertained themselves running around and skimming stones. On one occasion there had been so much rain that the river had burst its banks and the water had somehow got underneath the turf, which created a remarkable sensation when you walked on it, almost like jumping on a bouncy castle. The children thought this was fantastic and were leaping around when suddenly William's leg plunged down and a plume of water spurted up like a fountain!

Another popular holiday pastime was fishing; even now if we all go on holiday together we usually go on a fishing trip – and we always cook and eat whatever we've caught afterwards. A particular favourite when the children were very young was crabbing, using a bit of bacon or whatever else was in the kitchen as bait; other times our quarry would be sand eels, a sort of burrowing fish, which we grilled in the camper van until they turned bright pink. Once Thomas caught a small sea trout at Mothecombe that was big enough to feed the five of us for lunch: he was immensely proud, as you can imagine. On another occasion he hooked a five-pound Pollock. He was only six and was so excited, since this was a really big fish, and he was pulling it as hard as he could and managed to get it to the surface, but then my line got tangled up with his and the fish got away. He was in floods of tears, quite inconsolable! Thomas built on this early promise to become a very keen fisherman and would always love going to my parents at Charlcombe Farm to fish in their lake, which he had stocked with trout when he was a teenager.

At Mothecombe we would also prise mussels and winkles off the rocks to take back to the farm and cook for a starter before supper. Some of the other guests, who were often from cities, thought this was awfully odd, but we liked that sort of thing. I still eat them today because all the grandchildren like to gather them; we tease them out of the shell with a pin and then dip them in vinegar. The taste always transports me back to those happy days in Devon.

For several summers we went to Cornwall and stayed with a family called the Smiths at Hurdon Farm in Launceston. Margaret Smith was an excellent cook, who produced the

William and Tom uncovering seaside treasures.

most wonderful high teas, and was particularly proud of her Aga, which she'd had for several years but which still shone like the day she'd bought it because she used little cork mats to protect the enamel whenever she put a plate down. It was lovely to see an Aga looking so pristine. By this time the boys were older and more adventurous, heading off in the silage truck in the morning to help the farmer, and one day they decided they wanted to spend the night in the haystack. The other guests at the farm thought they were crazy to sleep in the barn when they had nice warm beds they could go to, but Margaret Smith provided them with sleeping bags and the barn was right near the house, so I was very happy to let them do it. Afterwards the boys admitted that they had been quite frightened, because they could see rats running around at the foot of the haystack, but they stuck it out all night and the next morning when Annabel raced out to see them Thomas started pelting her with rotten eggs that he'd found in the bales. Delightful boy!

Somewhere else that we enjoyed going on holiday was Salcombe, a pretty seaside town on the most southerly point of Devon, which I had first visited in my late teens because the Pattersons had a holiday house there. When we went back with the children we stayed in B&Bs and had the most idyllic time: paddling, making sandcastles and playing cricket on the beach. There was a wonderful bakery in the village called Upper Crust, where we went every morning to get fresh bread and croissants. Perhaps it was just the sea air, but everything they sold tasted especially delicious and one morning I got chatting to the owner, Jeremy, and asked if I could come and bake with him to learn some new techniques. His working hours fitted in pretty well with ours: we had been having supper at six o'clock because the children were so exhausted after a day on the beach. So I'd go to bed at the same time as them and have a kip until just before midnight when I'd walk down the hill to the bakery and start work, then would be back with a bag of croissants for breakfast. Paul thought that I had a screw loose, but it was what I loved to do; I was learning all the time and certainly didn't think of it as work. We had such delightful times in Salcombe that once the children had left home Paul and I bought a house in the town and we spend as much time there as we can.

Christmas was another special time of the year that we spent together as a family. We always went to my parents' house in Bath, along with my mother-in-law, both of my brothers and their families and in-laws. Dad was adamant that Christmas should be at Charlcombe Farm and, as it was really the only thing that was still expected of us, we all came home. However, I thought this was hard on Paul – although he never complained. We kept up the tradition until my father died at the age of eighty-four and then my mother starting coming to us instead. Nowadays I tell my children to go wherever they like at Christmas, as I would hate them to feel obliged to come home, but they still usually spend it with us.

We would always drive to Bath on Christmas Eve, the car overflowing with children, Granny Mop (Paul's mother), the dog and presents. As we drove along the A4 from Penn we would play car games like flip-flap and ting-a-ling (which is when you say 'flip-flap' every time you pass a letterbox and 'ting-a-ling' when you spot a phone box, and keep score); it was really just a way of shutting everybody up on the journey down there.

Once everyone had arrived, we always had Granny's famous Fish Pie for supper and then would gather round to sing carols, before heading off to Midnight Service at Charlcombe Parish Church. On Christmas Day, my sisters-in-law and I would vaguely help with preparing lunch, but Mum was extremely well organized and there wasn't much room in the kitchen. I would bring a trifle, and somebody else might do the pudding, but she produced everything else. Over the years we've tried every sort of bird on Christmas Day, but Mum would usually have a big turkey and I remember her telling me that when she was first married she would wait until Christmas Eve to buy her turkey as they were always so much cheaper.

Christmas at Charlcombe Farm was always a thrill, as the smells and decorations transported me straight back to the Christmases of my childhood. I think it's very important to keep up family traditions, especially when children are young. Mum would always decorate her mantelpiece with lots of boughs of greenery and little model doves, which is something I do to this day, and when they were at school my lot made Christmas decorations by cutting out the little cup-shaped bits from egg boxes, covering them with foil and threading them on a string to look like little bells, and we still hang these on our Christmas tree at home every year.

Having grown up surrounded by animals, I've always liked to have a pet at home – and soon after we moved to Penn we got a brown flat-coat retriever called Wellington and a cat called Primrose. It was lovely having a houseful of children and pets, and Paul and I were lucky that we could call on doting grandparents to help out if any of them needed looking after. I was not at all close to my mother-in-law – Granny Mop – in the early years of my marriage, although I was always respectful and did all the things a daughter-in-law should do, but I grew to become extremely fond of her and in her final years she came to live with us.

In the summer of Annabel's fourth year, Paul and I took

My mother-in-law, Granny Mop.

the boys to Scotland for a week-long holiday and Granny Mop came to stay to look after Annabel and Wellington. I made sure the larder was well stocked before we left and told Granny Mop that there was a lovely chicken in the fridge for her and Annabel's supper, and dog food for Wellington. As wonderful as she was with children, Granny Mop was not at all keen on dogs so, to make her life as easy as possible, I went to the butchers and got a big block of dog food made from compressed liver and lights (lungs) and other rejected bits of animal, wrapped up in greaseproof paper. You couldn't get tins of dog food in those days, so I thought this would be a more pleasant way of feeding Wellington for Granny Mop, rather than having to prepare the food herself.

When we got back from our week's holiday Granny Mop told me, 'I didn't touch the chicken, I saved it for you when you got home, but that pâté was delicious!' It took me a moment to realize what she was talking about. Well, I nearly died – the thought of my beautiful daughter eating dog food! But of course they were both absolutely fine, and I never told Granny Mop about her mistake – although having been through the war and rationing, I have no doubt it wouldn't have bothered her in the least. I'm still not entirely sure what Wellington ate that week.

Paul has always liked to walk the dog as early as possible – he's usually gone by six o'clock because he prefers to be out when everyone else is still in bed so that he doesn't have to stop for a chat – and after one such morning stroll with Wellington he returned with a duck egg he'd found by the village pond.

'How about we have it for breakfast?' he said, handing it to me.

'Oh you can't, there's a duck inside it,' I said, cradling the egg. I've always loved ducks. Then a thought occurred to me.

'I think I'm going to try and hatch it,' I said.

Deprived of his breakfast, Paul looked at me as if I was a nutcase, but once I've put my mind to something I'm not easily discouraged and later that morning I paid a visit to Mrs Griffiths, the local farmer's wife at Puttenham Farm, to get some hatching advice. She, at least, was rather more encouraging than Paul had been.

'That's a lovely idea, my dear,' she said. 'You want to put it somewhere warm and turn it every day, and you never know your luck.'

'I'll put it in a bowl next to the Aga where I keep my tea towels,' I said. 'It should be nice and warm there.'

'You do that,' smiled Mrs Griffiths. 'But don't forget to turn it and sprinkle it with water, then in twenty-eight days or so it might well hatch.'

And so I put the egg next to the Aga and every morning I religiously followed Mrs Griffiths' advice. Day after day I turned the egg and sprinkled it with water, until it became second nature and I'd lost count of the number of days it had been there. Then one morning, when I came down to the kitchen, instead of the egg there was a fluffy yellow duckling waiting for me amidst a load of broken shell. It really felt like a miracle! I lifted this dear little thing out of the bowl and ran straight upstairs to the boys' room. William was on the bottom bunk and I shook him awake and said, 'What do you think has happened? My egg's hatched!' I showed him the new arrival. 'I think we should call him Lucky,' I said.

'No, Mum,' said William sleepily. 'Call him Bloody Lucky.' And with that he turned over and went back to sleep.

Later that day I paid another visit to Mrs Griffiths and she told me how to look after the new arrival and gave me some chick food. I soon realized that our dear little duck only had one working leg – the other seemed to be stuck folded up beneath her body – so she couldn't walk properly. Poor little thing, I thought, let's take you to the vet and see what they can do for you. When we got to the surgery I sat in the waiting room with Lucky nestled in my pocket, surrounded by people with their cats and dogs, and when the vet opened the door to call me everyone looked at me in bemusement as if to say, 'But where's the animal?'

The vet explained that the duckling's leg probably got stuck to the shell while she was growing in the egg, and told me that there was nothing he could do to help her. Because she had to hop on one leg to get around the vet warned me that she might have a heart attack from the exertion and would most probably die soon.

The vet was wrong: Lucky not only survived, she thrived. When she was little she lived in a box in the kitchen then, once she was big enough to live outside, William dug a pond for her in the garden, lining it with polythene, and we made her a long, caged run – although she never really used it because the garden was fenced and gated and she couldn't fly because of her leg. She was quite happy just to wander around with Primrose and Wellington. In fact, it was just like having another dog or cat: you'd open the door in the morning and she'd be straight in, hopping around the kitchen. The only time Lucky was any trouble was when we had to find someone to duck-sit during our holiday when she was little. My friend Shirley Nightingale, who lived in London, kindly offered to look after her, and when I came to get her at the end of our holiday Shirley presented me with a photograph of Lucky swimming around in this huge great saucepan with an orange and a sauce boat sitting next to the pan. 'In the end I decided not to cook her,' she smiled.

We all adored our duck and she was very much part of the

Our one-legged duck, 'Bloody' Lucky.

family. William was particularly fond of her; one day I came into the living room to find him watching telly with Lucky sitting next to him.

'William, you can't have the duck in here because of the carpet,' I said.

'Don't worry, Mum,' he said. 'Lucky never makes a mess.'

It was only a little while later that I noticed that the bin was full of tissues.

Then one day when Lucky was a little over a year old we arrived home from a trip to London and found that our front gate had been left open after someone had made a delivery. She always used to run up to us when we came home, but this time there was no sign of our duck. We later discovered that she must have followed the deliveryman out onto the road. Lucky's luck had sadly run out.

# EXCEEDINGLY GOOD FISH PIE

My mother's traditional Christmas Eve recipe can be made up to 36 hours before cooking and kept in the fridge.

*Serves 6*

- 75g (3 oz) butter, plus extra to grease
- 1 large onion, roughly chopped
- 50g (2 oz) plain flour
- scant 600ml (1 pint) milk
- salt and freshly ground black pepper
- 2 tablespoons lemon juice
- 350g (12 oz) fresh haddock, cut into 1cm (½ inch) pieces
- 350g (12 oz) smoked undyed haddock, cut into 1cm (½ inch) pieces
- 4 large eggs, hard-boiled and roughly chopped

*for the topping*
- 900g (2 lb) potatoes, peeled and cut into even-sized pieces
- about 8 tablespoons hot milk
- about 50g (2 oz) butter

Preheat the oven to 200°C/Fan 180°C/Gas 6. Grease a shallow 2½ litre (4 pint) dish with butter.

Melt the butter in a pan on a high heat, add the onions and fry for few minutes, then lower the heat, cover and soften for 15 minutes. Remove the lid and increase the heat to drive off any wet. Sprinkle in the flour then add the milk gradually, stirring well and allowing the sauce to thicken, until all the milk has been added. Season, add the lemon juice and raw fish and boil for couple of minutes, stirring continuously, until the fish has just cooked. Gently stir in the eggs. Pour into the buttered dish and allow to cool.

For the topping, boil the potatoes in salted water until tender. Drain, add the milk and butter and mash with salt and pepper until lump free.

Spread the mash over the top of the sauce and fish in the dish. Score with a fork to make it look pretty.

Bake in the preheated oven for about 30 minutes, until the potato topping is crisp and golden.

## 13

By the start of the eighties, *Good Afternoon* had changed its name to *Afternoon Plus* (or 'A Plus' as it was known) and there were changes made to the programme's format as well. The producers wanted to keep a cookery element to the series and I was still keen to provide it, but I had grown tired of packing up my pots and pans for filming every time and so I came up with the idea of recording the programmes in my home. This would, of course, be far more convenient for me, but there would also be advantages for the production team: they wouldn't have to build the set from scratch every time, and there would be running water. Fortunately, the powers-that-be thought it was a terrific idea.

Rather than appearing alongside Judy Chalmers, for the first time I was presenting by myself, a prospect that scared me rather less than it would have done if I hadn't been on home ground. Gosh, it was wonderful being able to prepare everything ahead in my own kitchen, and such a relief not to have to worry that I'd left a key ingredient or a vital piece of equipment at home. Not only that, but I knew all my machinery worked and I could step out into the garden for herbs and veg! Nevertheless, filming away from the studio brought challenges of its own. As my work surface in the kitchen was in front of a window it was necessary to take the glass out before we started work, so that the two cameramen could film through the gap. Every morning before filming a carpenter would come and remove this big plate glass window, then twiddle his thumbs all day until it was time to put it back in again that evening. As a result, I was always exceedingly cold while filming, even though I had a blow heater at my feet, as I might as well have just been standing outside. (This proved to be excellent preparation for filming *The Great British Bake Off*, as the wind blows straight through the tent and it is rare that I'm not freezing!)

If I'm filming something at home today there will be just seven or eight people in the crew, but back then the team numbered something like thirty or forty and would arrive with two huge lorries of equipment, the wheels of which would sink into our drive, and they would erect huge tents on the lawn. And, of course, all these people were all over the house; I couldn't have imagined how much loo paper we would get through! By this time Paul had his gallery in the village, so he would escape off to work in the morning as soon as the crew started to arrive, but if it was school holidays and the children were around it was like the circus had come to town. The riggers, who were in charge of all the cables, taught the boys to play poker – and I think William actually won quite a lot of money!

Sometimes the unexpected happened. On one occasion when I was making chocolate cake, out of the corner of my eye I noticed Wellington's face pop up opposite me outside and, as I beat the mixture and said my piece to camera, that naughty dog nosed towards me through the window gap and ate the last piece of chocolate off the work surface. I just carried on, because I had learnt never to interrupt the action, but afterwards I asked the cameramen, 'Why didn't you tell me to stop? Whatever will the viewers say?' Thankfully he

The vast film crew for 'Country Cooking'.

reassured me that they had been filming straight down into the mixing bowl, and that nobody would witness Wellington's delinquency.

We filmed a number of television series at the Red House during the eighties, each one based on a theme, such as 'Cooking for Celebrations' and 'Country Cooking', under the stewardship of my wonderful producer at the time, Carol Jones. Carol and I are still in touch today, and here she kindly shares her memories of working together back in those days.

*Carol:*

In the 1970s and 1980s, Thames Television was the only TV network that produced daytime feature programmes in the afternoon. I became a researcher and later producer on *Afternoon Plus* in 1979 and took over responsibility for producing Mary's cookery programmes. She was always fully confident with her cooking, but hated doing intros to camera!

In 1980, we moved to recording on outside broadcast

cameras at her home in Penn, and these are the times I remember best. We always recorded the cookery series in the summer months and OB [outside broadcast] crews would be loitering outside my door in early spring, wanting to know the recording dates so that they could get themselves on the Mary Berry schedule! We're talking here of around thirty personnel, mainly male, who were not 'new men' exactly in the cookery department, but they loved the work and did get the most wonderful bacon baps at coffee break and (sometimes) a chance to savour whatever delectable dish Mary was producing that day. And then, of course, there was tea and cake in the afternoon. But mainly, I think the appeal of working on the programme had to do with the 'feel-good factor' – we were a very happy crew.

The Christmas programme was always recorded in summer and that brought even more joyous times – dressing the Christmas tree, decorating the dining room, spray snow on the windows, the smell of the turkey cooking with all the trimmings – although it was impossible to find red candles in the shops in the summer. On one occasion, when we recorded in the studio the camera wasn't picking up the lighting of the brandy on the Christmas pud, so we used turpentine instead. You could certainly see the flame then, bright yellow, as it leapt into the air and nearly set off the sprinkler system. I think we actually used that shot in the final programme!

The sort of food Mary was cooking on our programmes was for people at home who were preparing meals every day for their family and wanted some 'disaster free' recipes that they could produce, without the pressure of having to compete with Mrs X down the street who could rustle up cheese soufflés for ten while discussing Proust. Whatever Mary cooked on screen, ninety-nine per cent of the time the viewer could find the ingredients in their cupboards without having to disappear down to Sainsbury's to buy an omelette pan or seek out some foreign fruits. Not being a very adventurous cook, my role as programme maker was to ensure that the cooking process was easy to follow and that the final product really did look good enough to eat. Steam had to rise and meat pies had to be cut to reveal their juicy centres. Stews had to be ladled lovingly on to white plates and cream had to slide over warm apple pie. If the viewers couldn't smell and taste the food, our images had to be the next best thing. All of this was easy with Mary. Her recipes always worked and she never attempted any recipe that could cause problems for fledgling cooks, as she realized this would put them off rather than encourage them to do more.

As well as cookery, *Afternoon Plus* produced a number of feature programmes on dressmaking, knitting, health, etc. The viewers could write to us in response to the many subjects we covered and we produced endless literature on a range of subjects, but the most prolific were Mary's recipe books that accompanied her series: *Mary Berry's Recipes from Home & Abroad, Mary Berry's Country Cooking, Mary Berry Cooking at Home, Mary Berry's Complete Television Cookbook, Mary Berry Cooking for Celebrations.* I think we also had a correspondence section, with Mary answering cookery queries from the viewers. There was no Wikipedia in those days and so daytime television was the place to turn for answers and ideas on a range of subjects. Every Christmas, Mary would also produce a large fold-up sheet with preparation and cooking times for the Christmas dinner. When we stopped producing it my mother would refer each year to an old copy she had kept until it finally disintegrated.

Unlike the celebrity chefs of today, there was no ego involved with Mary. She wanted to share her love of cooking – it had nothing to do with image, or status, or wealth, and she is as straightforward today on screen as she was all those years ago.

I was not in the least bit famous at this time. Although I was appearing regularly on television and the books accompanying the series were selling well, in those days the powers-that-be didn't regard cookery as very important and as a result my programmes never appeared in a regular time-slot or even on the same day of the week, instead just popping up willy-nilly as if plugging random gaps in the schedule. Because of this inconsistency I didn't get much of a following, as nobody ever knew when the programmes were on; neither was I ever asked for press interviews nor mentioned in magazines. The really famous television cook at this time was Delia Smith.

Delia had brought out the first of her three *Cookery Course* books in 1978, along with the accompanying BBC television series, and thanks to their success she was very much a household name. Her recipes were inspirational and straightforward, and they always worked. Although I was continually frustrated that my programmes were never given a regular slot in the schedule, I wasn't at all envious of Delia's fame – on the contrary, I've always been full of admiration for her. Delia and I first met on press trips in the late sixties, when we were both starting out in journalism, and we kept in contact over the years. In 1975, she came to stay at the Red House with her husband, Michael Wynn-Jones, and their corgi, because Michael was doing some research on cartoonists and Paul has always been very interested in old prints and by this time had his gallery. We had a very happy weekend, during which Delia and I got chatting about our agents and comparing notes. Of course, you should never talk about money, but we found ourselves discussing the subject and Delia, who at the time was cookery writer on the *Evening Standard*, told me, 'You're giving far too much to your agent. Have you thought about changing agencies? A friend of mine, Felicity Bryan, the gardening correspondent on the *Evening Standard*, works for Curtis Brown. I'll have a word with her when I get home.'

Curtis Brown was (and still is) one of the biggest literary agencies, at the time representing the likes of Winston Churchill, so I thought nothing more of it, but a few days later a postcard arrived from Felicity that read: 'Delia says that you might want representing – I would be delighted to meet you.' With fear and trepidation I went to meet her in the agency's offices, we talked for a while and to my delight she agreed to take me on – and I've been with her ever since. Felicity always knows exactly which publisher to speak to about which book and has always been there for advice and support; I feel very safe with her. So I'll always be grateful to Delia for introducing me to my literary agent.

I've hardly seen Delia since because although I admire her enormously and she's done so much on television she is, compared to other cookery writers, something of a recluse. She doesn't come to any Guild of Food Writers events; in fact, the only time I ever see her really these days is on television at Norwich City football matches.

In these early days of food programming, the presenters were almost exclusively female home cooks, none of whom had ever worked in a professional kitchen, unlike the Jamie Olivers and Gordon Ramsays of today. In those days – and still to an extent now – there was a real division between the roles of men and women in the world of food. Chefs, on the whole, were male; Joyce Molyneux was one of the only female chefs at this time, cooking at The Hole in the Wall in Bath and The Carved Angel in Dartmouth, both of which restaurants I was lucky enough to visit. After Thomas's baptism we took the godparents and our family out for a special meal at The Hole in the Wall, which is where Joyce started her career with George Perry-Smith, and the food was amazing and very much ahead of its time, using wonderfully fresh, seasonal produce.

There is, of course, a very big difference between a home cook and a chef working in a large kitchen with a whole brigade to support him, each member of which specializes in a particular area, and the recipes they create will reflect these differences. I admire the likes of Heston Blumenthal, and can see his appeal to those with an ultra-scientific mind, but I really don't want to spend hours making mashed potato – and dry ice will never have a place in my kitchen. Also, chefs are forever deep-frying, but I have never done a deep-fried recipe in any of my books and never will do, because who wants a kitchen full of smoke? Once, on *Good Afternoon*, we had a fireman in the studio and he told me that most home fires start in the kitchen with a deep-fat fryer, so it seems foolish to take that risk. I, for one, am happy to save things like deep-fried chips or courgette flowers in batter for when I go out. And what's wrong with oven chips?

Fanny Craddock was the first television cook, but while she championed home cooking she didn't make it easy for anyone. Her recipes were rather unusual and complicated, featuring brandy, offal and cream in large volume, and were the sort of thing you would find in restaurants rather than for a simple family supper. Then, of course, there was Delia and myself, but most other cookery writers at this time plied their trade through books, rather than on television, because there just wasn't the appetite for food programmes that there is today.

While I was working with Carol Jones in the early eighties, we made a programme in which I interviewed cookery writers in their homes. There has always been a lovely camaraderie amongst my peers, a willingness to support each other and share recipes, and I already knew many of them from press trips over the years, so it was a very enjoyable project. One writer I interviewed was Jane Grigson, whom I had met a few years previously when I was doing freelance work for Spanish Olives while at *Ideal Home* (we had taken a group of writers on a promotional trip to Spain). Jane was an English scholar who was married to the poet Geoffrey Grigson and I had always admired her writing and envied her command of the language; not only that, but she was a delightful woman. The first thing that I noticed when I walked into her kitchen was a high chair, which surprised me, as I knew that her daughter Sophie – today a well-known cookery writer herself – was then in her teens. When I asked Jane about it she replied, 'Well, you never know who's going to drop in, do you? A lot of the young people in the village have babies, and it's so useful to be able to plonk them in the chair.' I thought that was lovely. For the programme, Jane made a Pithivier, a round French puff pastry pie, and I can still remember admiring the graceful dexterity of her knife as she cut the traditional pattern into the pastry. In her hall on a side table Jane had a collection of about fifteen candlesticks shaped like Roman columns, all covered with drips and rivulets of hardened wax. They looked delightfully informal, grouped together in a haphazard fashion, and they inspired me to start a similar collection of my own. I now have over forty, and every time I see one in an antique shop I'll buy it in Jane's memory.

We also went to film with *The Times* columnist Katie Stewart, who sadly passed away this year but has always been the cookery writer I've respected and admired the most, and with Prue Leith, who is still a good friend today. I remember having a poke around her kitchen and noticing that her pastry slab, which was made of marble and had rounded edges at one end, looked a bit like a gravestone; sure enough, when I lifted it up I discovered that it was engraved with the words 'Gone But Not Forgotten' underneath! Prue told me she had found it in a junk shop. I thought this was a splendid idea, but I did wonder how the poor chap it had once belonged to was doing without his headstone!

Carol and I spent a very enjoyable day filming with Mary Norwak, the cookery editor of *Farmer's Weekly*. Mary also contributed to numerous magazines and newspapers and was very well known at the time – especially for her traditional English cakes and puddings. It was a bitterly cold day when we went to visit her in her home in Norfolk and it was so wonderful to be welcomed into this glorious country kitchen, at the heart of which was a very old Aga. Later she made Drop Scones for us, but when we arrived there was a cat sitting on top of the simmering plate – obviously it didn't get as hot as they do nowadays!

Mary was a remarkably warm and friendly woman, well rounded both in personality and figure. 'Mary,' she said to me during our visit, 'never trust a thin cook,' – although on this point we had to disagree! She was very thrifty, using cheaper cuts of meat and offal in many of her recipes, and cooked with produce from her own magnificent vegetable garden, sending us home at the end of the day weighed down with armfuls of cabbages and leeks.

By this time, all three of our children had gone away to school. Thomas was a real daredevil, far happier climbing trees than he was sitting in a classroom, so when he was thirteen we sent him to Gordonstoun in Scotland, where they put a great emphasis on the outdoors, physical challenges and community service. The school, which counts Prince Charles amongst its distinguished alumni, has its own fire brigade (with two dedicated fire engines), mountain rescue unit and coastguard service, all staffed by pupils who attend genuine emergencies in the community. They even have their own boat, *Sea Spirit*, and every pupil spends time on board learning seamanship.

Paul and I would go up to Scotland to visit each summer half-term and would rent a thick stone cottage near the River Spey, where the children could swim and fish. During one such visit, we had just turned into the long driveway up to the school when we ground to a halt with a puncture. As Paul got out to survey the damage, a man pulled over and asked if he could help. 'I would be delighted to change your tyre for you,' he said eagerly. We thought this was a bit strange – he was unusually enthusiastic – but then he explained that he was the owner of a nearby garage, which had recently suffered a fire and the Gordonstoun fire service had arrived before the professionals from Elgin and put it out. 'It's thanks to them that I still have a business,' he said, 'so to think that I can do something for a Gordonstoun parent in return – well, I feel you've earned it.'

I had no reservations or worries about sending Thomas (or indeed any of the children) away to boarding school; I just thought how lucky he was to be going to a good school that offered all these wonderful activities. William was the most academic and diligent of the bunch, but even though he got into Radley, which we thought would have been more suitable for him, he wanted to go to Gordonstoun with Thomas, as he adored his brother.

Thomas was pretty wild at school; one evening when he was hungry he climbed in through the refectory roof to pinch some food. Another time he was caught smoking in the woods. But ironically it was William, my golden boy, who got into the real trouble at Gordonstoun. One night a group of his friends drove the school bus out of the grounds and William went along for the ride. When their crime was discovered and the headmaster confronted them the only one who owned up was William. However, the school knew who the guilty boys were and they were all expelled – apart from William, who was rusticated (suspended) for the rest of the term. I wasn't cross with him – he knew he shouldn't have let himself be led, and he was so ashamed that I felt sorry for him – plus it was just gorgeous to have him home for a few extra months. Having him on his own for that time, without the other two, meant that I felt we really got to know each other, and it was an opportunity I would later feel especially grateful for.

After attending New Gregory's School, like her brothers, Annabel then went to Godstowe in High Wycombe, although she didn't board until she was thirteen. She was very much like me at school: always in the mischievous brigade and with a rather chequered academic career. She went to a succession of schools; after Godstowe it was my old school Bath High

William on the banks of the Spey.

(now known as the Royal High School Bath) for three years and then on to the all-girls boarding school Cobham Hall, where she lasted for just nine months. But I'll let Annabel tell you more.

*Annabel:*

I wouldn't say that I was ever expelled from school; I prefer to describe it as 'asked to leave politely'! There was never a particular reason behind it and I actually got on very well with Mrs Cameron, the headmistress at Cobham Hall, but I was naughty and high-spirited and one does get a reputation. For the school, I think it was simply a case of 'we've had enough'.

I was always very much the good girl at home, so I think my behaviour at school was down to the fact that I'm pretty dyslexic. From a young age I struggled to understand what was going on in class so my exam results were the absolute worst, which made me think: 'Why bother?' But while, like Mum, I was not remotely academic, I excelled on the sports field and was also House Captain, so I suppose the school must have felt I could do something.

After I was asked to leave Cobham Hall, Mrs Cameron put me forward for an exchange program with an outward-bound school for naughty children in America. On arrival I was given the choice of sitting in a classroom or going on a three-week 'Survival Course' in the Arizona desert. For a girl who had spent most of her childhood outside, with a mother who had taught me everything there was to know about camping and survival skills, there was really no com-petition. And so a group of seven of us were taken to the desert where we spent the first week walking from sunrise to sunset with no food at all, just water. After the first week we were each given basic rations, including bags of rice, flour and lentils, were taught how to make a fire with a flint and then left to our own devices. I used to make 'ash cakes', as I called them, out of flour, water and raisins. We were sup-posed to keep a half-mile's distance between each of us at all times, but the boys (I was the only girl in the group) used to come and get coals from me, because I was the only one who managed to keep my fire going.

Within a few days we became aware of muffled explo-sions, and after a bit of detective work we found out that the US army were testing bombs in the desert nearby. We were all absolutely starving, as you can imagine, so the next time the boys came to get coals I suggested that we go and see if the army had any food to spare. The next full moon we all set off and after hiking up a hill we found the camp.

I crept over to the nearest tent and unzipped it; inside there were two soldiers – asleep, but with their guns still pointing to the heavens. I grabbed a chocolate bar and zipped the tent back up. A little further into the camp there were some steaks on a barbecue; the smell was too much for our hungry stomachs to bear, and we took about half of them (we didn't want to be mean) and ran back down the hill. Later that night we had a picnic at my camp and those steaks tasted like the most delicious thing I'd ever eaten. We hid the evidence of our contraband feast by burying the rubbish in the sandy soil and washing away all our footprints with water from the nearby stream, then dispersed with gloriously full bellies.

The next morning the course leaders pulled us from our tents, almost by our ears, and walked us a few miles into the desert and then made us sit down in a line. I remember seeing these huge shiny boots in front of us and I looked up, squinting into the sunlight, to see these enormous army officers.

'Y'all have nice steaks last night, boys?' one barked.

We flatly denied it, staring at the ground, but then they produced all the incriminating evidence we thought we had so cleverly hidden. Those officers were not at all happy that a bunch of sixteen-year-olds had stolen from the US Army!'


In May 1988, Paul and I decided to go house-hunting in the Cotswolds – we loved the area and were thinking about relocating there – with our neighbour and friend Joan Heath, who lived just down the road from us in Penn. On the Sunday evening we took Joan back to her house, Watercroft, where she had until recently lived with her late husband, Sir Barrie

Heath. We had tea in the morning room looking out over the courtyard that I had always admired (and rather envied). As the sun started to set, Joan turned to us and said, 'My house is going on the market tomorrow.' I looked at Paul and knew we were thinking the same thing – and then, at the next moment, a mouse ran from behind the sofa to the door. It seemed like a sign.

'We would like to buy it,' I said to Joan.

'Well, I'd like to look at the Red House,' she smiled.

And so that is what happened: we effectively swapped houses. Paul and I had to sell off the vegetable garden at the Red House so we could afford the extra for Watercroft, but otherwise it was as straightforward and gentlemanly as that. We agreed with Joan that rather than moving around all our things we would both leave all our respective curtains, carpets and light fittings – even our beds – in place. This was undoubtedly the sensible thing to do, although we thought

Watercroft, where we still live today.

we got the better end of the deal as ours were a bit tatty compared to Joan's. It was an extremely civilized way to move house, and we were then on hand to help each other deal with those niggly issues you always get with a new home, such as the idiosyncrasies of the boiler. Joan has a great flair for interior design and quickly glamorized the Red House; no more kicked paint!

A family called the McGregors lived in the house on the land that we had sold off from the Red House, and a few years later Joan swapped houses with them too, downsizing a little each time. It has been a very happy arrangement all round.

# WATERCROFT CHICKEN

This is a family favourite, named after our house, but also smart enough for a dinner party.

*Serves 6*

- 2 tablespoons lime marmalade
- 25g (1 oz) butter
- 6 chicken breasts, boneless and skin on

*for the mushroom farci*
- 150g (5 oz) button mushrooms,
- 10g (½ oz) butter
- 2 shallots, finely chopped
- 25g (1 oz) breadcrumbs
- 1 small egg, beaten (you may not need all of it)
- salt and freshly ground black pepper

*for the sauce*
- 200ml (7 fl oz) carton full-fat crème fraîche
- juice of 1 lime
- a lot of freshly chopped parsley
- salt and freshly ground black pepper

Preheat the oven to 200°C/Fan 180°C/Gas 6.

First prepare the mushroom farci. Chop the mushrooms finely by hand; then melt the butter in a pan, add the shallots, cook for about a minute, cover and allow to soften over a gentle heat for about 10 minutes. Add the mushrooms to the pan, toss quickly in the butter and shallot mixture and cook for another 2 minutes. Remove from the heat, add the breadcrumbs and egg, and season well (do not add all the egg if it seems too wet). Leave to cool.

Put the marmalade into a small saucepan and heat very gently; as it begins to dissolve add the butter and stir well until it is all combined.

To stuff the chicken breasts, carefully lift the skin down one side and, using a teaspoon, push the mushroom stuffing underneath then fold back. Put the 6 chicken breasts comfortably in a roasting tin and spoon the butter and marmalade mixture over the top.

Cook in the preheated oven for about 20–25 minutes until golden brown and the chicken is cooked through. Transfer the chicken to a warmed serving dish using a slotted spoon and keep warm while making the sauce. Place the roasting tin over the heat and scrape all the bits from the side, then add the crème fraîche and lime juice and stir well. Add the parsley, season to taste and serve with the chicken.

Paul and I by the lake at Charlcombe Farm.

Taken while I was Home
Economist at Benson's PR, a
job which taught me so much.

One of my first book signings.

A press trip with Spanish Olives to Seville – one of the perks of the job!

Tom with his head stuck in a book on holiday.

Annabel and Tom at their jungle-themed joint 18th and 21st birthday party at Watercroft.

The Aga Workshops, which got me back into the world of cookery after William's death.

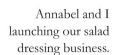

Annabel and I launching our salad dressing business.

Celebrating Mum's 100th birthday with the family.

Giving my grandchildren, twins Abby and Grace, their first baking lesson – what a joy.

My fantastic, life-long friends who have
been with me through thick and thin.

Four generations of our family: me with Mum, Annabel and her daughter, Atalanta.

## 14

When they finished school, none of our children had a clear idea about what they wanted to do next. While William stayed on at Gordonstoun to take A-Levels, Thomas left with just a few O-Levels and Annabel with none, but I wasn't concerned because they had big personalities and a strong work ethic so I knew they would be fine. Besides, after my school record I couldn't really complain!

After surviving – and thriving – in the Arizona desert, Annabel came home and spent a year at Evendine, a cookery school in Worcestershire. Having spent much of her childhood experimenting in the kitchen she enjoyed the course and did very well, graduating with her Cordon Bleu certificate, but she wasn't that keen on the idea of a career in cooking. I think her feeling was: 'Mother does that; too much washing-up.' To make up for her lack of qualifications, Annabel then went to the Oxford & County Secretarial College, colloquially known as the Ox and Cow, for a year's course in secretarial skills, but as this mostly involved sitting in classrooms it was not a huge success.

At sixteen Thomas left school and went to work in a residential estate agency in London with my friend Mavis Patterson. I'm not sure how much work he actually did, but she certainly gave him much guidance.

*Thomas:*

I started out as an office boy and was supposed to be learning the ropes from Mavis, but I don't think I was very easy to teach! Things went in one ear and out the other. I was still living at home and every morning before work Mum would always make me cooked breakfast in the Aga – eggs, bacon, the works – and then drive me to the station. I was pretty spoilt really!

After a while I was allowed to go out on client appointments and it all started to go to my head a bit. I used to rack up parking tickets, because I was an Important Businessman in a suit and my time was far too valuable to worry about petty things like parking! I'm afraid, rightly or wrongly, Mum and Dad ended up picking up the bills because they didn't want me getting into debt. One day I was meeting a client at a property in Chelsea and as I zoomed down this cobbled mews like some flashy yuppie in a Golf I got my shoelaces caught under the brake pedal and couldn't get my foot out to slow down, and I ended up ploughing into the front of the building at the end of the mews. Thankfully it was just a garage: if I'd been a few feet to the left I would have driven straight into an architect's office.

I worked at the estate agent's for eighteen months and then went to America and spent a year in Virginia playing rugby. I went out there with a friend and we had an absolute blast: rugby in the day and partying at night. Then when I came home I got a job in estate management at the Chelsea Harbour development, and I started to become a bit more useful.

Meanwhile, William worked hard at school and I was thrilled when he got a place at Bristol Polytechnic to read Business Studies. Always keen for adventure, he decided to defer his place and spend his gap year in Australia. A great friend of mine from Bath, Peter Turpin, lived in Sydney with his Australian wife Anne and they let William use their home as a base for his travels. William was determined to earn his keep while he was at the Turpins, taking on various jobs like gardening, hedging and waiting in restaurants, but I know that Anne was a wonderful support, caring for him and even procuring him a white shirt and black trousers for the waiter job. He spent some time travelling around with friends, but always came back to the Turpins.

The following September William started his degree course at Bristol Poly and from the start he absolutely loved it. He had grown into a wonderful young man: great company, sporty, good-looking and as kind and considerate as he had been as a little boy. During the first months of his course he managed to save a girl from committing suicide. With his life now in Bristol we didn't see much of him, so his trips home were always very special.

On Friday 20th January 1989, William came back to Watercroft for one of his occasional weekend visits. I hadn't seen him since Christmas, so was very much looking forward to his visit and was cooking his favourite supper: roast lamb, roast potatoes, mint sauce, redcurrant jelly – the works. We usually ate in the kitchen, but as Annabel was also home for the weekend from the Ox and Cow I decided to lay the table in the dining room to make it more of an occasion. Thomas was the only one who was missing; at the time he was living with the Nightingales in London.

When William walked in through the door on that Friday night he noticed the table in the dining room and assumed we had guests.

'Who's coming, Mum?' he asked.

'You!' I said. 'It's just so wonderful to have you home.'

We had a lovely supper and then, after Paul and I went to bed, William and Annabel stayed up together.

*Annabel:*

That night we sat in the drawing room and William went through all his old photographs. He showed me a picture of him and Thomas competing in a ski slalom in Wengen and explained that ever since then his lucky number had been their two race numbers added together. We talked about our memories of family holidays and growing up, and William told me all about his new life in Bristol. Then at around midnight he suddenly said, 'Oh, I want you to hear my new song,' and he dragged me over to the cottage, where Granny Mop lived, and proceeded to bash out 'Chopsticks' on the piano. 'Yeah, never heard this before,' I joked, squeezing up next to him so we could play it together. There was something about William that night – we had never been big on heart-to-hearts, but it was as if he felt he had to tell me all these things, to talk about his past and his hopes for the future. We sat up together, joking and laughing, until the early hours.

The next morning William came into my room at about ten o'clock.

'Come on, get up!' he said, flinging the curtains open. 'It's a beautiful day – don't waste it in bed!'

'William, it's Saturday . . . Leave me alone . . .'

But he carried on like that until I dragged myself out of bed. Later that morning Will told me he was going to drive the MG to the newsagent's, as Mum and Dad had the *Telegraph* delivered but he needed the business section of *The Times* for his course, and he asked if I wanted to go with him. As we were walking out to the car I picked up his moped helmet from the side and said, 'Why don't you wear this?' I'm not sure why I asked him to do that – I was probably just joking around – but William refused, so we got in the car, I tightened up his seatbelt for him and off we went.

You know how a January morning can be wonderfully crisp and bright? Well, that Saturday was just one of those days. After William and Annabel had left I made a start on lunch, which was to be at one o'clock sharp because Paul only had an hour's break from his work at the gallery. At ten to one Paul arrived home with his friend George, his great mentor in the antiquarian book trade, but as William and Annabel had yet to reappear they went out into the garden to have a walk round before lunch, while I sat in a pool of sunshine in the morning room and read the papers. It was a lovely spot, but I kept looking at my watch, wondering what was keeping the children and thinking it was really rather odd that they still weren't back, and then at twenty past one there was a knock at the door.

I opened it to find a policeman standing on the doorstep, and in that moment I just knew.

'Not good news for you, I'm afraid,' said the policeman. He was young but seemed composed. 'There's been an accident, and I have to tell you that William is dead.'

I don't recall my reaction. I think I went quiet, silenced by the shock of what he had told me; I certainly didn't scream or cry out. I just remember feeling extremely sorry for this young policeman for having to break the news to me.

'And Annabel?' I managed to ask.

'She's in Wycombe Hospital,' he replied, but couldn't tell me how badly she was injured.

And I just thought: 'Oh no. Not two.'

We went out to find Paul in the garden and then the policeman drove us to the hospital. As soon as we arrived someone brought us sweet tea; I never have sugar in tea – I don't even like tea very much – but that particular cup was very comforting. The nurses were so sweet and caring and their kindness calmed any impulse we might have had to shout or make a scene or argue against the fact of what had happened. We still had no idea what sort of state Annabel was in – and I feared the worst – so we asked to see her, and moments later I heard the sound of running at the end of the long corridor and then around the corner came this vision in a pink tracksuit, blonde hair flying about everywhere, and although she was a bit scratched and muddy she was fine. We still had Annabel; that, at least, was something.

Annabel went to her father and sat down without saying a word. It was terrible for her, just terrible. She had just seen her brother die and was clearly deep in shock.

Then someone asked if we would like to see William, and we said that we would. I suppose some people might feel that they wouldn't want to, but there was never any hesitation in my mind: I needed to say goodbye to him. We were shown into a little room that was white and clean and fresh, and there was William looking absolutely perfect, his body covered by a sheet, with no trauma visible at all. His little face was stone cold, but he looked so beautiful, so lovely – and when I dream, I dream of that.

He was killed instantly, so we were told. Annabel and I didn't talk about it much and they wouldn't let me read the newspaper reports in the aftermath, but there, in that little white room, William was perfect – and that's the memory I will always have.

*Annabel:*

William was being a typical nineteen-year-old in a sports car, tearing down the narrow lanes. As we went down a hill he started swinging the steering wheel from side to side, just mucking around. I remember that Bob Marley was singing 'No Woman No Cry' on the stereo. Although it was brilliantly sunny it must have been raining earlier because the road was wet and I yelled, 'For god's sake, William, slow down!' Then suddenly we were going towards a hedge, the car flipped upside down, landed on its roof and slid down the hill. I must have blacked out for a moment and when I regained consciousness there was smoke pouring from the engine. I looked across to William and could see he was in trouble, as there was a lot of blood.

Someone appeared from the neighbouring field and helped me out of the car – I think Bob Marley was still playing on the stereo in the wreckage – and then the ambulance came and I told them that I wasn't going anywhere without William and they literally had to carry me away, kicking and screaming, because I didn't want to leave my brother.

When we got to hospital they checked me over for injuries, but I seemed unharmed except for a few scratches, and then they gave me a cup of tea that I spilled all over myself because I was shaking so much; the shock, I suppose. When Mum and Dad arrived we went to see William together. I was wearing a gold bracelet and I took it off and put it on his body. That was the first time in my life I had ever seen Dad cry. It was the same sort of cry as when you're giving birth – a deep, primal wail. I hope I'll never have to hear it again.

Later that afternoon we all drove up to London to tell Thomas what had happened. That was almost the hardest part. We just told him straight: 'We have some very bad news. William has died.' I will never forget what he said to me: 'But we had so much to do, Mum.'

We drove back to Buckinghamshire that evening, each of us silent with our thoughts.

The next day – Sunday – we all went to church as usual, and during the service a memorial plaque on the wall happened to catch my eye. It read:

> In Honoured Memory of Frederick,
> William and George, sons of Alfred Busby,
> Clerk of this Parish, and of Emma his wife.
> They voluntarily gave their services to their
> country in 1914 and died for her in 1917.
> Frederick in Salonika, February 24 aged 24
> William in France, September 26 aged 21
> George in France, August 19 aged 19

I stared at that plaque and thought, I know how I'm feeling having lost one; how on earth would Emma have coped, having lost all three? After seeing that memorial, I would never dream of asking 'Why me?' Instead, I just tried to focus on how lucky I was still to have the other two. If William had been my only son – well, that would have been shattering.

Nevertheless, once the initial shock subsides you realize that the bottom has fallen out of your world. I couldn't cook, I struggled to sleep; we lived on soup for a long time and I ended up losing one and a half stone. I have our amazing friends to thank for getting us through those first weeks. Everyone was just so kind. People would pop in or phone to say, 'I'm not far away, can I come over?' Shirley Nightingale cancelled all her work commitments and moved in with us to run the house. She was wonderful: she dealt with the house-keeping, fielded calls, accompanied us everywhere and made us eat. We received so many lovely letters and cards from all sorts of people. Our friend and neighbour Joan Heath sent a note bearing an extract from the famous sermon by Canon Henry Scott Holland: 'Death is nothing at all . . . I have only slipped away into the next room . . . I am I and you are you . . . Whatever we were to each other, that we are still,' and even George Pinker, the consultant who had delivered William, sent us the most wonderful, warm letter. I would try to answer a few each day and our neighbour Sheila Inglis, who was helping me with the admin side of things, suggested I buy a box file and file each letter alphabetically together with a copy of my reply. 'At least you'll feel you're getting on with something,' she said, quite rightly. It was little things like that kept me going in those first awful days.

The Wednesday after William's death, the Millars, who lived in the village, rang up to say, 'We're having a family supper. Do come.' The impulse is to hide oneself away, but we went and it did do us good to be part of normal life again, and from then on whenever someone invited us out we always made the effort to go, however wretched we were feeling. Two weeks afterwards, Claire White rang and, knowing I was keen on gardening, told me she had tickets for the Chelsea Flower Show. 'We'll go together, have lunch and a day out,' she said. I accepted, despite not wanting to go at all, and of course it gave me something to look forward to. It really helped to be making plans, because it makes you realize that life goes on. Our friend Paddy Hopkirk told Paul he was going to start a new regular tennis four every Sunday, which meant that from day one Paul had to get out in the fresh air every week. They kept their Sunday date for years and years and played proper tennis – hard and to win, not like I play – and always finished up with a glass of something.

William's death changed my attitude to funerals: since then, I have never made a fuss about getting to them if I have a firm prior engagement, because I now know how much more important it is that you go and see people a week or a fortnight afterwards and just sit and listen while they talk. The very worst thing you can say to somebody is, 'You'll get over it.' I really wanted to sock anybody who said that to me because I didn't want to get over it, I didn't want to forget William – I was so lucky to have had him. You don't ever get over it, but you learn to live with it.

When the funeral director asked us about what sort of coffin we wanted and how many beautiful brass handles there should be I said, 'Let's have the most simple. It's just a little chap going to heaven. We don't need all this fuss.' Nevertheless, I was deeply touched by the number of people who came to the funeral. All of William's friends from school and college were there: the church was so full we had to get in extra chairs and afterwards everybody came back to Water-croft for fish pie. It was a beautiful service with simple white flowers and wonderful music, each piece chosen because it meant something to the family. The first hymn was 'Onward, Christian Soldiers', for which the music had been composed by Arthur Sullivan in the summerhouse at Watercroft when it was owned by Sir George Grove, the author of the original *Dictionary of Music and Musicians*, and the final piece was Rod Stewart's 'Sailing', because William loved to be out in a boat and that song was always playing in his bedroom. Paul, Annabel and Thomas all gave readings; Annabel read the wonderfully comforting words of the Henry Scott Holland sermon that Joan Heath had sent us in her letter.

I actually think William's death had a huge effect on his friends: they were extremely shocked because you could always rely on Will. He was the steady one, the shoulder you could lean on. It's now twenty-four years since he died and every Christmas there are flowers on his grave with a note from his college mates and girlfriends, and they still write and pop in to see me, which is amazing. They planted a tree for him at Bristol Polytechnic and we go every year to polish the plaque and plant primroses around it.

The funeral was a comfort to me. William's death deepened my faith; without its support, I really would have struggled. People who are Christian in their attitudes have been so kind and helpful and appreciative, which in turn has helped me to see how fortunate we've been, despite our loss. You have to count your blessings – and I have been extremely blessed. I had nineteen wonderful years with William and will always have those memories to treasure. He went out on a high: he'd had his trial for Scottish rugby schoolboys, he was enjoying college, he had hordes of friends – he was totally happy with himself. And you take comfort in the fact that at least Annabel was saved and that he didn't injure anyone else or leave behind a wife and children, which would have been ghastly. A cousin of mine died three months ago, after having been in a coma for twenty-six years as the result of a car accident that had killed his passenger. I have seen how something like that can be a terrible burden to a family, dragging on over so many years, so in that respect we were lucky to lose William. If William had ended up in a wheelchair, say, I'm quite sure he would have been at the Paralympics! He was the sort of person who loved life and would have turned any negative into a positive.

William's death has changed my life – and changed me.

On a fundamental level, it has made me realize what's important; little things just don't matter to me any more. I have
always collected knick-knacks, from mugs to candlesticks to
antique kitchenalia, and in the past I would be really quite
upset if one of my treasures got broken, but nowadays I can
drop anything and almost don't even notice. I've backed my
car into a wall and bashed Paul's car in the driveway, but we
just say, 'Oh dear, never mind.' It puts everything into per-
spective. While I rarely get angry, one of the things that has
annoyed me immensely since that day is when people discuss
their children's university results or what schools they've got
into. I just think, 'Well, at least you've got them. Really, what
does it matter?'

Losing William not only changed my attitude to life, it also
changed my attitude to death. I was with my mother-in-law,
Granny Mop, when she died, and while I wouldn't have
wanted to touch a dead person in the past, I found I was lifting her arm that was hanging off the bed and folding it gently
across her. Since those moments with William in the hospital
I'm not a bit nervous of it. And when my mother died
recently, at the age of 105, I was really quite matter-of-fact
about it. I just thought, 'Thank goodness for her.' I'm quite
ashamed to say that I didn't really grieve at all.

It was hard not to become too over-protective of Thomas
and Annabel in the wake of William's accident, as your natural instinct is to want to wrap them in cotton wool, but they
both love danger and I can't do anything about it. Thomas is
a fast driver and a daredevil, it's just the way he is made. We
recently went on a family holiday to Cape Verde and he was
out spear-fishing in rough seas for over four hours. He used
to use scuba equipment, but he's now trained himself to dive
down without anything and it's terrifying for me. During

the same holiday, Annabel and her husband Dan went off-roading on quad bikes without wearing helmets. When Annabel came back, her white dress covered in mud, she was bouncing up and down like a little girl, telling me what they had been up to, and I just said, 'I'm sorry, but I don't want to know.' I take some reassurance from the fact that they're both sensible and are always very safety-conscious for their own children.

Losing a child can destroy a family, but William's death undoubtedly brought us all closer. Paul and I were very quiet when we were on our own together; we didn't discuss it endlessly, because it had happened and we couldn't do anything to change that, but it was a great comfort for us both to have each other. Losing a child is one of the most terrible things that can happen to anyone, but I feel more upset for people who lose their other halves before their time; I think that must be dreadful. Paul and I were so lucky to have each other for support – it isn't your children's job to look after you. William's death was far harder on Annabel than it was on me. It really knocked her for six and affected her greatly – for years she was wild and up to all sorts of tricks – and I felt hugely inadequate because I didn't know what I could do to help her. Nowadays the Child Bereavement Trust, one of two charities of which I'm patron, along with the National Osteoporosis Society, are wonderful at helping in such situations, not only at looking after the parents who've lost a child, but also any remaining children. They get them together with other children who've lost their siblings or parents so you realize you're not the only one going through such a thing. In Annabel's case, it was only time that healed her.

Soon after William's death I had a phone call from the Ox and Cow saying that the college's fire alarm had been set off and would I please come and collect my daughter right now. When I arrived I asked Annabel why she had set off the fire alarm and she said, 'I didn't do it, Mum, but I did encourage the person who did.' So that was the end of the Oxford & County Secretarial School. It was the final term anyway.

*Annabel:*
Nothing was the same afterwards. You have this euphoric feeling of 'Oh my God, I'm alive!' – the realization that every second is precious, and I think that stays with you for ever more. So in that respect Will's accident brought me a positive attitude for life, although it wasn't evident immediately. I had a tricky time after he died because I was seventeen and your brain doesn't stop developing until you're older, so things weren't ever going to be rosy. When I got back to college I was still in shock, and I remember having to sleep with the television on for quite some time. I suffered flashbacks for many years and that was hard, but I never lost the feeling that I'd been given a second chance.

Mum comes from stock that doesn't analyze things endlessly – they keep calm and carry on in the face of adversity, even though they might be paddling like hell beneath the surface – and I'm very much a product of that. I could have easily moaned about what happened, but what good would that have done? Nevertheless, nowadays when people tell me about someone dying it can be difficult to be sympathetic, because you've been dealt quite a blow. You might be seen as hard, which is not intentional, but it's just the weathering of life. As Mum says, the little things in life don't matter any more.

I have very happy memories of Will, and it's undoubtedly made our family stronger and brought Thomas and I closer together. We'd always had a difficult relationship, but soon after Will's death we went on holiday together and I had it out with him. We had a huge fight then made up and this proved to be a turning point in our relationship. We have been extremely close ever since.

I miss William enormously, every single day, but he's not coming back. Even so, if he were to walk in here right now I wouldn't be in the least bit surprised; I would just say, 'And where the hell have you been, young man?' I think that's because as a family we have always talked about him, which in a way has kept him alive. If we're on holiday or at Christmas we'll say, 'Will would have enjoyed this,' and we'll always raise a glass to him on family occasions. There are framed photos of him all over the house and the grandchildren know all about their Uncle William. He will always be part of our family.

# FAMILY ROAST
# SHOULDER OF LAMB

It's a classic recipe and one I love to do for all the family on a Sunday. You cook the lamb and potatoes all in one dish, and it's easy to carve and serve.

*Serves 6*

- 1½ kg (3 lb) whole shoulder of lamb
- 3 large garlic cloves, sliced
- salt and freshly ground black pepper
- 2 large onions, thickly sliced
- 1 kg (2.2 lb) large potatoes, peeled and thickly sliced
- a bunch of thyme
- 750ml (1¼ pints) chicken stock

Preheat the oven to 220°C/Fan 200°C /Gas 7.

With a sharp knife make cuts into the shoulder of lamb on the top side. Stuff the holes with the garlic slices and season the joint with salt and pepper.

Scatter half the onions into a roasting tin or a 2½ litre (4 pint) shallow ovenproof dish and arrange half of the potatoes on top. Scatter half the thyme over the potatoes, pour on half the stock and season with salt and pepper. Repeat the layers using the remaining onions, potatoes, thyme and stock. Sit the lamb on top of the vegetables and cover the whole dish with foil.

Roast in the preheated oven for about 30–40 minutes or until the lamb is brown, then cover with foil and reduce the oven temperature to 150°C/Fan 130°C/Gas 2.

Return the lamb to the oven and slow cook for about 4 hours or until tender. Baste the lamb and vegetables halfway through cooking.

Carve and serve with the onions and potatoes and an extra green vegetable.

## 15

A year had passed after William's death before I felt strong enough to face the world again. While I hadn't been turning down offers of work during this time, neither had I been actively seeking them out; nevertheless, there seemed to be a fairly constant stream of requests for magazine articles, books and demonstrations and, because I was far from firing on all cylinders and can't type, I was struggling to cope with the workload on my own.

Throughout the eighties I'd had students from the catering course at Sheffield Polytechnic to help me out every now and then and one of these, Debbie Woolhead, was so good that she became my regular assistant in our final years at the Red House. She was a lovely girl and a brilliant help with recipe testing and development, but she left to get married and then, of course, the loss of William took over everything. Now, however, I was starting to take a more active interest in my career again, and it was clear that I needed a new assistant.

A good friend and neighbour, Joanna Drew, who lived near us in the village, had been coming in on the odd day to help with proofreading and admin – her help had been invaluable – and when I mentioned to her than I was looking for full-time assistance she told me that a friend's daughter was Cordon Bleu-trained at Winkfield Place in Windsor and might be interested in the job. The following week that girl – whose name was Lucy Young – came to Watercroft to meet me, and I liked her immediately. She was a little like Annabel, though a bit shy, but a warm, lovely girl, and from the way she talked about her parents and brothers I could tell she came from a happy and loving home. This last point was particularly important to me. After the past year I needed an assistant who would not only help with recipe development and organize my working life, but who would be able to fit seamlessly into our family. If the cat was having kittens or Paul needed a letter typed, they would have to be willing to muck in – and from that very first meeting I felt certain that Lucy would fit the bill.

We did have a few teething troubles. One of the first things I asked Lucy to do was to make a batch of meringues while I was out for the day, but when I came back I could see she'd been crying and later discovered the remains of all her numerous failed attempts in the bin. I just said, 'Oh gracious, I'm not cross in any way – we'll get through this together and soon you'll be the best meringue maker alive.' She was willing to try anything and was a fast learner, and eventually what she did was perfect.

As I had hoped, Lucy fitted in wonderfully well at home and, after a few weeks' trial, our arrangement became permanent and she has been with me ever since – not just as my assistant, but as my co-author, confidante and, in time, my best friend. I was mothering her to start with because she was very young and had a lot to learn, but nowadays she's more confident than I am. I trust her like one of my children, so she has total control of my diary and works alongside my agents to decide what I will, and will not, do; I don't have a mind of my own anymore! Lucy is very much in charge and knows who needs nurturing, who needs thanking and who needs ticking off; she keeps an eye on everything, but she always does it in such a lovely way that you will never hear anybody say a bad word about her.

Lucy and I.

As she has been such an integral part of my life for the past twenty-three years, I think I should let Lucy give her own account of our relationship. So over to you, Luc . . .

*Lucy:*
I was nineteen and doing part-time catering for weddings, parties and private events when Mum told me that her friend Joanna had rung to say she'd heard Mary Berry was looking for a new assistant. I was a bit young to remember Mary from television, as it was Delia who was dominating our screens at that time, but when Mum mentioned Mary's connection to the *Hamlyn All Colour Cookbook* I was immedi-

ately interested. As a family, we often had her Porc à la Crème recipe on special occasions, and I had always loved her lemon cheesecake, named Thomas's Flan in the Hamlyn book.

When the job came up, I was at something of a career crossroads: I knew I wanted to be producing plates of delicious food, but I didn't want to work in a restaurant or pub, nor was I keen on churning out hundreds of vol-au-vents for large events. So although I didn't for a moment think I would get it, I called Mary about the job because testing and writing recipes really appealed to me. I will never forget our first telephone conversation.

'Hello, it's Lucy Young,' I said nervously when she answered. 'I hear you're looking for an assistant?'

'Oh yes, do come and see me,' said Mary, her voice sounding strangely echoey.

We arranged a date and she gave me her details, and then Mary said, 'Let me just find something to take down your phone number, I'm in the bathroom,' which explained the weird acoustics. After failing to find either pen or paper, she told me she was going to write it down with lipstick on a piece of loo roll, and I just thought, 'I'm going to like her.'

A few days later I came to Watercroft for the interview – although it was really more like an informal chat in the living room. Mary was fifty-five at the time, and I remember being immediately struck by how glamorous and pretty she was. I had already told her about my Cordon Bleu training, but she didn't ask me about cooking or food; she was far more interested in my family life, about my parents and three brothers and if I liked animals. She actually seemed very similar to my own mum, in terms of her kindness and how important her family obviously was to her. As we chatted I started to relax and feel a little more confident, but then Mary asked if I had ever used an Aga. I told her I had not, and with a sinking feeling thought, 'Well that's it – I'm not going to get the job.'

A few hours after I got home that afternoon the phone rang: to my surprise, it was Mary.

'You remind me of my daughter,' she said to me. 'Would you like to come and work for us?'

On my first day I was terrified, as it was really my first proper job (I had worked in a pub, but only because I had been going out with the barman) but Mary went out of her way to make me feel like I was part of the family. I asked what I should do first and she said, 'Oh, you can empty the dishwasher.' The message was very much: just muck in – and so I did.

Nevertheless, for the first week I was unsure about whether I was going to cut it. I was so painfully shy that I didn't really speak or sit with the family at lunch, and Mary, who is a perfectionist, was quite strict with me. I was nineteen and a bit slapdash, so she was always picking me up on things, just as I would do with someone now. I remember I stuck some stamps on to envelopes in a bit of a wonky fashion, and she asked me, 'Why wouldn't you put the stamps on straight?'

'I don't know really,' I said. 'Does it matter?'

And Mary said, quite rightly, 'Well, it does really. First impressions.'

I know now that one of the few things that Mary can't abide is slovenliness and laziness: she has an enormous appetite for fun, but when you're working she expects you to do so to the best of your ability.

On my second day, Mary was going out and before she left she said, 'Could you please make a batch of meringues and line a flan tin with some pastry?'

'Yes, yes, absolutely no problem,' I said. This, at least, was something I felt I could definitely do.

The first batch of meringues I produced collapsed. After the second lot were also a disaster I began to panic. I had made meringues at college and they were fine – what on earth was going wrong? Mary had already taught me how to use the Aga, so that wasn't the problem. (I know now that I was adding the sugar too quickly.) Anyway, the fourth batch was just about passable and so I put all my failed attempts in the bin and covered them in rubbish to hide them from Mary. Thankfully my pastry came out fine, but I couldn't find a rolling pin to roll it out. I searched the house high and low wondering if this was some sort of test, thinking, 'Surely Mary Berry must have a rolling pin somewhere . . .' But in the end my search proved fruitless and so I used a milk bottle instead.

The following day I arrived at work and Mary said, 'Oh, I liked your meringues – although I preferred the ones that were in the bin.' To my relief, she found it really funny. She didn't care that I was rubbish at meringues; it was more important to her that I had been determined and kept going until I had got them right. And at least the flan case had turned out fine. 'Did you find the rolling pin?' Mary asked me. When I told her I hadn't, and had used a milk bottle instead, she was delighted. 'Brilliant!' she said. 'Initiative!' Because that's what Mary likes: people who get on with things, and don't make excuses. (It turned out the rolling pin was in a stupid place, and is still there today!)

It took about a month for me to find my feet in the job. Luckily Mary's style of cooking was exactly the way I cooked – or rather wanted to cook. It was basically home cooking: really nice food, but nothing that's going to wear

you out with the effort of making it! Over those first weeks
I began to realize that what Mary was looking for was someone who was going to take the initiative and pre-empt her
requests, so I stopped waiting to be told what to do by her
and became more proactive. If she went out for the day
with Paul I'd make sure there would be a cottage pie waiting
for them when they came home, so Mary didn't have to
worry about making supper. I would make a hot lunch for
Granny Mop, Mary's mother-in-law, every day and take it
over to her cottage. I could see that here was a family that
was very like my own family, which helped me to settle in.
Tom and Annabel were often around, which was great
because we are all similar ages – Annabel is two years
younger than me and Tom's a year older. And as Mary and I
got to know each other, I began to feel like we might become
good friends, rather than just colleagues.

Whatever she might say, Mary is a workaholic – she loves
work and loves her family and friends. The first thing Mary
will say when she comes in is: 'Did anyone ring?' When I ask
that question I mean did any friends or relatives call, but Mary
wants to know if anyone got in touch about work. Mary's
ethos is that if someone is paying you to do something, you
do the very best you can. She is the softest, kindest, loveli-
est lady, but I can see that when she's talking business she
can be tough. I have learned so much from her, not just in
cooking but in life skills too – Mary is so generous with her
knowledge, which is an amazing quality, but I think I might
have taught her to listen to others a bit more. Sometimes I'll
say to her, 'You were a bit harsh to so-and-so,' and she'll say
with a smile, 'Was I? Well, they should have done it properly
the first time.' Mary has a wonderful dry sense of humour

and we laugh a lot. While she's the best at praising someone if praising is due, she will just as quickly point out if something's not good enough – but when you're seventy-eight you have certainly earned that right. Mary isn't too keen on small-talk, as she has so much on her mind, but she listens to everything that is said. And people might be surprised to know that she is actually quite shy: if you put Mary in a situation that's not work-related she can be quiet.

Mary and I tell each other everything. She is like my second mother; in fact I will often slip up and call her 'Mum'. I hope I will always work for her – we joke that when she's in a nursing home I will turn up there every day with a flask of hot soup! I love Mary dearly: she is my mentor, friend and a huge part of my life.

Although I was starting to take an interest in my career again when Lucy joined us in early 1990, I didn't want to be going up to London for work because Paul had his gallery in the village and it was important for me to stay close to him. I wasn't ready to face the big, bad world on my own just yet. I needed to find a job I could do from home, but what could I do? I loved making television programmes, but I wasn't at all in demand at this time – and I'm not very good at pushing myself forward – so that wasn't an option. I also loved giving demonstrations and knew I was good at it; I don't like showing off, but if I can do something well, I want to share it. In 1988, I had been asked to write *The Aga Book*, a cookbook that was given away to everyone who bought an Aga, and had really enjoyed the job. (This book is still going strong; I think we're on the fifth edition now.) I had learned an awful lot about Aga cooking over the years and knew there was a growing interest in the techniques – I had also done an Aga video to accompany the book – so it occurred to me: why not start an Aga cookery school?

Lucy thought it was a splendid idea and we sat down together and came up with a formula for a series of day-long Aga cookery workshops. Although I do think an Aga makes your life easier, it does take a bit of getting used to as it is quite a different way of cooking, the main difference being that you can't vary or control the heat in an Aga like you can in a conventional oven. On the top you have two hot plates: a very hot boiling plate on the left and a cooler simmering plate on the right. There are two-, three- or four-oven Agas available, but in all the models there is a roasting oven, which is around 220 degrees centigrade (gas mark 7), and a simmering oven at 150 degrees centigrade (gas mark 2). The bigger models have additional warming and baking ovens. So if you want to cook something at, say, 180 degrees (gas mark 4) we would teach that you would have to start it off in the roasting oven and then move it down to the cooler oven. Cakes can be tricky, as you have to move them around and use a cold sheet (a metal sheet that you put in the oven to lower the temperature), and simple things like Yorkshire Pudding require a different approach. So our initial aim, with the first workshops at least, was to explain the basic techniques of Aga cooking and demonstrate recipes for kitchen suppers and easy entertaining.

When we were planning the workshops my main concern was that we should spoil everyone rotten and give them a really lovely day. I had been on similar courses in other people's homes, not just for cookery but also gardening and flower arranging, and they always seemed to be held in some distant annexe or drafty barn while you were barred from the rest of the house, but I felt that if I was inviting people into my home it was important to welcome them like I would any other guest. I didn't want any rooms to be out of bounds; I felt people should have free rein to be able to go into our bathroom and wander around the garden. Only our bedroom was kept closed.

So that was the basic premise: I would open up my home and demonstrate recipes on my Aga. There was no official endorsement by Aga, I just hoped that because of the success of the book and video there might be people out there who would want to come. To drum up interest, I wrote to all my journalist friends and invited them to two separate press days of Aga cookery demonstrations in July and then roped in close girlfriends to help get everything ready and make sure it all ran smoothly. But although we planned everything in meticulous detail, we had no long-term strategy or any idea whether the concept would appeal to paying customers. In that respect, we were really just winging it.

On the morning of the first press day, my friends Jenny Hopkirk and Sheila Ingles went to collect the journalists at Beaconsfield station to chauffeur them to Watercroft. I'll always remember Jenny giving her car a final polish before setting off! Among the invitees were Katie Stewart, Cookery Editor of *The Times*, Philippa Davenport of the *Financial Times*, Thane Prince of the *Telegraph*, Moira Fraser from *Good Housekeeping* – all the biggies. It was really lovely, because everybody was so pleased to see everyone else (cookery journalists have always been good pals) and I didn't find the prospect of teaching my peers in the least bit intimidating because after owning an Aga for many years and doing an awful lot of research for the book I was confident in my skills. Besides, most of the cookery writers who were attending didn't actually own an Aga themselves.

*Lucy:*

In the run up to the press days I just remember feeling how important it was that we got this right: if the cookery school was going to work, then these first two days had to be perfect.

Before the journalists arrived, Mary was very focused, but she doesn't actually get stressed, and once she's got a wooden spoon in her hand she's as calm as you like. She started the morning with a two-hour demonstration in the main kitchen, while the other helpers (who were good friends) and I were prepping and chopping all the ingredients for the recipes in the small test kitchen out the back, then it was lunch in the dining room with lots of wine and chat. The recipes that Mary demonstrated were the sort of thing you would cook at home, rather than elaborate restaurant food, and I think the journalists loved that simplicity. To our relief, everyone seemed to have a wonderful time and Mary was thrilled that all her friends had supported her and seemed to think her cookery school was a good idea. At the end of the two days I remember being on a high, with a real feeling of, 'Wow, we did it.' We were exhausted, but really chuffed it had worked so well.

Soon afterwards these amazing articles began to appear in the press and our phone started to ring non-stop with people enquiring when the next Aga Workshop would be. Caught off-guard by the response, we just picked two dates at random, the 3rd and 4th September, and then when those dates quickly filled up we added another two, and it just grew

Me demonstrating one of the Aga Workshops.

from there. We never advertised the Aga Workshops – it was all word of mouth – but over the next sixteen years more than 14,000 people from all over the country would come through my kitchen.

# RASPBERRY MERINGUE ROULADE

Hopefully you will have better success with this than Lucy did with her first meringues!

*Serves 8–10 slices*

- 5 large egg whites
- 275g (10 oz) caster sugar
- 50g (2 oz) flaked almonds

**for the filling**
- 300ml (½ pint) double cream
- 350g (12 oz) raspberries

**to serve**
- icing sugar
- extra raspberries

Preheat the oven to 200°C/Fan 180°C/Gas 6.

Grease and line a 33 x 23cm (13 x 9 inch) Swiss roll tin with non-stick baking parchment.

Whisk the egg whites in a large, clean bowl with an electric mixer on full speed until very stiff. Gradually add the sugar, a teaspoon at a time, and still on high speed, whisking well between each addition. Whisk until very, very stiff and glossy and all the sugar has been added.

Spread the meringue mixture into the prepared tin and sprinkle with the almonds. Place the tin in the preheated oven and bake for about 12 minutes until very golden. Then lower the temperature to 160°C/Fan 140°C/Gas 3 and bake for a further 20 minutes until firm to the touch.

Remove the meringue from the oven and turn almond side down on to a fresh sheet of non-stick baking parchment. Remove the paper from the base of the cooked meringue and allow to cool for about 10 minutes.

Lightly whip the cream, and fold in the raspberries. Spread the cream mixture evenly over the meringue. Roll up the meringue fairly tightly from the long end to form a roulade. Wrap in non-stick baking parchment and chill well before serving.

Serve dusted with icing sugar and more fresh raspberries if liked.

## 16

We held the Aga Workshops on Tuesdays and Wednesdays every week throughout the year during school term time. In the winter I would pick six different topics for the following year's sessions and we would then repeat them on a loop, because if we'd had a different subject for every day the amount of research would have been impossible. For example, in 1998 the workshops on offer included: 'Making the Most of the Aga', 'More Adventurous Aga' (I and II), 'Flavours of the Mediterranean', 'Masterclass for All Seasons' and 'Aga Favourites'. Then in the run up to Christmas we would offer a series of extremely popular festive-themed courses, including 'Traditional Christmas' and 'Sensational Flavours for Christmas'. The workshops constantly evolved, as I strongly believed that each one we did should be better than the last, so we added more recipes or changed the presentations and in the end we became really rather good at it. Nevertheless, the basic model and aim of what we wanted to achieve in the workshops remained pretty much unchanged from day one.

In our brochure, which gave details of the day's schedule and costs, I laid out our mission statement as follows: 'The Aga Workshop is all about Aga know-how and technique, in other words getting the most out of your Aga. My aim is to encourage and inspire those who have been brought up with an Aga, to help new Aga owners gain confidence and to master the art of Aga cookery. I will demonstrate the short cuts and show how to use the roasting oven not only for roasting and baking, but in the true Aga tradition for grilling and frying – unlike a conventional oven when the hob is used.'

There was a terrific amount of preparation involved in the workshops, most of which was organized by Lucy with the help of an assistant. Almost from day one we took on a student from Leith's (Prue Leith's cookery school, which offers a training similar to Cordon Bleu) who spent a period of eleven months with us, from September to July, shadowing Luc. Over the years we had nine students with us who came straight from college. We provided them with a real introduction to working in a kitchen: they would prep, weigh, chop, help with demonstrations, wash up, sweep the floor – whatever was needed – and then at the end of their time with us they would go off and get a proper job!

*Lucy:*
On the Monday before each workshop we would do the shopping and prep the demonstrations, laying out a tray for each recipe with all the ingredients weighed out and labelled in bowls. Careful preparation was the key to success. We would rearrange the furniture in the house, setting up twenty chairs in the kitchen (Mary insisted on canvas director's chairs, rather than the uncomfortable plastic variety), lay the tables, put fresh flowers around the house, chill the wine, sweep the courtyard and bake the shortbread for the punters' arrival. Another part of my job was typing up recipe handouts to give to everyone to take home at the end of the day, which was done on a typewriter so if there were mistakes – tough! My office was in the cleaning cupboard under the stairs – although 'office' might be an overstatement, as it was really just a phone, typewriter and pen! It was

so cramped that the typewriter used to hit the wall every time I reached the end of the line. Looking at one of our handouts from March 1999, from a workshop entitled 'Fresh Ideas for the Aga', the recipes include Marinated Canon of Lamb, Parma Risotto, Chocolate and Strawberry Summer Tart, Crispy Duck with Blueberries and Thai Prawns with noodles. We always cooked with ingredients in season and tried to use modern ideas. We had about ten recipes in each workshop, so there was a lot of work involved and I did seem to spend an awful lot of time in the cupboard under the stairs. Email hadn't been invented yet so everything was done by letter or phone call.

On the morning of the workshop everyone was told to arrive at ten o'clock and leave their cars in the church car park opposite Watercroft, where one of the girls would be standing, rain, snow or shine, to point them in the right direction. We had to have twenty people attending to make it really worthwhile – and any more than this wouldn't fit in the kitchen – but I would usually book in twenty-two because I assumed a few people wouldn't turn up. So we often ended up with twenty-two attendees, which used to drive Lucy mad! The moment people arrived they were given coffee and shortbread in the morning room, while the girls were all scurrying around getting things ready for the first recipe, and then at half past ten everyone was shown into the kitchen where I would start the demonstration. I would do about six recipes in two hours and then there would be a general discussion and tasting of what I had prepared, so people could see if they liked the dishes enough to make them at home.

At half past twelve everyone would go back into the morning room while we set out lunch, during which time they could browse in our shop – well, really more a table at the end of the hall. We had set this up in response to people asking, 'Could I have a signed book?' or 'What's that saucepan you were using?' and we sold my books, which I would sign, branded aprons and my favourite pots and utensils. Everyone seemed to want to go away from the day with a little something, so it was really quite lucrative – which was very welcome as there were quite a few staff to pay: six of us in total on Aga days.

We had a great team over the years. As well as Lucy and myself, we had several ladies from the village who worked part time: Margaret Cook, Judy Bicknell and Cheryl Dyer, a good friend and local caterer Rebecca Reed (who would always say she had 'come for the fun'), our Leith's student, and Sue Meigh, who kept us washed up and tidy, plus my wonderful friend Penny. We all got on like a house on fire. It was Penny who would run the shop and take care of the profits, because she was the one who could add up, and Margaret and Judy would put all the purchases in bags ready for when people went home. Pete came in twice a week to help with the lifting of tables and chairs and is the best handyman. Testing the recipes over the years was a dedication to duty. We would employ ex-Cordon Bleu cook Izzie Forrest to come down from Scotland for a week every January and Lucy, Izzie, Lucinda Kaizik (one of our Leith's students who ended up staying on) and I would spend a week devising new recipes and ideas. Jane White, who lived in the village, kept us on track with our accounts – which was wonderful as Luc and I don't do figures! We have now been joined by Kathryn Demery as well, who has taken over from Jane. My team is so important to me.

Lunch was served in the dining room and would be a big dish of something like lasagne with salad and then pudding, accompanied by as many glasses of wine as people wished – although I don't ever remember anyone taking advantage and getting too drunk! We had quite a long break at lunchtime, because everybody wanted to go out into the garden, to have a look round and stretch their legs, and then we used to start up again at half past two for another hour of demonstrations with three or four more recipes. In the early days I would do the afternoon session as well, but in 2004 Lucy took over. Everybody loved her, as she had a young outlook and fresh approach to Aga cooking. 'I really didn't want to do any demonstrating at the beginning and was very scared,' she remembers. 'I'm still in touch with quite a few punters now and they say, "Oh gosh, at the beginning you were so embarrassed you used to go bright red!" But then, of course, you do it day in and day out, you get used to it and start to enjoy yourself.'

The workshops were tremendously popular: we were full or overbooked for every single one. I had stuck firmly to my principle of treating everyone like a welcome guest, and I think people really appreciated the fact they could taste everything we demonstrated, as well as having a specially prepared lunch. My only rule was that there was no bagging of seats when people arrived, because someone had warned me that people would arrive earlier and earlier to make sure they could sit where they wanted. Instead, I would announce, 'I want the short people at the front and the tall people at the back,' and nobody ever objected. We did get the occasional tricky customer, but on the whole everyone was lovely; we really did spoil them, and I think people responded to that. The atmosphere was so friendly that people would often come back year after year; we especially looked forward to seeing our 'frequent flyers', those punters who came religiously twice a year for sixteen years, including lovely Carol Rymer, who would come down from Yorkshire with her sister Mo Barker and a gang, and Elizabeth Holland-Bosworth from Sussex, who was an absolute delight and would come en masse with about eight of her friends. Mrs H-B was a larger-than-life character who would arrive with a basket on her arm full of little presents for all of us: candles, boxes of chocolates or olive oil from her own estate in Italy. It was a real joy to see these groups and we loved getting to know them.

The audiences for our workshops were usually all female, but occasionally we had a few men, which really changed the dynamic because men tend to be far more technical in their approach to cooking: women want to know about the practicalities of a recipe, whether something can be made ahead and how long it will keep for, while men want to know the scientific explanation for why something curdles, or why celery stays crisp and leeks go soggy. Once we did a special workshop just for men ('once' being the operative word here!) for a friend's husband, Dermot Clancy, and his pals, and it was hysterical. Unlike the women, who would stay in their seats, listening and taking notes, these chaps were jumping up and standing next to us, saying, 'Can I stir that?' or 'Oh, let me have a look!' It was lovely having them there, as they were such good fun, but gosh they were hard work!

I really can't remember any disasters over the years, although that was probably because we put so much work into the planning and preparation. A few people fell ill while they were here (although not as a result of my cooking, I should add!) but we put them upstairs in one of the bedrooms until they felt better. Lucy remembers: 'That was always a bit challenging, as you did feel sorry for them. I would go and check on them every now and then.'

We had a few celebrities attending our workshops along the way. There was the actress Patricia Hodge, who was delightful, the television presenter Anthea Turner and the novelist Joanna Trollope, famous for her 'Aga Sagas', who came a few times and we just adored. After her first workshop she sent me the most delightful letter thanking me for the day. 'You can't imagine how much I enjoyed Tuesday,' she wrote. 'Not just what I learned (a huge amount, which I am fervently applying) nor all those lovely people, nor that delectable lunch, nor even the chance to have a little invisible holiday, but almost above all the treat of being at Watercroft. I hope you noticed that we were all silently vowing to go home and make our domestic lives more Maryish with all those colours and flowers and warmth and welcome, without anything being studied or self-conscious.'

Another familiar face at the workshops was Fern Britton, who used to live next-door-but-one to Watercroft, and who is just as lovely as she seems on television – but with much more of a naughty streak! Fern was presenting the hugely popular *Ready Steady Cook* on television at the time, and as we would both be invited to appear at the BBC Good Food Show at the Birmingham NEC – me to do a demonstration and Fern to conduct a live version of *Ready Steady Cook* – we used to travel up there together. The minibus would arrive at five o'clock in the morning and we'd all pile in, Lucy, Fern and myself, then we'd make several other stops to pick up Raymond Blanc and whoever else was appearing at the show and we would chat all the way up the M40 while Fern did her make-up. At this time I was always booked into one of the

smaller, subsidiary theatres; it is only now, since the enormous success of *The Bake Off*, that I'm doing the big
audiences. In those days the main theatre was the preserve
of the great (male) chefs of the time such as Rick Stein and
Gary Rhodes.

It was at the Good Food Show that Lucy and I first became
aware of the term 'celebrity chef', when Jamie Oliver arrived
on the scene in the late nineties. Gradually, the audience
started to change; rather than sedate groups of housewives,
there would now be crowds of young girls waiting to see
Jamie, screaming and wanting autographs. While my demonstrations were always popular and well attended, I had
nothing like the level of interest that these new celebrity
chefs were attracting, although all that changed after the first
series of *The Bake Off*. For the past couple of years I have
been absolutely stunned by the audience's reaction when I
appear at the Good Food Show or similar events. People will
be screaming, giving me presents and asking for photos; at
last year's Cake & Bake Show I even had to be accompanied
by security! Forget Beatlemania – this was Berrymania. I had
never seen anything like it and it was really quite daunting.

It's easy to forget how much cookery on television has
changed over the past fifteen years or so, probably since
Jamie Oliver arrived on the scene. Today cookery programmes are very much seen as entertainment: take Nigella,
for example, who everyone loves watching because she's
exciting and unpredictable – and very beautiful too. I hope
that I entertain people, but for me what's far more important
is that when they have watched me make a recipe, they go
and try it for themselves. I was in Waitrose today and the girl
on the checkout said, 'Oh, I made that Easter meringue you
did on telly last week.' I asked how it went and she replied,

'Absolutely wonderful. Mine was a bit lopsided, but the family thought it was delicious.' That makes me very happy indeed.

I do think Jamie has done wonders for food in this country: he's managed to get families cooking together and he's encouraged young people into the kitchen. Not only that, but he's a genuinely lovely man. Whenever we run into each other at shows or exhibitions he always makes an effort to come over and say hello. 'Here comes the Aga Queen!' he'll say. I think he treats me a bit like his mum – as does James Martin, another lovely chap who has his feet firmly on the ground and bridges the gap between chef and home cook.

In terms of other TV cooks I admire, I love Michel Roux Junior dearly. He knows his stuff inside out and although he's a Michelin-starred chef, he is able to cross the boundary between fine dining and family cooking, which is quite unusual. He is an enchanting man and I always love working with him, but I don't often watch him on *MasterChef: The Professionals* because, while I like the characters, I'm not so keen on the food: it's just too busy. Raymond Blanc is excellent too, and I love the way that he runs Le Manoir Aux Quat'Saisons. I was walking through the kitchens with him one day and could see how much his employees respect him. There was a guy taking the shells off prawns the wrong way round, and Raymond stopped and very patiently showed him the correct method. Instead of leading by shouting and swearing like some chefs, he does so with kindness and smiles; his employees know he is there to support them. There should be no place for bullying in a kitchen.

I think Nigel Slater is brilliant – although funnily enough I prefer to read his books than watch his programmes, as he writes so superbly. And we must never forget Delia, because she effectively set the standards that the rest of us now work to: her recipes were inspirational, effective and always worked.

The Aga Workshops took over the house and our lives for sixteen years, but I loved doing them and, of course, it helped me greatly to have something to focus on in the wake of losing William. In the midst of the hard work, we had a lot of laughs. One particular workshop fell on 1st April and when Lucy arrived that morning, shortly before everyone was due to turn up, she found me sitting in a chair with my arm in a sling and a dejected air. 'I'm so sorry, Luc. I've broken my arm,' I told her. 'You're going to have to do the workshop for me.'

Well, Lucy's face was just a picture. 'But I can't!' she stuttered. 'I don't know what I'm doing . . .' It was only then that I whipped off the sling and said, 'April Fool!'

Later that morning I was in the middle of demonstrating a cake and when I went to crack the eggs I discovered that they had been hard-boiled: no prizes for guessing by whom!

Although we never advertised, our courses got wonderful write-ups in the *Sunday Telegraph*, *The Sunday Times* and the *Mail on Sunday*, who wrote that 'Mary Berry is to Aga what Pavarotti is to opera.' And alongside the workshops I was still doing other work as well, writing books and magazine articles and giving charity demonstrations, but as much as I wanted to do more television I just hadn't been offered the opportunity. It had been ten years since my last series for ITV; I was clearly very much off radar. Still, I held on to the hope that one day something might come along, in the way that it often had during my career, and in 1994 it did. At the end of one of our workshops, Frances Whitaker came over and introduced herself to me. She told me that she was a BBC producer, and asked if I would be interested in filming a new series to go with my latest title, *Mary Berry's Ultimate Cake Book*. Well, as I'm sure you can appreciate I was absolutely thrilled to bits!

I was in very safe hands with Frances, who was the producer who first introduced Delia to the BBC in the early seventies and has since then worked with virtually every television cook and chef out there, from Gordon Ramsay to Nigel Slater. Because of the tremendous success of *The Great British Bake Off* it's now hard to believe that at the time certain people at the BBC were sceptical about the success of a television series based entirely around baking. Nevertheless, the series went on to be a hit and the book has sold over a million copies and become my most successful book after *The Complete Mary Berry*.

*Frances Whitaker:*

I had never met Mary before, so when the BBC approached me to produce a television series to go with Mary's *Ultimate Cake Book* I booked myself on to one of her Aga workshops. With most chefs I've worked with over the years I have usually gone to watch them give a demonstration before agreeing to work with them, because you can tell whether or not someone has 'it' in terms of working on television just by looking at how they handle food. Some chefs have a particular sort of respect for the ingredients and, perhaps it is a coincidence, but those who handle the food sympathetically are the ones who are going to make good television. After all, the viewers are going to be focused on their hands: if they're slapping everything around it doesn't mean that they're less skilled, but it does look less professional.

Of course, I knew that Mary had already done a great deal for ITV, but it had been about ten years since she had last been on television and a huge amount had changed during the time in terms of the style and technique of programme making – audiences were expecting more and demanding more. But Mary was very good at explaining things and answering people's questions, and, more importantly, at handling the food, so after the workshop I introduced myself and we set up a screen test.

One of the biggest challenges for Mary was to make the transition to a brand new way of working. Compared to when she started out in television, the style of presentation had become far more informal and the pace of how long you could stay on a particular shot had speeded up. Audiences were far more visually literate and better at taking in information, which meant you could be demonstrating one thing but talking about something slightly different at the same time in a way that the audience wasn't able to assimilate before. For example, instead of telling viewers that you were now beating eggs into sugar – and then doing it – you could be giving them a useful tip for keeping eggs fresh or some other information about the recipe. So Mary had to learn how to physically perform a task, and focus on getting that right, while talking about something else: a bit like patting your head and rubbing your stomach at the same time! But she took to it like a duck to water. Smiles were hard to come by at first, as you're not thinking, 'I must look as if I'm enjoying myself' when you're preparing food, but she got better at it, and although I knew Mary was very nervous you wouldn't have known it.

Mary and I did two series together – *Mary Berry's Ultimate Cakes* and then *Mary Berry at Home* in 1996 – and we had great teams working on both. Mary spoiled everyone. She would always have breakfast waiting for the crew in the Aga when they arrived in the morning: bacon, scrambled eggs, croissants – the whole lot! Lucy was always on hand to help with the prep and we also employed a brilliant home economist called Caroline Liddell, who had worked a lot with Delia so knew all about television timings. When time is so short you need to have three lots of each ingredient ready and waiting so if something goes wrong and you have to do a retake you haven't got to wait for somebody to weigh out 500 grams of flour. Also, every recipe had to be tested and double-tested to get everything right, not just because Mary is a perfectionist, but because this was for the BBC, so each recipe had to be absolutely infallible as if something didn't work there would be a backlash.

Mary and I chose the recipes for each series together. I would look through the manuscript of her book to make sure we had a broad range of techniques and food within the series. It's vitally important that the finished dish looks appetizing on screen, because without taste or smell all the audience has to go on is the appearance, so I'd often cook the recipes myself at home first, just to see what the end product looked like. Brown food doesn't work well on television, so you generally don't want more than one brown recipe per programme.

Working with Mary was a real pleasure – especially compared to some people I've worked with – but the shooting schedule was pretty intensive because the budget wasn't terribly generous: I think we filmed the entire eight-part series at her home in under two weeks. We were cooking several recipes a day and would work out the schedule so that Caroline and Lucy would be a stage ahead, prepping for the next recipe, while we were filming the last. Often we would film different parts of the recipe out of sequence, because if something needed three hours cooking time we couldn't have it ready for nine o'clock in the morning.

As we were so short of time the whole team had to work together seamlessly. Before each shot Mary would rehearse by going through the motions without actually cooking, so that the cameraman knew exactly what was going to happen, then we would shoot it once or twice as necessary with me sitting by her feet all the while double-checking the method and ingredients. The trend in food programming at the time was for everything to look absolutely perfect, the thinking being that if the expert couldn't get it looking absolutely right what hope had the people doing it at home, so I was always checking with Mary if she was happy with the way a dish looked, and if she wasn't then we'd start again, or pick it up halfway through – whatever would be the most cost-effective and labour-saving way to do it.

We were shooting with two cameras, one focused on the food and the other on Mary, and there would be a monitor in the prep kitchen where Lucy and Caroline were working, so if they saw that Mary needed an egg or 200 grams of sugar then they could whizz it straight in. For the cake series when we filmed the finished recipe, known as the pack-shot, we would try to choose somewhere interesting to present it rather than just having it sitting on a plate on a table. Because Mary has such a beautiful garden we would often do it outside, but neither of the directors knew anything about plants so often Mary would say something like, 'It would be really nice to do this by the thyme,' and she'd get very upset when we'd go out there and find they'd set up the shot by the mint!

The first series went out on BBC One in the afternoon, just after *Neighbours*, and – despite the reservations of the powers-that-be that people wouldn't want to watch cakes – we had fantastic viewer feedback. People wrote in to say how lovely it was to see Mary back on television and how delicious and easy she made everything look. We had people telling us that they were going away and making the cakes from the programme, having never done so before, and so we realized that we must have been speaking to the right people and saying the right things, which for a programme maker is extremely rewarding.

# THE BEST EVER SHORTBREAD

This is the shortbread we made for the punters to enjoy with coffee at every Aga Workshop. My recipe has semolina in it for extra crunch.

*Makes 48 pieces*

- 350g (12 oz) plain flour
- 350g (12 oz) butter
- 175g (6 oz) caster sugar
- 175g (6 oz) semolina
- demerara sugar to sprinkle on top

Preheat the oven to 180°C/Fan 160°C /Gas 4.

Whizz all the ingredients together in a food processor until the mixture combines to form a dry dough. Then turn the mixture out into a 46 x 34 x 5 cm (18 x 13 x 2 inches) traybake or roasting tin and press down with the back of a spoon so the surface is level all over. Sprinkle with the demerara sugar.

Bake in the preheated oven for about 45 minutes, or until the shortbread is pale golden and just cooked, turning the tin around once. Cut into 48 triangles while still soft. Leave to firm up and then remove from the tin.

## 17

While the loss of William narrowed my horizons for several years, for Thomas and Annabel you could say it almost had the opposite effect. In the years after their brother's death they both spent a great deal of time abroad: Thomas went to live in Australia and Annabel spent two years travelling around Asia. It was quite difficult for me to stand back and watch them go out into the world when my every impulse was to keep them close, but my children had always been fearless and loved adventure and I knew it was important to let them spread their wings, however much I might want to have them at home.

In 1993, Thomas went to stay with our friends the Turpins in Sydney, just as William had done before university, and he landed a well-paid job with Manpower, for whom he had been working back in London. But Thomas had always had a yen for the great outdoors and, after saving enough money, he applied to an agricultural college near Darwin to study Stock and Station Skills (farm and animal management). Following the six-month course, he got a job at a cattle station in the Northern Territories. From his phone calls home, it sounded as if he had found his calling.

*Thomas:*
I worked as a stock-hand or jackaroo – an Australian cowboy – and would ride out every day to round up all the cattle on the station. There were seven of us working on a farm

that was two and a half million acres (the size of Greater London), and between us we would take care of all the branding, castrating, de-horning and mustering of the cattle and breaking in the horses. The cattle station held its own rodeo, so we would practise bull riding in our spare time. For a young man who loved the outdoors it was a wonderful life. I had good friends, a great little dog – an Australian cattle dog called Ellie – and was very content. I don't think I grew up until that time in Australia, and I would probably still be there now if fate – and the authorities – had not intervened.

Over Christmas in 1996, Paul, Annabel and I went out to visit Thomas. We had planned a family holiday in Cairns, but first I was very keen to see the cattle station where Thomas had been working. We flew to Darwin and drove for miles and miles into the outback until the road ran out and there was just a sandy track. I was petrified we would get stuck, because every time we stopped the tyres would sink into the soft dirt, but to my relief eventually we arrived at a house in the shadow of a huge barn that was quite literally in the middle of nowhere. There was Thomas, looking excessively well: brown, slim and as happy as Larry. I asked to see where he slept and he took me to the barn where there was a row of what looked like little horseboxes, each containing just a bed and small table, all of which had air conditioning apart from the very last one, which belonged to him. But he explained that he spent most of the time sleeping out in his swag (tent) with the cattle, so it didn't matter at all.

The farm manager's wife welcomed us into her home, bringing out a tray of coffee and homemade biscuits on an immaculate tea set. She told me about her 'yard' (garden to us) and how she had planted every single blade of grass with her fingers because it wouldn't grow naturally; she seemed very proud of this little patch of green.

The house itself was rather bleak inside, with just a Rexine sofa and a couple of chairs on a bare wooden floor, and I felt quite sorry for this woman who, with her hard-won grass and dainty china teapot, appeared to aspire to the life of a suburban housewife yet lived miles away from anything like civilization. She had two young sons whom she had to teach at home, because they were too far from any schools, and once a year the state funded her to stay in a hotel in Darwin where she would go to learn the next year's curriculum. Yet she seemed very content with her lot and the two boys appeared to have a wonderful life, with endless space to play in and the animals for playmates.

The farm manager's wife told me that when she took the jackaroos their meal out to the barn, the only one who ever thanked her was Thomas. 'And he pays me for doing his washing,' she said. 'That bit of money makes all the difference.' I was very proud of him for that.

*Thomas:*
When I first arrived, I had a six-month visa to stay in Australia, but I been out there for two and a half years when the authorities caught up with me, the week before Mum, Dad and Annabel arrived for their visit that Christmas. I begged the officials to let me stay for another two weeks, as my family would be getting on a plane to see me any day and, amazingly, they were really decent about it and told me that as long as I booked my flight home they would give me a bridging visa for the extra two weeks.

Not that I mentioned any of this to Mum and Dad while they were in Australia for their visit, because all I'd have heard from Mum was: 'What are you going to do when you get home?' Mum had wanted me to stay in London and be a smart businessman and had been badgering me about when I was coming home for most of my time in Australia. So I didn't say a word about being deported and at the end of the holiday I waved them off – 'Hope to see you soon!' – and then turned up on the doorstep at Watercroft two days after they arrived home.

As soon as Thomas got home, much to my disappointment he started making plans to return to Australia, but a month later something wonderful happened: he met a girl at a party in London and fell for her almost instantly. Her name was Sarah Farrell, she was a wedding gown designer and was not only very beautiful, she was charming and clever and wonderful fun. Sarah's father was a vicar and she came from a large and loving family in Liverpool; you can still hear her accent when she says words like 'bath' and 'raspberries'. (The Farrell family are huge Everton fans and the only time I've ever heard Sarah speak her mind was when Thomas found her a second-hand car and it was red. 'I can't have a red car,' she told him, ever the Blues fan. 'It's Liverpool's colours!')

The first time I met Sarah I asked her, 'You don't want to live in Australia do you?' And when she told me that no, she was quite happy in London, I said to Thomas, 'Right, we're keeping her!'

A year after they met, Thomas asked Sarah to marry him in Hyde Park on the very same spot that Paul had proposed to me all those years before, except Thomas took a backpack with a bottle of champagne and two glasses with him to

Tom and Sarah's wedding – what a happy day.

mark the occasion – times move on, don't they? Keen to do
things properly, Thomas wanted to ask Tom Farrell, Sarah's
father, permission to marry his daughter. By this time Thomas
had trained as a tree surgeon – still his profession today – and
was doing some tree work at his future father-in-law's church
in the City of London. Terrified that Reverend Farrell might
refuse, Thomas asked for Sarah's hand while they were sitting together in his old truck, which had a faulty handle on
the passenger side. He joked afterwards that he wouldn't
have let Tom Farrell out until he had said yes! They were
married six months later, so Sarah could fulfil her dream of
a summer wedding. The ceremony was at our local church in
Penn, with Sarah's mum giving her away and her dad conducting the marriage, followed by a reception in a marquee in
our garden at Watercroft, so it truly was a family affair.

*

As I have said, when William died Annabel had understandably found life very difficult and became even more free spirited. She was unable to settle at anything. I was very worried for her, of course, yet at the same time I was well aware that she was not really herself because of what she had been through, so really we just let her do what she wanted and get it out of her system. And I was sure that she would be fine in the end, because even as a very young child Annabel had been very sensible and marvellous in an emergency. One time when we were living at the Red House she had noticed smoke coming out of the window of the flat over the garage where Paul's mother, Granny Mop, was living. I was working in London, but Annabel stayed calm, called the fire brigade and then rushed over and put the fire out herself.

After the Ox and Cow secretarial college, she worked as a chalet girl for several seasons in Meribel, Val d'Isere and Verbier, which she loved, and had a stint at the London College of Fashion. However, she had been dying to go travelling and so she set off with a friend and a backpack and spent much of the following two years exploring India and the Far East. I didn't hear much from her during this time – and what I did hear used to terrify me! When she was in India she ventured off into the countryside by herself and stayed with rural families to learn about their food, which I thought sounded highly dangerous for a young girl on her own. A week or so before she was due to fly home from India, I got a phone call from Annabel from a bank in Delhi. 'Mum, I'm so sorry, I haven't got any money left and I don't have any food.' Well, you can imagine I was absolutely frantic – my daughter on her own in the middle of Delhi without a penny! I contacted various places but nobody would transfer money to a bank in India, because they said it couldn't be guaranteed, but Coutts, whom I've banked with since I was nineteen, told me that it was no problem at all and that the money would be there that afternoon. It might be an expensive place to bank, but at that moment, gosh, I was grateful that I did!

When Annabel arrived home a week later her hair was extremely short and she had a ring through her nose. Although I spotted the latter immediately and just thought, 'Oh dear,' I didn't say a word, as Paul obviously hadn't noticed Annabel's new accessory – because I'm quite sure he would have voiced his opinion on the matter. As we chatted away to her in the kitchen, thrilled to have her home, Paul suddenly said, 'Darling, I think you've got a little something on your face . . . Just give your nose a wipe . . .' I thought that was so funny! Anyway, the nose ring was never mentioned and later that weekend it quietly disappeared.

*Annabel:*
I absolutely adored going travelling. I wasn't the sort to just hang about on a beach and do nothing, I would visit six countries in six months and explore. If you're spending time in different countries you do get absorbed into their culture, and I'm a great believer in wearing local dress so you're less likely to get hassled. When I came home from India with my nose pierced and Mum didn't say anything I initially thought, 'Well? Come on!' But then I realized it was actually quite brilliant, as after that I stopped trying to shock her.

I then went to Bali for six months and while I was there I set up a clothing label. It didn't really go anywhere though, because for me the fun was in making the collection, rather than dealing with the numbers side, but it sparked my interest and when I came back from travelling I set up a novelty candle business called Cosmic Candles. I started out making them at home with a friend, but when we realized there was potential to make money we got a grant from the Prince's Trust that allowed us to set up in a studio in west London. Things grew from there. We sold our candles to shops, at festivals and craft shows, and it was a good little business.

One day in 1994, Annabel, then twenty-three, was having lunch with Paul and me in the kitchen at Watercroft. As usual, there was a bottle of my homemade salad dressing on the table, made to my mother's original recipe with a few tweaks of my own, and during lunch Paul and Annabel suggested that we start selling it commercially, as our family and friends had always remarked on how much they had enjoyed it. The Aga Workshops were taking up most of my time and so I said that I was too busy, but Annabel, who as a child had loved the dressing so much that she would drink it straight from the bottle, piped up and said, 'I'll do it, Mum.'

She had already proved her talent for business with Cosmic Candles and so I was very happy to let her take it on – although rather worried about the potential mess in my kitchen! With fifty pounds from her savings, Annabel went to the East End in London and got some bottles with corks and bulk-bought ingredients from the Cash and Carry, then took over my kitchen in the evening to make up batches of the dressing. She handwrote each label herself, with 'Mary Berry's Salad Dressing' and 'Secret Recipe' surrounded by a pattern of flowers, and Paul helped her to hammer in the corks.

Annabel started by selling the dressing in our little shop at the Aga Workshops. Although each batch varied because she didn't measure out the ingredients very carefully it still tasted pretty good and we were selling about twenty bottles a week. Encouraged by the positive reaction, Annabel took a stall at the Royal Show in Warwickshire and made 350 bottles to take with her. I thought this was rather over-ambitious, and assured her that it didn't matter if she didn't sell very many, but she sold every last bottle. From there on she began to take bottles of the dressing to festivals and county shows to sell alongside her candles. She was already a familiar face at such events; she had bought a VW camper van with the proceeds from Cosmic Candles and in the evenings she would have parties with a barbecue and candles. She later traded the camper van in for a very cheap and highly unreliable Winnebago that would frequently break down on the motorway, leading to all sorts of dramas because the AA could rarely do anything to help since it was so enormous. We should have known that Winnebago was going to be trouble, because when she first brought it home Paul opened it up and found a robin nesting in the back!

*Annabel:*
Slowly but surely sales of the dressings overtook the candles and I left the candle business to my partner to dedicate myself to the dressings. Soon after my success at the Royal Show, a competitor complained about the labelling on my bottles, trying to push me out of business, and before I knew it I had an official from the Trading Standards Agency knocking at the door.

Of course, the problem was that I hadn't listed any of the dressing's ingredients on the label (apparently just writing 'Secret Recipe' wouldn't cut it!) and had been sealing the corked bottles with sellotape, but the Trading Standards

people were terribly nice and told me everything I needed to
be doing and so, rather than closing the business down,
whoever dobbed us in effectively put us on the road to
becoming a proper brand. I sat down with Mum and Dad
and we arranged for the labels to be made by a factory and
eventually the production of the dressings was taken over
by Baxter's in Scotland.

Our company 'Mary Berry & Daughter' started with the
original Salad Dressing and my Mustard Dressing, which I
had also made all my married life, and then Annabel and I
developed other recipes that had proved popular within our
own family to add to the product range. Our first official
sales outlet was Lakeland, a company I knew well, having
used their kitchen gadgets and equipment throughout my
career. The Rayner brothers, who run the business, never
asked for bank references when we did business. 'We know
you, lass,' they told me, 'and we like your dressings.' From
there we began selling to supermarkets, starting out with
Waitrose, and now our dressings and sauces are available
everywhere from farm shops to Fortnum's. Our latest
addition to the range is an oriental sauce that was heavily
influenced by Annabel's travels, making the most of the
trend for Asian fusion food. Paul is heavily involved in the
company as well, and it is lovely to have a truly family
business.

I was delighted when twelve years ago Thomas and Sarah
announced they were expecting twins, not only because I
was terribly excited about becoming a granny (and twice
over!) but because I knew what a hard battle it had been for
them to get there. Thomas would be dashing home between

jobs, covered in dirt, to get to their numerous hospital appointments in time. But our joy at Sarah's pregnancy quickly turned to anxiety when tests showed that there was a problem with one of the babies. Initially the doctors thought that one of the twins had a very high chance of suffering from Edward's syndrome, a chromosomal abnormality that means the baby won't live for more than twenty-four hours. One of the indicators of this condition is that the baby has clenched palms and so Sarah was rushed off for a scan. When both babies showed up on the ultrasound with their hands open, as if they were waving to us, it was a huge relief. However, it was not all good news: the doctors now believed that the baby was likely to be born with Down's syndrome.

Thomas and Sarah are both strong Christians and I know that their faith was a particular comfort to them during this time. They were offered an amniocentesis test, which would have given a more definite diagnosis, but because it came with a risk of miscarriage they refused. While it was a great comfort to know that both babies would live I did wonder how they would cope raising a potentially ill child, but I will never forget Thomas's response when I told him how sorry I was. He just said, 'Well, isn't it lucky that this baby is coming into our family?' And it was true. Thomas had been such a naughty boy when he was younger – as wicked as can be! – but he had grown into the most wonderful husband, and I just knew he would make an incredible father.

When Sarah was nearly thirty-eight weeks pregnant she went into labour and gave birth to two beautiful baby girls, Grace and Abby, and despite the doctors' warnings they were absolutely perfect.

After the birth, Thomas wanted to remain in the Radcliffe Hospital with Sarah as she was so exhausted, but they told him there weren't any facilities for visitors to stay. 'Then I'll sleep on the floor,' he said. 'I'm not leaving my wife.' That night Thomas camped out next to Sarah's bed and helped with the twins.

Paul and I were so thrilled to be grandparents – and the joy that those children brought to their parents was just wonderful to behold. Sarah would come to stay with us and she'd still be in her dressing gown at half ten in the morning, content to sit on the floor with these two little girls for hours, playing with them and loving them. Then Thomas would arrive back from work and he would just sit and look at them: they were very special.

Compared to my own childhood, when my parents were generally of the attitude that children should be seen and not heard, Thomas and Sarah love nothing better than spending

Tom, Sarah and their treasured girls in Salcombe.

time with their girls; in fact they don't really like to be away from them at all! Abby and Grace are the greatest of friends and when they're here they'll get out the cards and play on the floor together or will go outside and make a den. It's sweet to watch – and how lovely that they'll always have a friend in each other.

Thomas and Sarah now live near Oxford, but when they were newly married they moved into the cottage next to Watercroft where Granny Mop had been living before she died. One evening they had a dinner party and among the guests was a mutual friend of theirs, Dan Bosher. Apparently Dan looked across the table at Annabel, who was also at the party that night, and knew straight away that here was the girl he was going to marry.

In the past Annabel's boyfriends had often been quite artistic types who had bare feet and long hair and weren't very good at getting up in the morning, prompting frequent mother–daughter conversations that usually ended with Annabel saying, 'But Mummy, you don't understaaaand . . .' I was quite sure it was just a phase and that it would pass; still, Paul and I were delighted when Dan appeared on the scene. He is the sort of son-in-law that any mother would love to have: he is enthusiastic and hard working, loves sport and he is very thoughtful – he always rings on my birthday morning, and not because Annabel is prodding him. How lucky we are to have him! But he's not a pushover, which is important because Annabel is strong and loyal but can be quite a handful.

Dan designed Annabel's engagement ring with their friend Nessie, whose company Robinson Pelham designed the earrings the Duchess of Cambridge wore on her wedding day. Before starting the design, Nessie asked Dan what came to

Annabel and Dan on their wedding day – what joy they bring.

mind when he thought about Annabel. 'Chaos,' he replied, and the beautiful ring she eventually produced certainly has that element to the design. Dan proposed to Annabel while they were on holiday in Africa and they married at Holy Trinity Church, Penn, the following year. Interestingly, Annabel got married at exactly the same age I did – thirty-one – and went on to have her three children at the same age and in the same order. Isn't that spooky? Her children are eight, five and two now. There are the two boys, Louis and Hobie, who are little monkeys but absolutely great, and then Atalanta came along, which was a huge joy. I think Annabel would have walked out if there had been a third boy! I must admit that it did take me a little while to get used to their unusual choice of names. When they rang to tell us Hobie's name I asked what the inspiration had been behind it.

'Is it after Hobie Cat, the sailing boat?' I asked. 'Is it *Holby City*?'

'I don't know, Mum,' replied Annabel. 'We just liked it.'

I did think, 'Why couldn't it have been Charles or James or Edward?' There are plenty of good English names. But Hobie it was – and it suits him just perfectly.

Annabel, Dan and their gorgeous children.

# PASTA AL FRESCO

This is a wonderful pasta recipe that I came up with in the nineties as a great option for kitchen suppers. The dry-cured ham usually comes in packets of between 70g and 100g (2½ and 3½ oz). Asparagus tips are the short thin asparagus spears sold in supermarkets but not usually available in greengrocers. Serve the dish with chunks of fresh bread and fresh green salad leaves.

*Serves 6*

- 350g (12 oz) penne pasta
- 225g (8 oz) asparagus tips
- 150g (5 oz) Parma ham, Spanish Serrano ham or Black Forest ham, snipped into pieces
- 350g (12 oz) small chestnut mushrooms, sliced
- 200ml (7 fl oz) full-fat crème fraîche
- about 50g (2 oz) Parmesan cheese, grated
- salt and freshly ground black pepper
- a good handful of chopped parsley

Cook the pasta in a large pan of boiling salted water, over a high heat, as directed on the packet until al dente. Three minutes before the end of cooking add the asparagus tips. Drain then refresh in warm water and set aside to drain again.

Fry the Parma ham in a large non-stick frying pan without any oil until crisp. Remove half of the ham and keep warm.

Add the chestnut mushrooms to the pan and mix with the remaining ham for a moment, then stir in the crème fraîche and half the Parmesan cheese. Season with a little salt and pepper (go easy on the salt as the ham is salty). Bring the sauce to the boil; meanwhile return the cooked pasta and asparagus to the large pan. Tip the contents of the frying pan over the pasta and asparagus and stir well, until piping hot throughout, and check the seasoning.

Sprinkle over the remaining Parmesan, reserved ham and some parsley. Serve at once.

The *Bake Off* team at the BAFTAs. Friends for life.

On *Loose Women* – Paul and I do love a laugh together.

A promotional photo for *The Great British Bake Off*. Don't touch the cakes!

Paul and I filming the Easter Masterclass *Bake Off*.

The *Bake Off* tent.

Messing around with the gang.

Mel on set for *Bake Off* series three.

Me sporting my famous bomber jacket.

A day out at Windsor with Paul, Tom and Annabel to receive my CBE.

Celebrating my investiture with my brother Roger, sister-in-law Margaret, Paul, my brother William and sister-in-law Avril.

With Cousin Robin, a tower of strength to me.

Celebrating the publication of my
*Complete Cookbook*, which has sold over
one million copies.

Making a very emotional speech
upon receiving a lifetime achievement
award from the Guild of Food Writers.

What a pile – the books I've written over the years.

My wonderful family.

At the National Television Awards, adopting my classic pose with my hands behind my back to hide my bat wings!

# 18

By 2006, demand for places on our Aga Workshops was at an all-time high, despite it being our sixteenth year of operation. By the end of January, all of our courses were full to the brim and there were already people trying to book for the following year before we had even had a chance to think about dates. My cousin Robin Buchanan, my mentor and my accountant – to whom I am very close and who is always there to lend an ear and give sage advice – had been asking me for years when I was planning to retire, and for the first time the prospect seemed quite appealing. I was seventy-one and the workshops required a lot of hard, physical work; I had loved every single day of them but I wanted to be able spend more time with Paul, the family and my grandchildren. Also, Lucy and I found that we were having to put in even more each year – more recipes, more ideas – to keep the workshops fresh and interesting for the large number of people who came back year after year. It had reached the point where we were running out of new things to do with chicken.

In addition to Lucy, by this time we had another full-time assistant for the workshops, Lucinda Kaizik – now McCord – who had come to us as a Leith's student in 2001, but rather than leaving after eleven months had ended up staying full-time for six years because she was such a gem and had fitted into our team so well. Around the time that I was having doubts over the future of the workshops, Lucinda announced to Lucy and me that she was thinking of leaving to go travelling with her boyfriend, Johnny. For the past few years the workshops had been running like a well-oiled machine, because we had all got into such a routine, and we really couldn't face the thought of starting all over again with a new student and having to show someone else the ropes.

So I said to Luc, 'We've had a good innings – do you think it's now time to stop?' To my surprise, she told me that she had been thinking the same thing. It was a tough decision, but it was a relief that we both agreed it was the right one.

At the end of that year we had our very last Aga Workshop at Watercroft. Everybody was rather upset about it, and Lucy and I missed the events a lot because of all the wonderful friendships we had made, but Paul was pleased – he was a

Lucinda, Lucy and Me.

bit tired of having to creep around the house on workshop days! Lucy actually continued to give her own Aga workshops for a period, but she did them in other people's kitchens: she would set off at the crack of dawn with Lucinda (who had decided not to go travelling after all!) and demonstrate the recipes on someone else's Aga for a group of their friends. Lucy would still work for me when she was not on the road, as well as finding the time to write her first solo cookery book.

For me, however, the idea was now to slow down – to play tennis every Monday, spend time with the family and go on lots of garden visits with friends – and for a couple of years at least this was the way that it worked out. Suddenly my life became a lot quieter and I was happy with that, although I was still writing books, doing a few charity demonstrations and popping up on television every now and then (on programmes such as *The Alan Titchmarsh Show*) and as a guest on the radio.

I enjoyed the radio shows immensely. In the early nineties I had been the guest on BBC Radio 2's *Debbie Thrower Show* on the first Monday of every month in the lunchtime slot. Debbie is a delight and I loved every second of our time together. We would have a listeners' phone-in where I answered cooking queries and give recipes on a theme for that month according to the season. Apparently my chocolate cake was the most requested recipe on the radio ever after one of the programmes! Luc often came in with me too and both of us would be on air discussing recipes, which was great fun. I also have a real soft spot for Chris Evans on Radio 2 – I think he's a genius. He is immensely talented and has always been so lovely to me; the energy he puts into his programmes and his life is great.

I have always loved *Woman's Hour* on Radio 4 and its pre-senters, Jenni Murray and Jane Garvey, and consider it a huge honour to be invited on the programme, so I have always accepted with great pleasure whenever they have asked me to be a guest. I first appeared on *Woman's Hour* back in the eighties, when I was asked to do a series of programmes on basic cookery skills alongside the then presenter Sue McGregor. There were no permanent cooking facilities, so I arrived at the radio studios to find a fold-out card table covered with green baize, next to which was a Baby Belling tabletop stove – and next to that a fire warden stood holding a fire extinguisher, who remained in position for the entire programme. I felt rather self-conscious, knowing that he was going to be stand-ing watching me cook, although I'm thankful that he never had to do anything more than just watch.

You might think it strange going to the trouble of cooking on the radio, as people obviously couldn't see what was going on, but Sue McGregor was very skilled at bringing the scene in the studio to life for the listeners, and you could also hear the sounds from the Baby Belling in the background as I cooked. I did enjoy doing those programmes – I think it's the teacher in me coming out – and Sue was such a lovely person to work with. I remember her arriving at the studio one day with a plas-tic bag full of empty honey jars for me, having brought them in on the tube, and she said, 'I hate to throw things away, and I know someone who'll use these to make jam.'

On one occasion I was invited to appear on *Woman's Hour* alongside Hugh Fearnley-Whittingstall and Women's Insti-tute judge Jill Brand as part of a group discussion on what makes the perfect Victoria Sandwich, a subject I was sure I knew something about after making thousands of them over the years. We were all asked to make a Victoria Sandwich according to our own recipe and bring it with us to the studio; I made mine using the all-in-one method with Stork, as I had done ever since I started baking, whereas Jill Brand had made hers with butter using the creaming method, as did Hugh, who used butter and eggs from his own very superior tree-laying hens. As soon as we arrived at the studio our cakes were taken away from us for a panel of independent testers to taste and decide which was best, and it was only then that I thought, 'You stupid fool. You've been promoting the all-in-one method for years – if either of the other recipes wins then you're going to look like you don't know what you're doing!' I was terribly worried, as it felt a bit like my whole reputation was resting on the verdict, but thankfully they thought Hugh's tasted a bit eggy and, to my immense relief, my Victoria Sandwich was declared the winner.

I had actually met Hugh Fearnley-Whittingstall once before, when he had come to one of our Aga days. I thought he was enchanting, although in his newspaper article about the workshop he described me as 'a charming and sprightly lady in her early seventies' – and I was only sixty-five at the time. I didn't say a word, but we had a great many Aga Workshop regulars asking if I had noticed Hugh's mistake. He actually wrote a very sweet letter to me apologizing for getting my age wrong, and I replied saying he was totally forgiven. He's young, you see: anybody over sixty must have seemed ancient to him.

While the intention was to wind down my career during this period, if a particularly interesting project came along I would usually make an exception. When my agent told me that I had been asked to be a cookery lecturer on board the *Black Watch* cruise ship on a two-week jaunt around the Caribbean – and that Paul would be able to join me on the

trip – I very happily accepted. I have always loved visiting
the Caribbean (my cousin lives in Barbados) and the cruise
sounded very well organized. The *Antiques Roadshow* expert
Bunny Campione was also going to be on board discussing
antiques, while the MP Edwina Currie would be talking about
her books. I sent the organizers the recipes I planned to demonstrate together with a detailed list of ingredients, which I'd
tried to keep as local as possible with lots of tropical fruits
because we were to set sail from Barbados, and they said it
was all absolutely fine. So imagine my concern when we got
on board and I went to the kitchen to find they had nothing
that I'd asked for: no fresh fruit, no spices – in terms of raw
ingredients there was just a sack of flour and a sack of sugar.
I had to dash out and find a market at the first place we
stopped to buy everything myself. Not only that, but there
were no scales and not even a proper tablespoon, so I had to
guess all the measurements in the recipes. It was an absolute
disaster. They had asked me if I would demonstrate recipes,
but there was no mobile cooker so I had to prepare a dish in
front of the audience, someone would rush it to the kitchen
to be cooked by the chef and then bring it back when it was
finished. I don't know how I managed to create a single thing,
but somehow I did. I felt bad for the audience because they
had been told I would be demonstrating cookery and in the
end I just spent most of the time talking. It was horrendous.
I have been asked to do similar things since then, but I always
say, 'Never again.'

   Yet despite these occasional forays into the world of work,
for the first time in my life I found my career slipping down
my list of priorities. Hobbies suddenly became a possibility,
so Paul and I took an antiques restoration night class together,
because we seemed to have so much furniture that wasn't

quite perfect. We restored a harp that had been stored at South Lawn with the pianos during the Bath Blitz, but which the owner had never come to collect at the end of the war, and a hall desk that was missing a leg. In the course of repairing this desk we made a rather grisly discovery: inside a secret central chamber was a mass of tiny curled bones, which we worked out were the tails of rats or squirrels. At one time there had been a bounty on them and the desk's previous owner had obviously been collecting the tails in order to receive the bounty payment. They must have been a hundred years old, at least; needless to say we immediately threw them away!

What I was looking forward to most in retirement – well, semi-retirement – was spending more time in the garden. Along with food, gardening is my biggest passion in life and although this time round I've devoted more time to the cooking, in my next life I think that gardening will take priority.

Like many people I discovered my green fingers fairly late in life. My literary agent, Felicity Bryan, always used to say to me, 'When your children grow up you'll become interested in gardening,' and I had always laughed this off because I was so busy I couldn't imagine having the time, but of course she was absolutely right.

When we lived in London we had our tiny yard that was too shady to grow very much and then when we arrived at the Red House I had very little spare time and I'm afraid the lovely two-acre garden with its vegetable patch and weeping beech tree, the branches of which arched over like a leafy green tent, was predominantly a football pitch. As the children grew up, however, I began to take an increasing interest in what was happening in the garden and, from learning on the job with basic weeding and pruning, my confidence grew and I started to add to the garden with the help of Ma Block, the mother of my great friend Penny and a brilliant gardener.

Ma Block was a marvellous lady, whom I used to grill about garden matters whenever I went to her house in Little Gaddesden for Sunday lunch. She would tell me when it was seed time and what seeds I should buy, and could usually solve any gardening dilemmas I might have. On one occasion when I had invited her and Pa Block to Penn for lunch they arrived with a trailer full of horse muck for our garden. As Ma Block shovelled it out of the trailer my husband rushed over to help but – despite being a granny – she was adamant that she would do it herself. (She was very fond of Paul, but she didn't think he was any good at getting his hands dirty.) 'Well, can I get you a drink then, Ma?' asked Paul. And without even looking up from her muck-spreading she said, 'You know it's a whisky.'

By the time we moved to Watercroft, our present house, I was confident enough in my abilities to make more ambitious changes to the lovely three-acre gardens – although this has been very much a long-term project. There was a grass walkway through a series of arches that we turned into a rose walk by taking out every single perennial plant (and all the perennial weeds along with them) and replanting with roses. We now have 350 different types of rose bush in the garden and my favourite variety is Chandos Beauty, which has a beautiful pinky-white bloom and a wonderful scent. It was bred by Harkness, the specialist rose nursery, which is situated in Hertfordshire, not a million miles away from us here in Penn. There was a wild meadow with all sorts of different grasses, cowslips and daisies – a great haven for wildlife – and Paul put paths through it to make the area easier to enjoy.

We wanted to put in a hard tennis court, because the whole

family love to play – plus there would be the added bonus of slightly less lawn to mow! There was an area of the garden that had actually once been used as a tennis court, where now grass didn't grow at all well, but we decided against rebuilding it in that spot as it had particularly beautiful views over the countryside and it seemed a shame not to make the most of them. Instead, we transformed the old tennis court into an Italianate garden. I'd had the idea after going to visit Sutton Place, a Tudor mansion in Surrey, from which I returned home in ecstasies over the garden. I told Paul all about the stunning topiary and yew hedges and suggested we do something similar at Watercroft. 'We could plant hedges all the way around the old tennis court to enclose it and have some sort of design in the middle,' I said to Paul. 'Then we could put our urns at the entrance.' We had bought two magnificent stone urns after Paul's former boss at Hiram Walker, who had become a great friend, left us a small legacy in his will – we had felt that rather than put the money towards the gas bill it would be nice to have something to remember him by.

'Well, don't just talk about it,' said Paul, handing me a piece of graph paper. 'Get busy with the design.' So I did and, since Paul liked what I had drawn, I ordered the yew trees and got to work. Like my father I've always been a doer, rather than a talker; Thomas is the same, except he wants everything right now!

That was eighteen years ago and our Italianate garden is now well established and most attractive. Annabel had her wedding in a marquee within its hedges and on a sunny day you can be standing there and see all the way to Windsor Castle – although whenever we take visitors there it's never sunny and they think we're mad. Thomas and I were down there on the afternoon of the Windsor Castle fire and we saw this great plume of billowing smoke, which was quite frightening and, of course, I felt immensely sad for the Queen.

When we arrived at Watercroft there was already a large clay-based pond, fed by natural springs, but we took out the bull rushes from around the edge because we wished to make it bigger. This was a huge risk because the rushes provided the pond with stability, but thankfully one that worked out. As you may have gathered, I am very fond of ducks and ducklings and I was keen to colonize our pond with diving ducks – such as Rosybills, White-eyed Pochards and Tufted Ducks – as well as the wild ducks that it already attracted. I had recently done a demonstration for Waitrose organized by a friend and colleague Rosemary Moon at Leckford, the John Lewis estate, and while I was there I was taken around their beautiful water garden, Longstock Park, and introduced to a man called Mike Stone, who was one of the garden's creators. Mike retired from Leckford the following year and came to help us at Watercroft with the planting around the pond, advising me on the best plants to buy and where to put them. Sadly, he has now died, but he was a brilliant plantsman and I have a lot to thank him for. Nowadays we have fish in the pond too, but they're not expensive carp: friends' children have given us goldfish won at funfairs and those that have survived the heron have grown to be a good six inches.

For me, one of the great joys of the garden is being able to pick flowers for the house. My mother always had lots of fresh flowers at home, simply but boldly arranged and augmented with greenery; even when she was 105 she would go outside a find a few primroses or daffodils to put in a vase. Mum's passion had a great effect on me, although I have nothing like her talent for flower arranging.

Me with Mum, aged 105.

Like her, I prefer flowers to be in season – and spring flowers are my absolute favourite. On Paul's birthday in March this year we had thirteen people for lunch (I don't mind thirteen as long as the last one's in a high chair) and I decorated the table with a little posy of snowdrops at each place. At Easter time I pick branches of anything that's coming out, usually hazel or hawthorne, put them in a vase and hang little Easter eggs from them. The grandchildren help me decorate them; it's almost as much of a tradition as putting up the Christmas tree.

There's a definite correlation between people who own an Aga and an interest in gardening, so some of the workshops we offered at Watercroft combined the two – such as 'Aga Fast Food/Creative Gardening' – for which we enlisted the expert help of Sarah Raven, who lives at Sissinghurst in Kent, one of the most beautiful gardens in the country. It was Sarah who suggested that I put in a picking bed at Watercroft, a small area in the vegetable garden dedicated to growing flowers for the house, and I find it so useful. I grow rows of fragrant yellow-white narcissi, both the Bridal Crown and Silver Chimes varieties, tulips and alstroemeria in a rainbow of different colours (no orange though, as I'm not keen) and glorious dahlias. I used to hate the big, showy dahlias that you would see at village fêtes, but the small-headed varieties are marvellous because they go on and on. I also grow hellebores, which provide a welcome splash of winter colour outside and are perfect for decorating your table for a kitchen supper – you can float the heads in a shallow glass bowl along with some of their leaves. This not only looks beautiful, but when sitting down you can see over the top to chat. I love irises for the blue of their blooms, particularly the Mary Barnard variety, which is the deepest violet-blue, and often pick these from the garden when they're still in bud so that they open in a warm kitchen. The same applies to forsythia: if you bring the budding branches into the house then they will flower more quickly than they would outside and provide the most magnificent bursts of sunshine yellow, although I have to reassure Paul that 'those pots of sticks' I've put in the dining room will honestly turn into something spectacular!

Sarah Raven advised me always to pick flowers straight into a bucket and then leave them sitting there for a while in the cool of the day so that they draw up the water, while my mum used to put her arrangements outside at night, which helps them last longer, and every evening when I do the same

I think of her. I'm sometimes lucky enough to be given bouquets, which I'm always very grateful for, although I get quite ratty when you find things like gerberas and chrysanthemums shoved in amongst bunches of spring flowers. To me, chrysanths mean crisp autumn mornings and chilly, dark evenings and seem horribly out of place at other times of the year. Another bugbear of mine is lisianthus – the delicate flowers always look so lovely, but whatever I do I can't seem to make them last, which I find incredibly frustrating. I think lilies are beautiful, but they're a disaster because of the pollen since I'm not very good at remembering to snip the stamens out of them. I always seem to be wearing a white silk shirt and the stains are a devil to get out.

Of course, another one of the joys of a garden is being able to grow things to eat. I have an extensive herb garden including flat-leaf and moss-curled parsley, dill, lemongrass, sorrel, rocket and many more, and we grow a whole range of vegetables from beetroot to courgettes to fennel. There is a small greenhouse for tomatoes, cucumbers and the odd melon, and among the different fruits we cultivate is a fig tree – although sadly I'm the only one in the family who seems to enoy eating them!

For me, the most rewarding part of gardening is watching things grow. I find it terribly exciting in the spring when the first colour starts to appear in the garden: the blue of the hyacinths, white crocuses and yellow daffodils. Apart from the winter, when nothing much happens out there, I would happily spend every moment of my time in the garden, but as that is just not possible these days we have two gardeners, Kevin and Simon, who are here twice a week. They always come in for coffee at eleven o'clock so we can chat and catch up – it's wonderful to know that they love the garden as much as I do. Kevin has been with us for so long that he automatically knows what I want without me having to tell him.

Every year we open up our garden at Watercroft as part of the National Gardens Scheme. Originally we would do this on the first two Sundays in July and Lucy and I would lay on tea and cakes for the visitors, but when I started appearing on television again in the nineties we were getting huge crowds, 400- or 500-strong, and so the parking – and catering – became unwieldy. On one occasion we had to go to our local Waitrose and ask if we could use their freezers to store the 600 scones we had made for the teas. So now we open the garden by appointment for groups of twenty or so at a time – usually gardening groups. We have tea in the glasshouse where we keep our pots of pelargoniums, which is just an old metal-framed greenhouse and not at all posh, but it has a lovely vine growing inside, old weathered oak doors and a very pretty floor. We talk about the gardens and tell people the history of the house and it's always very enjoyable.

Also, once a year we open the garden for our local church, Holy Trinity Penn, to hold a plant sale. It's always in June, so the *Bake Off* team know that I can't film on that particular Saturday as it's imperative I'm at home for it. Although the sale is organized by the church, we all muck in and even my granddaughters Abby and Grace have a little stall selling their homemade fairy cakes. Local friends and supporters of the church do wonderful teas, all the plants for sale are donated by keen gardeners and it's such a happy occasion whatever the weather.

In 2009, I was invited to the Guild of Food Writers' annual awards ceremony at Lincoln's Inn in London. I've been a member of the Guild for years, which is virtually a *Who's Who* of everyone involved in cookery writing and broadcasting, and I have always supported them, although I don't get to the meetings that often as they are always in London. Anyway, I remember the drive up to town because it was a blisteringly hot June day and Lucy, who was accompanying me, seemed quite jittery and I couldn't work out why. When we got to the venue it was, as always, lovely to catch up with all these familiar faces and I was enjoying the ceremony. Then we reached the point in the proceedings when they announced the Lifetime Achievement Award. This is a particularly special honour because it isn't given out every year and in the past had been awarded to such luminaries as Marguerite Patten and Katie Stewart – so you can appreciate how astonished I was when I heard them read out my name! With tears in my eyes I made my way up to the stage, feeling completely overwhelmed. To be recognized in this way by my peers, people whom I admire hugely myself, was the greatest of honours and I think possibly my proudest achievement in my career. (I later found out that Lucy had been told I was to receive the award six months before and had been under strict instructions to make sure I attended the ceremony – hence her nerves on the day!)

Being presented with the Lifetime Achievement Award by the Guild of Food Writers felt rather like the closing of a chapter: I might now be in the twilight of my career, but I could look back at what I had achieved over the years and know that all the hard work had been worth it. It was a wonderful and very fitting way to mark my retirement. But then, just a few months later, came the telephone call that would completely change my life.

# ROASTED FIGS WITH PARMA HAM AND GOAT'S CHEESE

This recipe was the invention of Brenda Berners Price. We were on holiday with Brenda and her husband Peter in Portugal and there were wonderful figs at the market. We so enjoyed cooking together with me as the sous chef for a change! I have often prepared this dish since we starting producing figs in the garden at Watercroft. Use vacuum-packed dry-cured ham because this comes in convenient even-sized slices.

*Serves 8*

- 200g (7 oz) roll of goat's cheese, e.g. Capricorn
- 8 fresh figs, all the same size
- 16 slices Parma ham

**to serve**
- a little green salad, dressed

Preheat the oven to 220°C/Fan 200°C/Gas 7.

First freeze the goat's cheese until firm – for about an hour.

Cut the tops of the pointed stems off the figs. Stand them upright on a board and cut a cross in each fig down not quite to the base.

Trim the ends off the chilled cheese roll and cut into 8 slices. Then cut each slice in half to give 16 half moons. Cut 8 of these slices in half again widthways to make quarters. Lie each slice of Parma ham out flat, trimming any excess fat.

Put the eight halves of cheese into each fig where you have made the cross. Use the quarters to fit in either side so the complete cross is filled with goat's cheese.

Wrap each fig in two pieces of Parma ham, so the join is on top of the fig in a cross shape, and squeeze the join of the Parma ham to seal.

Roast in the preheated oven for about 6 minutes, until the cheese has melted and the ham is crisp. Do watch them closely while they are cooking.

Serve at once with a small dressed green salad.

# 19

The telephone call was from Fiona Lindsay, my television agent. Fiona is head of Limelight Management and has been dealing with all my media work for about twenty years. It's a wonderful family team and Fiona and Alison look after us very well – anything we are not sure about they can sort out! They deal with all the financial side of bookings, which is wonderful as I cannot bear talking about money. It was Felicity Bryan, my literary agent, who recommended Fiona to me for my TV and media work. I really am so blessed to have them both by my side – or at the end of the phone – when anything uncomfortable or exciting crops up. Fiona was ringing to tell me that the BBC had been in touch with an idea for a new television series that they thought I might be interested in. The programme was to be along the lines of a cake competition at a traditional village fete and they wanted me to be the judge.

I immediately thought, 'Well that's right up my street,' because if there's one thing I know about then it is cakes. Over the course of my career I must have made practically every single cake that has ever been invented (there are a few from abroad I haven't tried yet, but we're all still learning, aren't we?) and have researched the subject inside and out in the course of writing my many cake books. And I do like doing television; I enjoy making programmes and think I'm quite good at it – although I had assumed that apart from the odd guest appearance my television days were largely behind me (it had been over ten years since my last series). But as chuffed as I was to be asked to be part of this new programme I had been short-listed for many projects over the years that had never come to fruition, so I didn't get too excited. (Sure enough, I later found out that the production company had pitched the idea four times before it had been accepted, so I was right to be cautious.)

Anyway, there was a bit of back-and-forth between Fiona and Emma Willis – the commissioning editor at the BBC – and Love Productions, the company who were making the programme, and to my absolute delight I was offered the position of 'the judge' (just the one at this stage) on the first series of *The Great British Bake Off*. I had been with Fiona since the eighties, and for years she had earned virtually nothing from me as I wasn't doing much television, but she always had time for me. One of the reasons I was so thrilled when I got the job on *Bake Off* was because I felt I could at last pay Fiona back for all her support. Despite the potential workload I didn't have any reservations about accepting the job, which was unusual because I had been very much picking and choosing projects during the previous few years. When I talked to my husband Paul we both agreed that this was just the time of my life that I could commit to something like this: I no longer had the children to look after, and Paul loves a bit of a peace and quiet when I go away to work – as long as I come home eventually! I thought it was a brilliant format and after meeting the team at Love Productions – headed up by Richard McKerrow and Anne Beattie – I felt they were so nice and gentle and keen for me to just be myself that I knew working on the programme wouldn't be at all stressful.

When I was first approached about the programme the

focus was very much on cakes, but early on in the development process there was talk of including bread. 'Well, if
that's the case,' I told them, 'then we'll need to get another
judge, because I'm not a great bread maker at all.' I thought
it better to be honest at the very beginning and I'm glad that
I was, because in the end the programme has become really
quite bready, hasn't it?

The producers set up screen tests for me with four different bakers, a couple of whom I had met before, including
a chap called Paul Hollywood. Paul and I had appeared
together on a programme called *Great Food Live* on the now
defunct Carlton Food Network; I had been a guest and Paul
had been a guest presenter. The programme's host, Jeni Bar-
nett, was terribly funny and cheeky and I could remember
that we all had a great time together.

After the screen tests the producers asked me who I had
liked the best, but I was adamant that my own personal
preference was irrelevant: it was far more important that
they – Love Productions and the BBC – decide which of the
men worked best with me on screen. I didn't want to be
responsible for choosing, in case it ended up being a disaster!
Nevertheless, I was delighted when I was told that they had
selected Paul – as was Lucy, whose response, when I told her
who the other judge would be, was: 'Paul Hollywood? Ooh,
he's dishy!'

For the first series the idea was that we would film each
episode at a different location around the country with a particular connection to baking, for example Sandwich and
bread, Derbyshire and Bakewell tarts and Cornwall and pasties, although this concept was dropped for subsequent series
as scouting locations and travelling around involved too
much work for the production team.

I remember being horribly nervous on our first day of filming. I had judged cake competitions at village shows before, but if you took away the pastel bunting and marquee then this was completely different. The presenters Mel Giedroyc and Sue Perkins were absolutely delightful, clever and so full of fun, and that helped me to relax a little. (To this day they are so brilliant at what they do and are just lovely to me, and I shall always value their friendship.) You rather imagine that you're going to have a briefing before the programme, but the producers were keen that Paul and I should just be ourselves, and so they didn't give us any guidance on what we should say or how we should act. They had put together this wonderful format of the three challenges (the Signature Bake, in which the contestants show off their speciality, the Technical Bake, in which they are all given the same recipe to test their skills, and the Showstopper, when they must pull out all the stops to produce a professional-standard masterpiece) and were happy to let the action unfold naturally from there. Neither has the team ever tried to influence our judging decisions in any way. In the second series we had three girls in the final and in the third it was three men; I'm sure the producers would have preferred a mixed bunch, but the decision on who goes through is purely down to what they achieve with their baking on the day.

If you watch those early programmes you will see that Paul did a lot more talking than me, partly because I was so scared, but also because I felt that I mustn't interrupt him – although nowadays I wouldn't hesitate to do so! It was apparent from day one that there was going to be a good cop/bad cop element to our judging (obviously with me as the former) but Paul and I were never encouraged to assume particular roles: there is nothing fake about how we appear on camera.

I was gentle with the contestants from the start, as my aim was to be encouraging and constructive, but also because I was terrified I might upset someone. I can't bear to see people cry and the thought that I might reduce people to tears with something I said was just awful. I was also keeping in mind the viewer at home, whether that was a child or an adult, as I wanted them to enjoy the programme and be inspired to have a go at baking. For me, much of the success of the series is down to the fact that we teach as well as entertain.

After the first weekend of filming, I remember Lucy asking me what I had done. 'Well, I tasted cakes,' I told her. I was still very much finding my feet and the whole thing had been rather a blur. It wasn't until after the second or third weekend that I said to Luc, 'Do you know, I think that this might be really, really good.'

There is something rather magical about the process of baking, of putting your heart and soul into creating something beautiful and delicious for people to enjoy, and even in these early days of filming I felt that *The Bake Off* was capturing that spirit. Then, when I finally saw the broadcast programmes, I was hugely impressed with the skill of the team in editing and polishing the finished product. Nevertheless, at the start I had absolutely no idea how successful the series would be – I don't think any of the team did really, although we all very much believed in the format.

Once the first episode of a new series has aired there is always a nervous wait for the viewing figures, which are released the following morning. Right from the start I remember being surprised at the size of the audience – over two million for the first show – and then, of course, with each episode the viewing figures went up and up, until by the second series it was five million, and that really was most exciting. As

I write, we are currently in the middle of filming series four in the grounds of Harptree Court in Somerset, which was also our location for series three.

Although *The Bake Off* appears on television from August, we begin work on the programme in the first weeks of spring. There's quite a lengthy audition process involved to whittle the thousands of people who apply down to twelve contestants, and Paul and I are involved from the early stages. Once the producers have got their longlist of finalists, Paul and I will take part in two-part screen tests with each of them: first of all they are asked to bring two baked items of their choice for us to taste, and then they will come in a second time with a loaf and scones. Paul and I decide who goes through based entirely on merit; as ever, neither the BBC nor Love Productions try to influence us. After the screen tests, the chosen few will go off to see the psychologist, to check they can cope with the pressure of filming twelve-hour days, until we have got down to our twelve final bakers.

We film each episode over a long weekend, so that the bakers don't need to take too much time off work. In the morning I'll arrive on set at seven o'clock and go straight into make-up with the lovely Jo Penford, who has done my hair and make-up since series three. I'm always fussing about my hair, because it's as flat as anything and Jo knows to give it a bit of oomph. I usually wear only a bit of pink lippy but for TV Jo adds a few extra lashes to brighten my eyes and colour to my face as I look pale and uninteresting naturally. It is lovely to chat to Jo in the make-up chair but twenty minutes is my limit as I can't sit still for long.

Before each series I will go shopping for my *Bake Off* wardrobe. I've got increasingly more confident with my look and now wear much more colour than I did at the start;

nevertheless, I was absolutely flabbergasted about the fuss made over the floral bomber jacket that I wore last year. I can only think that people were watching me and thought about their old granny who might also be around the same age. The main reason I chose that famous floral bomber was because when I saw it on the rail I thought, 'Ooh yes, lots of room under there for warm layers.' I get immensely cold while filming as the wind blows through the break in the side of the tent, so the crew always get me long-sleeved thermal underwear and I have two hand-warmers in the back pockets of my jeans that they keep heating up in the microwave for me. I'm very spoilt! I do always wear trousers, not just for their warmth but because I don't like being different. Mel and Sue both wear jeans so I do too, usually a pair from Marks and Spencer as they fit me better. That's a bit silly isn't it? But I do like to fit into the pack.

I admit that I'm a perfectionist in my career, but not in other areas of my life – and certainly not when it comes to my appearance. I'd wear the same things every day given half the chance. Clothes have never been high on my list of priorities, but I'm learning to have fun with my look. Three years ago I was wearing A-line, mid-calf-length skirts with twinsets and pearls every day; now, I've just found a bright yellow biker jacket with zips that I plan to wear on this year's *Bake Off* – and I liked it so much I bought one in blue, too!

As reluctant as I am to think of myself as a 'style icon', I would love to think I could inspire older women to make the most of themselves. These days, there's no reason to be dowdy. I do look at people in the street and think, 'Gosh, I wish you'd cheer yourself up a bit!' I don't have style rules as such, but I think there are certain guidelines that women might find helpful as they get older. A few years ago Barbara Hulanicki, the founder of Biba, wrote a piece in the *Telegraph* about being a 'Stylish Seventy-Something', which I tore out and kept. (I'm a great one for hanging on to things that look useful.) One of her suggestions was that older women should carry their handbag with a straight arm, rather than hung over the top 'like Margaret Thatcher'. I'm not sure if it's right or wrong, but I've been doing it ever since.

Cashmere polo necks are one of my wardrobe staples, not only because I get so chilly but because my husband Paul says I've got scraggy around the neck, which is quite right. My granddaughter Grace was sitting on my knee one day and asked, 'Granny, why do you have those two great hollows in your neck? Mummy doesn't have them.' I thought it was really sweet! If I'm not in a polo neck, I'll usually wear a scarf or a chunky necklace. Annabel found me the most beautiful one in Turkey, a thick, collar-like band of pearls with a little dangle underneath. You can find quite similar styles in Accessorize – great for covering up the scraggy bits!

I tend to buy my dresses a size too big, as I don't like clothes to be clingy. It's fine to have a more fitted look around the arms, but I do like things to move round your bottom and be comfy. Every skirt I buy is too big in the waist – I get a size 12 to fit around my hips – but I have a wonderful lady called Val in the village who adjusts things for me. She'll take my sleeves up so they don't get covered in flour and even adjust the neckline on a dress the better to accommodate a necklace.

During filming Paul and I will be in the main tent with the bakers for everything except the Technical Challenge. During the Signature Bake and Showstopper we will be wandering around the tent, observing the contestants' technique, finding out what they've been up to and talking about the recipe. When they tell me that they're using one of mine I just think, 'Gracious, I hope it works!'

When you're walking around you sometimes notice someone doing something wrong; we've had people pick up sugar instead of salt or make a glaring error with the technique. Obviously you can't say anything at the time, which I find terribly hard as my instinct is always to help, but when we taste the end product I will bring it up: 'I did notice that you were adding the butter when it was far too hot and so it was likely to separate.' We will tell the contestants if something doesn't taste good, or if they've tried to be too clever by putting together unusual flavour combinations, but I try to be as constructive as possible with my criticism, and praise them for the things they have done well.

While the bakers get to grips with the Technical Bake, Paul and I go to the small tent next to the main one to discuss what we will be expecting from the contestants' efforts and to review what a perfect example of the recipe should look like. In the first series Paul and I would make this ourselves, but nowadays we have three wonderful home economists, Faenia, Georgia and Becca, who create the bake for us according to our recipe. We will usually be with them as they finish it off, perhaps doing a bit of piping, but they are great experts. I'm always popping into the test kitchen to chat to Faenia and Georgia and they are extremely kind to me and bring me mugs of homemade tomato soup to warm me up! They really are a great combination and at the end of a long day's filming they will often use any leftovers and bake a scrumptious pizza or tart for the crew.

I am always gobsmacked by the bakers' dedication and skill, and by the results of their efforts. They all have different strengths, whether that is decorating or flavour combinations, and it is wonderful to see how they develop throughout the course of the series. These are very busy people – teachers, surgeons and full-time mothers – yet they still find time to put their heart and soul into the competition. And I'm always astonished at the way they use the internet for research and to source all sorts of unusual ingredients, different spices and cake finishes.

Looking back, I'm afraid that all the bakes tend to merge into one a little so it's difficult to pick a standout recipe, but we have had some very wonderful chocolate cakes in our time. There have also been some interesting wellingtons: you usually think of beef, but we've had unusual fillings like sea bass with puy lentils and lamb and rosemary, which worked very well indeed.

I always try to taste a decent piece of everything the bakers produce, so I do end up eating an awful lot during the course of a day's filming. When I go back to our hotel in the evening – Ston Easton Park, a glorious place with superb light food – I won't have a pudding with supper and I will eat something small the next day to compensate. I do get asked a great deal how I manage to stay slim while eating so much cake, and it's really just by being very, very careful. Having been much bigger when I was younger, it is important to me that I don't gain weight. I'm now a size 10–12, but before William died I was a stone heavier and a size 14 and, while it was grief that initially caused me to lose the weight, I have since been diligent about keeping it off.

I know that metabolic rates can vary, but in my humble opinion your figure is generally a representation of your diet and lifestyle. Staying slim is largely down to education and self-control. You can have a very interesting and varied diet, but you don't need a huge portion and you certainly don't need a second helping – and as you get older, you need even less. Rather than deny myself anything, I prefer to have tiny portions of beautiful food: a small piece of wonderful cake or a sliver of quiche with crispy bacon and a nice bit of asparagus. You just learn to have a little of the very high calorie ingredient, which is what provides the flavour.

I find the success of *The Great British Bake Off* staggering really, and I'm very proud to be involved in such a phenomenon. Last year's final attracted an audience of over seven million and the format has now been sold to something like twenty countries around the world. Even my own family are hooked: during the second series I had a phone call from my granddaughter Gracie, then eight, absolutely sobbing. 'Granny, why did you send Janet home?' she asked, between sniffs. 'We love Janet! You were wrong!'

Nevertheless, I'm still not entirely sure why the show has captured the public's imagination in the way it has. There is the appeal of baking, certainly, and the fact that viewers are learning something from us as well as being entertained. I also think that people respond to the fact that it's a very positive, warm programme. Many other reality shows on television can be quite bullying and aggressive, but we wanted *The Bake Off* to be an antidote to that: there would be no bad language, harsh words or, hopefully, tears. Paul Hollywood and I are always very much on the contestants' side and desperately want them to do well, so if there are disasters, as there can be in any kitchen, we try our best to be fair. Perhaps the oven has gone off or the scales haven't been quite accurate, but I'll always try to encourage them to keep going.

'Well, what do you think you can do about this?' I might ask. 'If you're quick, you'll have time to make another one.' And I'm always so relieved when they manage to salvage their efforts. In last year's quarter-final, James had planned to make an idyllic gingerbread Scottish barn, but when it began to collapse in on itself he very cleverly changed the design to make a tumbledown shack, complete with sugar-spun cobwebs. What a terrific idea! That really amused us.

From day one, Paul and I have respected each other's opinions and areas of expertise. He is a professional baker and a brilliant bread maker, whereas I am a home cook. When the chips are down, I have the decision on cakes and he does on bread; it's not something that is planned it just happens naturally – although that's not to say that we always agree. We once argued for four hours about whether someone should go through.

Paul and I usually have supper and a drink together with Sue and Mel back at the hotel after filming to chat and catch up on life, but we don't socialize outside of work. We are both very family orientated, so as soon as a series is over we go our separate ways, but we do get asked jointly to events like food shows and then that's really quite fun being back together. Paul is such a showman and I'm always really glad that he's alongside me. I do have to tell him to be quiet sometimes, but I like and admire him a great deal, and don't even mind that he calls me 'Bezza'! Paul's absolutely obsessed with his Aston Martins and is always very kindly offering to drive me to the location when we're filming, but if you have that sort of car you will drive fast and while I used to love motoring, nowadays I certainly do not like speeding through the countryside – even with Paul.

*Paul Hollywood:*

From the moment we first met on *Good Food Live*, Mary and I just got on. I thought she was fantastic on camera and was really happy when I found out we would be working together on *The Bake Off*.

We knew our judging roles from the start: I came at it from the bread angle, Mary came from cakes and we met in pies, puds and pastries. It was effortless and enjoyable, although none of us knew that we were sitting on something that would take off in the way that it has.

I've learnt a great deal from Mary about the way that home bakers work. I've always prepared things in bulk so it has been very interesting to watch her attention to detail. She's got unbelievable energy: we all get knackered after a long day's filming, but she'll still be going. She's like the Duracell Bunny! We always dine together in the evening and then she'll be at the bar with us, having a drink and a laugh. She's just one of the lads. It helps that her daughter-in-law is a Scouser, so she gets my sense of humour.

Mary's husband Paul has thanked me for taking care of her, and she does lean on me when we're in public together, but when I stay at her house she looks after me brilliantly. She's like a mum to me: my TV mum.

Without a doubt there's been a huge increase in the number of people who approach me in the street since I started appearing on *The Bake Off*. If I'm in a supermarket they tend to just touch me on the shoulder and tell me how much they love the programme – and they nearly always ask if Paul Hollywood is as tough as he appears and whether his eyes really are that blue. To which I reply: yes he is and yes they

Paul Hollywood and I finishing a live event.

are, but both the man and his eyes are delightful! Or they might ask me about soggy bottoms, which are something of a bugbear of mine and seems to have become a catchphrase. For the record you can avoid this problem by making sure the pastry is nice and thin, baking it blind – making sure you put it on a hot baking sheet – then drying it out before you put the filling in. Hopefully that should put an end to all soggy bottoms!

As Lucy is usually with me when I'm out and about, she has witnessed this great upsurge in attention since I started appearing on the show.

*Lucy:*
The first series of *The Bake Off* came as quite a shock, because people started talking about Mary to a degree that I had never seen before, and we were getting so many more emails about her and requests for interviews, but her

current level of fame – the real explosion in popularity – all started last year with her floral bomber jacket. That was when the interest seemed to switch from Mary Berry, the judge on *The Great British Bake Off*, to Mary Berry the celebrity (although I know she hates that word!). Suddenly, people were talking about Mary's clothes and make-up and describing her as a 'style icon'.

To begin with, she found the whole concept hilarious; one day she said to me in complete disbelief, 'The *Daily Mail* want to come and do a feature on my wardrobe!' We had a good laugh about that one. But now I think she's quite enjoying the attention – and, of course, her clothes have become fabulous and far more modern. Mary still doesn't like a fuss – she hates spas and beauty treatments and only gets her hair and nails done so she looks neat on television – but she is having a lot of fun with her style these days.

When Dermot O'Leary appeared in *Heat* magazine dressed up as Mary in the floral bomber jacket I had to explain to her not only what *Heat* magazine was, but who Dermot was. It didn't mean much to her, but she had a giggle and said, as she always does, 'Luc, it's not going to last.'

In January this year, Mary was invited to the National Television Awards to present an award with Paul. She had originally been planning to wear an old ball dress, a navy number with puffy sleeves that she'd had in her wardrobe for years, but while it looked gorgeous it wasn't quite right for the red carpet, so she ended up borrowing a sleeveless electric blue gown and the press coverage was astounding, with her photo on all the front pages, because she just looked about fifty years old.

The first time she was mobbed at one of the food shows she was still in shock when she got home. 'Luc, I've never known anything like it in my life,' she said. Nowadays she is often accompanied by security when she appears at the shows, because they can then move her quickly through the crowds, although the reality is that she can't step outside her door without attracting attention. We stopped at a service station on the way to Salcombe recently and as she walked to the ladies there was this ripple of whispers – 'There's Mary Berry, there's Mary Berry,' – and then people starting asking for photos and autographs. Mary is so polite that she always obliges. Later that trip we went to the pub for a quiet supper and six people came up to us while we were eating to ask for photographs; everyone recognized her – and that never used to happen. People used to stop for a chat in our local Waitrose, but whereas before it was middle-aged ladies who'd say, 'I made your chicken recipe last night and it was very nice,' nowadays it will be people of all ages going, 'Oooh, you're on telly!' And since *The Bake Off* that's been the big difference really.

I'm afraid to admit that since *The Bake Off* I have got heartily sick of eating cake and nowadays I rarely have it at home – and if I do I always prefer something plain without a fancy filling or buttercream icing. Paul my husband loves proper cakes, but for me a slice of golden Madeira cake or a piece of crumbly homemade shortbread is just perfect.

There was talk of going to America to do *The Bake Off* over there, but not for me: I'm firmly here with my husband Paul and the family. Nevertheless, I plan to be a judge on *The Great British Bake Off* until I get the sack. It's enormous fun and I love every moment of it. I really am very, very lucky.

# SEVILLE MINTED CHICKEN

I came up with this dish in the mid nineties, but it's still a favourite recipe today. It's perfect for a special family supper.

*Serves 6*

- 12 chicken thighs
- 4 tablespoons thick-cut marmalade, chopped
- 1½ tablespoons mint sauce from a jar
- 3 garlic cloves, crushed

### for the sauce
- 2 level tablespoons cornflour
- finely grated rind and juice of 1 large orange
- 400ml (⅔ pint) chicken stock
- salt and freshly ground pepper
- a little gravy browning

Preheat the oven to 200°C/Fan 180°C/Gas 6.

Arrange the chicken thighs in a large roasting tin. Measure the marmalade, mint sauce and garlic into a small bowl and mix together. Spoon over the chicken.

Roast in the preheated oven for about 35–45 minutes until tender, basting once.

Remove the chicken from the roasting tin, place in a serving dish and keep warm.

Skim the fat from the tin and put over a low heat. Slake the cornflour with the orange juice and rind in a bowl. Pour the stock into the roasting tin, bring to the boil, then add the corn-flour mixture and bring to boil again, stirring until thickened. Check the seasoning, stir in a little gravy browning and serve with the chicken.

## 20

The year 2012 was a very big one for me. *The Great British Bake Off* was awarded a BAFTA for Best Television Feature and I was presented with an honorary degree from Bath Spa University in recognition of my contribution to cookery (which was particularly thrilling, because I didn't exactly leave school with flying colours!). But the cherry on the cake was being awarded a CBE in the Queen's Birthday Honours List.

The notification letter arrived in the post one morning. The envelope bore the royal crest, which I noted with great excitement, and when I opened it I was in shock. 'Oh my goodness gracious me!' I thought. I had to Google what becoming a CBE – Commander of the British Empire – actually entailed; it was one of those moments that you wished your parents were still alive to see.

As the big day approached, my wonderfully opinionated friend Mavis Patterson marched me off to Knightsbridge. I had mentioned to her what I was planning to wear for the ceremony – a very smart outfit I already had in my wardrobe – and she had said, 'Oh no you're not. Your mother would insist that you buy something new.' With her help, I found a lovely pale blue dress and coat by Stewart Parvin: frightfully expensive, but beautifully made and very correct.

My husband Paul and the children accompanied me to Windsor Castle, where Prince Charles was to present the honours as the Queen was suffering from a bad back. Before the ceremony began all of us attendees were briefed on what to

RECIPE FOR LIFE · 325

do and say when we had our moment with the prince, and then we were gently herded into a line. I would have loved to be one of the last to go up, as I was hoping to be able to copy how the other ladies curtsied, but there were only a few people in front of me and unfortunately most of them were men. When it was my turn I did my best, looking straight in Prince Charles's eyes and doing a little bob, although you're so over-come and confused that you forget everything you've been told, but the Prince was just lovely – what a smile, and what presence! We talked a little about his wife, who's the president of the osteoporosis charity that I'm a patron of – although in truth I couldn't actually hear him very well. He was standing above me on a dais and has got a very soft voice.

I'm immensely proud to have been made a CBE, but I don't ever use the letters after my name, unless someone has included them in correspondence to me.

Our day at Windsor Castle was actually my second audi-ence with royalty that year, as a few months earlier I had been fortunate enough to be invited to the Palace to have lunch with the Queen and the Duke of Edinburgh. When I first got the call to invite me I had thought it was a joke. Thomas answered the phone and said, 'It's Buckingham Palace for you.' Well, I just assumed he was taking the Michael out of his mother. Then I took the call and they said, 'It's Bucking-ham Palace here. Her Majesty would like you to come for lunch.' 'Gosh,' I thought, 'how lovely!' The man on the other end of the phone was Charles Richards, Equerry to the Queen and Deputy Master of the Royal Household, but even then I really didn't believe it until the official invitation arrived in the post.

Usually I choose my own outfits, often with the help of Annabel or Lucy, but on this occasion I decided to see a

EⅡR

*The Master of the Household*
*has received Her Majesty's command to invite* —

Mrs. Mary Berry

*to a Luncheon to be given at Buckingham Palace*
*by The Queen and The Duke of Edinburgh*

on Tuesday 28th February 2012

*at 12.50 p.m. for 1.00 p.m.*

*The reply should be addressed to:*
*The Master of the Household,*
*Buckingham Palace, SW1A 1AA.*

20/1/12 Yes

Dress: Lounge Suit
Day Dress

personal shopper. I was very busy at the time with *The Bake Off*, so I went to John Lewis and met with a lovely girl called Victoria. The invitation from the Palace had specified 'day dress' and I told her that I wanted an outfit that wasn't too short, tight or trendy. When I arrived she had all sorts of things waiting on a rail for me and, at the very end of the selection, was a blue dress. I tried it on and liked it immediately – and then I noticed it was in the sale. Even better! One hundred and fifty pounds reduced to thirty-five pounds. John Lewis: 'never knowingly undersold'. We waltzed round and got some navy tights and navy suede shoes and I thought it was a thoroughly civilized way to go shopping.

On the day of the lunch, I was driven to Buckingham Palace and we went straight through the front gates, past the sentries and right up to the front door. There I was walking up the red-carpeted stairs to the Palace, and all I could think was: 'I'm not going to fall over.' I was terribly nervous, but all the butlers or footmen were nodding their heads as I went past and were really very helpful. My mother had only recently died at the age of 105 and I was wearing one of her brooches, as it was on occasions like this that I really missed her. She would have been the first person I would have wanted to phone afterwards to say, 'Gosh, the Queen was wearing comfortable shoes!' But I'm fortunate that I'm very close to my sister-in-law Margaret Berry and we often discuss how much Mum would have enjoyed hearing about all these exciting things.

I was shown into the most magnificent gilt-decked room with huge windows overlooking the garden, where the other lunch guests were assembling. There were ten of us altogether, including the Children's Laureate Michael Morpurgo, the cyclist Mark Cavendish and a lovely girl who was a Chief Constable in the Surrey police. We were offered champagne and wine, but I stuck to apple juice from Sandringham as I was determined not to be drunk when I met the Queen.

In the room with us there were an awful lot of equerries or whatever you call them, looking terribly smart and very similar in dark suits and immaculately clean shoes, all standing upright in a very military fashion. I noticed that one of these chaps had a long sheet of paper with all our photographs arranged in the order in which we would be standing to meet the Queen. I had seen her in person once before, back in 1951 when my parents took us to the Festival of Britain. The whole of the royal family had been there and I was standing right at the front of the crowd when they walked past. I was just a child, but I remember thinking how tiny they all were, especially Princess Margaret, and what perfect skin they had. They looked so special, so immaculate – and so obviously royal.

And now, over sixty years later, when the Queen walked in to meet us I was no less impressed. The presence that she had! A more elegant, beautiful woman I can't imagine. Her skin was still absolutely remarkable. She was wearing a lovely blue dress and a huge smile and you warmed to her immediately. And – why do I always look at shoes? – she was wearing very, very shiny, very well-loved shoes. (And yes, they did look comfortable.)

When we went into lunch I was placed on Prince Philip's right. It was an oval dining table, just like we have at home only larger, and the interesting thing was that the Queen and the Duke sat opposite each other in the middle of the table, rather than at either end as you'd expect, which when you think about it is far more sensible as it means everyone can enjoy their company. And I thought, 'I'll get home and try that!'

Etiquette dictates that a gentleman starts talking to the lady on his right, so Prince Philip chatted to me first. No, he doesn't watch *The Bake Off*, but he is a great barbecuer. He told me he barbecues game and stuffs the birds with haggis, but he said that you need to add a little bit more breadcrumb to the stuffing because haggis is greasy. And I thought, 'Here's a man who knows about barbecuing . . .'

We had a starter of langoustines followed by Lamb with Winter Vegetables and Boulangère Potatoes, but this was one occasion where the food wasn't the most important part. That was watching the Queen, and drinking in every detail of the whole wonderful occasion. Everything in the room looked so precious. There were the most gorgeous arrangements of seasonal flowers, and the glass, silver and china were just beautiful: the table was literally sparkling. While we were eating I noticed a little silver box by the Queen's right hand, but its function only became apparent at the end of the meal. Throughout lunch the corgis had been rushing around the room and the Queen would occasionally look over and say, 'Be quiet! Be quiet!' You felt as if you were at a very posh family lunch. And then, once we'd had our pud, she opened the little silver box and gave each of the dogs a treat, before they were taken out of the room. It was just lovely.

I've still no idea exactly why I was invited to that wonderful lunch, but there's no doubt that the remarkable success of *The Bake Off* has given me so many exciting opportunities that I otherwise might not have had. I took Clare Balding's memoir with me on holiday to Barbados and enjoyed every moment – and then a few months later I was lucky enough to be invited to be a guest on her Radio 2 show on Sunday morning. When I'm on the red carpet at events all these famous people will come up and say hello; I've had newsreaders telling me how much they like my Lemon Drizzle Cake! It's certainly not just celebrities, though; when I give a talk or sign books I get to chat to the most interesting people. I remember going to a Women's Institute function and a small lady came up and asked if I would sign her book. She said that her name was Britannia, and when I commented on how unusual her name was she drew herself up to her full height, which must have been all of five foot, and announced, 'I'm a Romany Gipsy.' She told me that she'd been on the road her whole life, living in a caravan, and that although her husband had just bought a bungalow they still had the caravan out back and that was where she felt most at home. 'There's one disadvantage to being a gypsy,' she added. 'I've never learned to read nor write.' And I thought, 'How strange that I'm signing a book, yet she won't be able to read it.'

Amongst the opportunities that I have had since *The Great British Bake Off*, one of the most interesting and enjoyable has been filming a television programme about my life. I must admit, when the BBC's Emma Willis (who also commissioned *The Bake Off*) first approached me with the idea for *The Mary Berry Story* – a two-part programme about my life – my initial reaction was one of complete surprise. I couldn't believe that anybody would be that interested in me: I had a normal upbringing, I didn't excel at school – there was nothing particularly remarkable about my life, and certainly not enough to fill two hours of television!

Despite this, I am so glad that I agreed to Emma's suggestion because I enjoyed filming the programme immensely. The production company was Love Productions, whom I knew so well from *The Bake Off*, and I was working with a great team: director Scott Tankard and cameraman Sam Montague. It was lovely to look back over my life and revisit places from my younger days, including my childhood home in Bath and the Paris Cordon Bleu. We went back to film at my old school and it was a huge pleasure to be able to walk through the front door for the very first time, because only prefects and sixth formers had been allowed that privilege when I was at school – and of course I had been neither. I instantly recognized the black-and-white tiles outside the headmistress's office, as I had spent such a lot of time waiting there when I was a pupil, and it was wonderful to be invited inside by the current headmistress and to be greeted with smiles, rather than the stern countenance of Miss Blackburn! In my day there had been a green light outside the office that flashed when you were permitted to enter; the light was still there but the current headmistress hadn't known what it was for, so I was able to explain its purpose to her. It was quite a novelty for me being inside that office and not feeling like I had done something wrong!

The other part of filming I particularly enjoyed was visiting Bath Spa University, where the Vice Chancellor, a charming lady called Christina Slade, had unearthed my exam results from my time at Bath College of Domestic Science. We also spent a morning in the archives at the Council Chambers in Bath, where they produced all sorts of fascinating reports and newspaper cuttings about my father.

After the programme was broadcast we had the most amazing response. People wrote to me with their own recollections of the places and people we had talked about, including three viewers who had been patients in the Orthopaedic Hospital at the same time as I had been there recovering from polio, and their letters reminded me of things that I had long forgotten. It was a real joy to read everyone's memories.

I have been extremely lucky that people in the press have largely been very nice about me. One journalist, Allison Pearson in the *Daily Telegraph*, wrote: 'All I want for Christmas is Mary Berry.' Isn't that sweet? I admit I really would be mortified if people started saying nasty things about me. There was an unpleasant patch earlier this year after I was asked about feminism in an interview, and some people accused me of not being supportive of women. It was very frustrating, as that's not how I feel at all, and I think the problem was that I wasn't entirely sure as to the exact definition of 'feminism'. I would much rather people look at my career if they want to know my views, as I think it proves that I have never been anything but strongly supportive of women. In my generation, women and men traditionally had very different roles, but things are changing and I'm certainly not against that. I always welcome women in positions of authority, just as I'm delighted to see husbands staying at home to raise children while their wives are the breadwinners, which I come across increasingly with colleagues in the television industry.

I was lucky enough to have been invited to this year's BAFTA Television Awards ceremony since, for the second year running, *The Great British Bake Off* was nominated for Best Feature. To our astonishment and delight we had won the award the previous year – which had taken us all by surprise because when we had arrived at the Royal Festival Hall, Perks (aka Sue Perkins) told me that there was no way we would win because we were sitting too far back in the auditorium. 'They would never have put us here if we have to go up on stage to collect the award,' she said confidently. 'There are too many stairs to fall down.' And so we all just relaxed and enjoyed the evening.

To be quite honest, I don't remember much about the ceremony itself, but what I do recall is my huge excitement at seeing all the famous faces and beautiful dresses on the red carpet. I was astonished by how tall everyone was, which is probably because when you see presenters on television they are usually sitting down! Alex Jones from *The One Show*, looking a million dollars in a bright yellow dress, literally towered over me. I'm not very good at recognizing famous people so I kept muttering to Mel and Sue, 'Ooh, I think I know her – who is she?' And they would tell me it was Billie Piper or whoever. I can completely understand why people come up to talk to me, thinking they've met me at bridge, as I had exactly the same feeling that night at the BAFTAs: 'I'm sure

I've seen you before somewhere . . . Oh yes, you read the news!' I was totally star-struck and loved every minute.

So when they announced that *The Bake Off* had been awarded the BAFTA it took me completely by surprise. We all tumbled down the steps to get to the stage – Mel and Sue, my co-judge Paul Hollywood and the wonderful team from Love Productions – and I had no idea what to do once I was up there, so I just stood behind everyone else and smiled and smiled, trying to take it all in. It was a wonderful moment and I felt absolutely proud and honoured to be involved in the programme's success.

Then I heard that we had been nominated for a second time this year and my first thought was: 'Ooh, how exciting!' Closely followed by: 'Whatever am I going to wear?' The previous year I had simply worn the best dress in my cupboard, but I was aware that my clothes were under a bit more scrutiny these days. That said, I really couldn't believe it when the *Guardian*'s weekend supplement listed me as number two in their list of 'The 50 Best-Dressed Over-50s'. I just thought, 'Good gosh, they should see me slopping about on a Monday morning in a tracksuit before playing tennis . . .'

Everyone had loved the electric blue gown from a label called Damsel in a Dress that I had worn to the National Television Awards earlier in the year, so that was who I went back to for my BAFTA outfit. I chose a navy satin dress that was quite clingy, so that I didn't trip over the hem, with a matching jacket to hide my flabby arms. (Paul Hollywood is always going on about old ladies' bingo wings, so I wanted to cover them up!) I got a lovely Susie Pringle necklace to go with it and wore a pair of sturdy navy shoes. Everyone else had these tiny heels that I would just have fallen off, so I thought I'd go for the sensible option and hope that my dress would hide the rather unglamorous footwear.

On the day of the BAFTAs I had invited friends to Sunday lunch with my husband Paul and me at Watercroft, completely forgetting that although the ceremony doesn't start until the evening you have to be there earlier in the afternoon to do press interviews on the red carpet. I wouldn't have dreamt of cancelling lunch, but because I was going to be whizzing off I kept things simple, cooking Fillet of Beef (a gift from Aune Valley Meat in Devon, who are based near my family's holiday home in Salcombe and whose tea room I had opened the week before) with Jersey royals and asparagus, then Summer Pudding to follow. Delicious.

By the time we had finished eating I only had about fifteen minutes to get ready for the red carpet, as I was being picked up at quarter to four. The absolute best thing about my new-found fame is that I am driven on all work occasions by David, who is great company and looks after me royally. It is such a treat, because it feels like I have spent my whole life trying to be on time – dropping off and collecting the children, getting to interviews, coordinating appointments – and that has always been a major stress in my life, especially in the days before satnav. Nowadays, even if I'm doing something for charity, I'll say, 'Yes, I'm very happy to do it, but please will you fetch me and bring me home.' It's the greatest luxury.

Mel, Sue and our producer Amanda Westwood were all congregating at Mel's house before the ceremony, to have a bit of a party and get their hair and make-up done by Jo Penford, but while I too had been invited I couldn't make it in time and had to get myself ready. Luckily, we had been filming *The Bake Off* the day before and so Jo had already puffed my hair up a bit and I still had on the three little strips of false lashes, so I just gave my hair a bit of a boost and applied my usual make-up: Max Factor Age Renew foundation, powder and English Rose lipstick (colour 510).

Paul Hollywood was staying in a hotel just around the corner from the Festival Hall, where the ceremony was to take place, so I picked him up and then we stepped on to the red carpet together. It took the pair of us about twenty minutes to walk from one end to the other, as we were stopped by so many journalists. Most of the time I had no idea where they were from but they all asked nice questions, nothing beastly, mainly about *The Bake Off* and what I was wearing (which made me glad I hadn't just pulled something out of my wardrobe!) and they all wanted to ask Paul about the American version of the show, which he had just finished filming. It was pouring with rain so people were holding huge transparent umbrellas over us to keep us dry, while at the same time trying to keep them high enough so they wouldn't be seen on the telly. As we were being interviewed I kept wanting to turn my head around to see everyone else arriving on the red carpet. There was Sienna Miller looking gorgeous in a pale blue sparkly dress, Paul O'Grady, who was up against *The Bake Off* with his programme about dogs and who I'd very much enjoyed chatting to at the BAFTA nominations party, and the lovely Clare Balding, who was due to receive a special award that evening. I congratulated her and she told me that her parents were there to watch her receive the award – 'I know Dad will be very emotional,' she smiled – and I thought that was so natural.

When we finally got into the reception I just stuck with Mel and Sue, who kept saying, 'Are you all right, Bezza?' They really are my guardian angels. The champagne was flowing and of course I had a glass, although just the one, as I thought I had better stay under control!

This year we were seated much closer to the front, in row E, which was lovely because Graham Norton was presenting the ceremony and he gave me a wave from the stage. I had been a guest on Graham's Saturday morning show on Radio 2 and I don't know when I've enjoyed doing a programme more, so when I was asked to appear on his television chat show last Christmas I immediately agreed. As well as Paul Hollywood and I, the other guests were the comedian John Bishop and actors Billy Crystal and Hugh Jackman. Billy Crystal had me in stitches. I've got nothing but admiration for John Bishop, after he raised huge amounts of money for Sport Relief last year, and as for Hugh – wow. You've never seen a dishier man! He was amazing and funny and just such a heart-throb. I was wearing a feathery cardigan from Phase Eight and was glad that I had chosen it, because I was the only girl amongst all these handsome men and I do think it's nice to be a bit different.

If anything, I was even more star-struck this time than I

had been at the previous year's BAFTA ceremony, but I was more confident too. Having said that, I was quite sure that *The Bake Off* wouldn't be taking home the BAFTA for the second time in a row. As Sue said, 'We've got no chance, Bezza.' I didn't mind at all though – I was just glad to be invited. The evening flew by, and then it was time for the category in which *The Bake Off* had been nominated: Best Feature.

'And the BAFTA goes to . . . *The Great British Bake Off.*'

Well, I was too stunned to move. Paul was straight out of his seat and bounding up to the stage, but I thought I'd better take it slowly as I didn't want to do a dramatic fall. Mel and Sue, who are our stars and without whom the whole programme would collapse, gave a speech and then Paul said a few words. Before the ceremony Mel and Sue had been asking what I would say in the unlikely event that we won, but I hadn't prepared anything. I just came forward and managed to say, 'Thank you . . . It's wonderful.' Not for the first time in the past few years – a period of my life that I had assumed would be spent pottering around my garden rather than waltzing down red carpets and signing autographs – I was virtually speechless.

But while it is tremendous fun to be able to dip one's toe into the world of celebrity, to borrow beautiful dresses, go to parties and have all sorts of interesting people want to talk to you, at the end of the day my life really hasn't changed at all – apart from having to be careful not to leave the house looking too scruffy! Perhaps it's because I became famous later in life, but my friends are still the same, I go to the same places and enjoy doing the same things, and if I'm not working, my daily routine is just as it has always been. My husband gets up at six o'clock and I'm straight behind him, as I don't like to stay in bed once I'm awake. Once Paul is dressed we will make the bed together and then while he walks the dog I reply to letters and make a start on breakfast. I wouldn't like a lie-in – I can always think of too many things that need doing. I'm very much a list person: my memory has never been brilliant and if I don't write things down I'm in real trouble. I even make a list before making a phone call, so I don't forget the points I wish to make, and when I go to the doctor I make a note of what I'm going in for because I can get so engrossed chatting to our lovely lady doctor at our wonderful village surgery that I forget to ask for my pills!

If I'm at home during the day, Paul and I – and whoever else is here – will stop at one o'clock for lunch. We have a rule that we never discuss food at lunchtime, because it would be very easy for Lucy, Lucinda and I – who will generally have spent the morning testing recipes – to continue the conversation over the meal, but it's really not fair on Paul to have this continuous dialogue about food. I don't watch cooking programmes in the evening for the same reason. When we're at home, lunch is purely social – and when I say lunch, I mean soup in the winter (made from homemade stock from bones) and salad in the summer. Preparation wise, lunch should be a non-event, taking no more than ten minutes to get ready.

On days when I'm very busy, Lucinda (who's now been with us for thirteen years) will leave Paul and me a Cauliflower Cheese or something for supper, or will shop for the ingredients so I can prepare it myself. I allow myself one glass of wine every night with supper – and it's a very large one! I love to find something on television to watch at eight o'clock, especially documentaries or drama series like *Downton Abbey*, but I do prefer a happy ending and I can't bear noise and fighting and extreme bad language, which I realize is because of my age. By nine o'clock I'm upstairs having a bath, ten o'clock is watching the news in bed and then it's lights out. As long as I've got everything that's in my head written down on a list I'm asleep as soon as my head touches the pillow.

Once a week I play tennis with three very special girlfriends – Di, Margaret and Annie – although it's far more about gossip and laughter than it is the tennis itself. Before the game we'll sit in the kitchen drinking coffee and chattering away and sometimes Paul will walk through and ask how tennis was, and we'll have to say: 'We haven't actually been out yet.'

Every two months Paul has a long-standing arrangement with his friends to meet up on a Friday to play poker and very early on we wives decided that we certainly weren't

The tennis girls.

going to stay in and cook for the men, so we now all go off to the pub or cinema or theatre while our husbands are playing cards. It's a guaranteed opportunity to see very good friends – Jenny Hopkirk, Janey Shepherd, Charlotte Dinan, Alison Gibbs, Ann Love and Laila Smith – and I try never to miss it, since it is always tremendous fun. On one such occasion a few years ago we booked a table at Heston Blumenthal's pub, the Hinds Head in Bray, which is about ten miles from .Penn. I offered to drive, as I thought I was familiar with the route, and so five of us squashed up together in our car with Laila sitting in the boot. We had a very noisy dinner with excellent food and some jolly good gossip and at the end of the evening all piled back into the car in extremely high spirits. Anyway, just as we were coming out of Bray I got to a junction to find a 'no right turn' sign where I had been planning to turn right. 'Well, that's nonsense,' I announced. 'That's the way we need to go!' My friends were egging me on, telling me to ignore the sign and take the right turn, and so I did – and a moment later a police car appeared and waved us down.

The policeman asked me to step out of the car on to the pavement. Everyone in the car had fallen silent.

'Do you realize you turned right at a "no right turn"?' the officer asked me.

'I do,' I said. 'But I know the route and I think the sign is wrong.'

There was a stony silence from the policeman. He then looked in the car and saw how overcrowded it was and when he lifted up the boot to find Laila all squashed up he became even sterner.

'Everybody has to wear a seatbelt – so that's three points on your licence. Have you been drinking, madam?'

'Yes,' I said. 'I've had one glass of wine.'

So I was breathalyzed and, although I was sure that I couldn't be over the limit, I was terribly worried at the prospect of getting points on my licence. To my relief, however, the policeman eventually let me off with nothing but a slapped wrist.

'You're not over the limit,' he said. 'And you didn't know these roads, but you do now. Please drive home carefully.'

It was a very subdued journey home. Jenny, who was sitting in the front, had just been made High Sheriff of Bucks – imagine the scandal if we had all been carted off to the police station! Ann and Charlotte were extremely quiet too. You will appreciate why I haven't been the first choice to drive on our nights out since then.

Because I'm so busy at the moment holidays are particularly precious to me, especially the annual trip Paul and I take with our children and grandchildren. Annabel and my daughter-in-law, Sarah, usually decide where will we go, and it's always somewhere hot: we've been to Italy, Portugal and this year it was Cape Verde, off the west coast of Africa. Although actually this was Thomas's choice because he had been spearfishing there before. We had two little houses on the beach: Paul and I stayed with Thomas and his family in one, and Annabel was in the other with her lot, which worked well as her two boys are very lively! We went swimming and sailing, enjoyed family meals together, and played volleyball every evening on the beach. There are never any arguments and nobody gets their knickers in a twist. Of course there are differences of opinion that everyone has to share and sort out, but we never quarrel and I dearly hope we never will. We all care about each other, so arguments are something very much to be avoided.

In recent years Paul and I have been to Barbados for a fortnight to stay with my much-loved cousin Robin. It's a huge treat. Paul and Robin play golf while I sit in the sun (I do like a tan, although I'm careful to cover my face) and read the pile of books I have been intending to get through all year. I will usually read five, if not more, in a fortnight; I like anything by Maeve Binchy and Joanna Trollope, and I like a good autobiography as well – the most recent one I read was by my friend Prue Leith, and it was really pretty racy!

Sadly, Robin lost his wife Naomi quite recently and, as she was a great entertainer, I like to step in when we stay and help him do a dinner party in great style for forty or so friends. To me, this really isn't a chore. I just follow in Naomi's wake: she always used to make Fish Pie, so I do the same, going to the market for the fish and borrowing pots and pans from neighbours. Everyone lends a hand, with Robin always taking care of the pud himself: raisins soaked in rum poured on vanilla ice cream. Robin has always been there to advise me since my father died, so I'm just pleased there is something I can do for him to say thank you.

I'm often asked what motivates me to keep on working, but really I just feel extremely lucky to be offered these opportunities. Being in a studio, being interviewed about my specialist subject, is meat and drink to me. I love teaching people how to cook, because I want everybody at home to get the same success and pleasure from a recipe as I do, and it is this desire to share my skills and enjoyment of cooking that runs through everything I do. One of the things I love best is when people bring a copy of one of my older books, such as the *Hamlyn All Colour Cookbook* or *Fast Cakes* for me to sign, and it might be missing a cover and the pages will have turned brown and be covered with scribbles and splodges. It is occasions like that when I think, 'Oh, I'm so glad I do what I do.'

I believe the success I've had in my career has been down to grabbing hold of every opportunity that came my way. If I could give any advice to the young it would be to get as much experience as possible in your chosen field and be willing to go that extra mile so that you stand out – and, as Judy Chalmers always told me, to make sure you do it with a big smile! I've got a lovely runner on *The Bake Off* at the moment – she makes me coffee, warms my hot water bottle and never leaves my side – and because she's made such an effort, I let people know how good she has been. I have also been fortunate to have such a wonderful husband, family and friends who have always supported me in my career. My brothers, Roger and William, have recently started to tell me how proud they are of me, which is thoroughly unlike them and very lovely! Thomas and Annabel write very sweet things in my birthday cards, and they accept that I can't always make the children's plays or netball matches because of my work, although I do try to do what I can. I have given a fairy cake demonstration at Louis and Abby's school and was part of a 'food awareness day' with Abby and Grace's classmates.

*Annabel:*

We're so proud of Mum, but we've always kept her feet on the ground and within the family unit nothing has changed. We have a meal together at Watercroft at least once a week and we joke about how famous she is and take the mickey. She's not as available for babysitting as she used to be, but she's always the one who gets out the diary and goes: 'Right, when can I have the children?' Although her schedule is very busy, it's still very important to her to be a granny.

Today, Mum and I get on better than we ever have before. You're a product of your parents and we increasingly lean towards each other as we realize how similar we are. I've only known a working mother, so I've never expected to be a kept wife. We're all quite driven, because we've never been allowed to laze about.

Nobody could have predicted how *The Bake Off* would take the country by storm, but I can honestly say it's only improved the family. I think Mum is enjoying life more than ever: she loves what she does and doesn't see why she should slow down. She is incredibly motivated. Mum doesn't talk about her polio much, but I suspect that coming through that had a profound effect on her. She must have had the same feeling that I had after William's death: 'I've been given a second chance.'

*Thomas:*

Mum's been reasonably well-known as long as I've been here so you get used to photographers and film crews, and so to us her current fame is really just a progression. I can see that Mum's very excited about it, which is brilliant, and she's really good on telly. If you've got a passion in life you want to put your heart and soul into it, so I don't think she thinks of it as work.

Going to Windsor Castle to watch her receive her CBE was amazing and we are all very proud, but at the end of the day she's just Mum. She hasn't changed, but that's because it hasn't been overnight fame. She loves the fun of going out to exciting events and meeting new people. She'll come in, all excited, and say, 'I met Gary Barlow today!' But she's kept her moral values and knows what's important in life: as much as she enjoys all these showbiz events, she likes nothing better than a family meal with all of us.

I can't think of any ambitions I have left that I wish to achieve. It is wonderful in one's twilight years to have something like *The Bake Off* and all the wonderful opportunities that has brought me, and I am so looking forward to doing my own series, *Mary Berry Cooks*, next year, when I'll be back demonstrating the sort of recipes I cook at home every day of the week – which is really where it all began for me. I am thrilled to be asked to do all these exciting things, and don't take any of it for granted for a moment. My only real regret is not working harder in English lessons at school: oh how I wish I could write like Jane Grigson or Elizabeth David!

I have been immensely lucky to enjoy my life enormously. Looking back, I consider the arrival of my children to be the most special thing that has happened to me, especially because it was a shared event with my husband Paul. You feel immensely blessed each time a child or grandchild arrives: they're a gift to you, but one you know you'll have to give up – although I definitely haven't given up mine, as they are always popping in! Yet beyond that, I do think the most exciting time of my life is right now – and how many other people, at the age of seventy-eight, are lucky enough to be able to say that?

# WONDERFUL APPLE CAKE

Perhaps it's not a show-stopper, but once you've tried this you will never make apple pie again! Serve warm with cream and/or custard. It is an excellent way of using up windfall apples. If preferred, you can use a little grated lemon rind instead of the almond extract.

*Serves 6 generously*

- 225g (8 oz) self-raising flour
- 1 level teaspoon baking powder
- 225g (8 oz) caster sugar
- 2 large eggs
- 1 teaspoon almond extract
- 150g (5 oz) butter, melted
- 350g (12 oz) cooking apples, peeled, cored and sliced
- 25g (1 oz) flaked almonds

Preheat the oven to 160°C/Fan 140°C/Gas 3.

Grease and line the base of a 20cm (8 inch) deep loose-bottomed cake tin with non-stick baking parchment.

Measure the flour, baking powder and sugar into a bowl. Stir in the eggs, almond extract and butter. Beat well until smooth.

Spoon half the mixture into the base of the cake tin. Arrange the apple slices on top and spoon the remaining cake mixture in blobs over the top of the apples. Sprinkle with the almonds.

Bake in the preheated oven for about 1½ hours until golden brown and shrinking away from the sides of the tin.

Release the sides from the tin and leave the cake to cool for about 15 minutes, then turn out and serve warm.